# Land in Dār Fūr

UNION ACADÉMIQUE INTERNATIONALE

INTERNATIONAL ACADEMIC UNION

*FONTES HISTORIAE AFRICANAE*
*SERIES ARABICA III*

Series published under the editorial direction
of J. O. Hunwick with the assistance of Y. F. Hasan,
J. F. P. Hopkins, V. Monteil and M. Zouber

Published on the recommendation of the International Council for
Philosophy and Humanistic Studies with the financial assistance of
Unesco and of the Norwegian Research Council.

# *Land in Dār Fūr*

## *Charters and related documents from the Dār Fūr Sultanate*

Translated with an introduction by
R. S. O'FAHEY and M. I. ABŪ SALĪM
with
M.-J. and J. TUBIANA

CAMBRIDGE UNIVERSITY PRESS
CAMBRIDGE
LONDON NEW YORK NEW ROCHELLE
MELBOURNE SYDNEY

PUBLISHED BY THE PRESS SYNDICATE OF THE UNIVERSITY OF CAMBRIDGE
The Pitt Building, Trumpington Street, Cambridge, United Kingdom

CAMBRIDGE UNIVERSITY PRESS
The Edinburgh Building, Cambridge CB2 2RU, UK
40 West 20th Street, New York NY 10011–4211, USA
477 Williamstown Road, Port Melbourne, VIC 3207, Australia
Ruiz de Alarcón 13, 28014 Madrid, Spain
Dock House, The Waterfront, Cape Town 8001, South Africa

http://www.cambridge.org



First published 1983
First paperback edition 2003

*A catalogue record for this book is available from the British Library*

Library of Congress catalogue card number: 82-4186

ISBN 0 521 24643 1 hardback
ISBN 0 521 54563 3 paperback

Now, with very few exceptions which have just been explained, they (i.e. medieval legal documents) were, till the thirteenth century, invariably drawn up in Latin. But this was not the way in which the realities they were intended to record were first expressed. When two lords debated the price of an estate or the clauses of a contract of subjection they certainly did not talk to each other in the language of Cicero. It was the notary's business later to provide, as best he could, a classical vest for their agreement. Thus every Latin charter or notarial record is the result of a work of translation, which the historian today, if he wishes to grasp the underlying truth, must put back, as it were, into the original.

Marc Bloch, *Feudal Society*
I, 77–8.

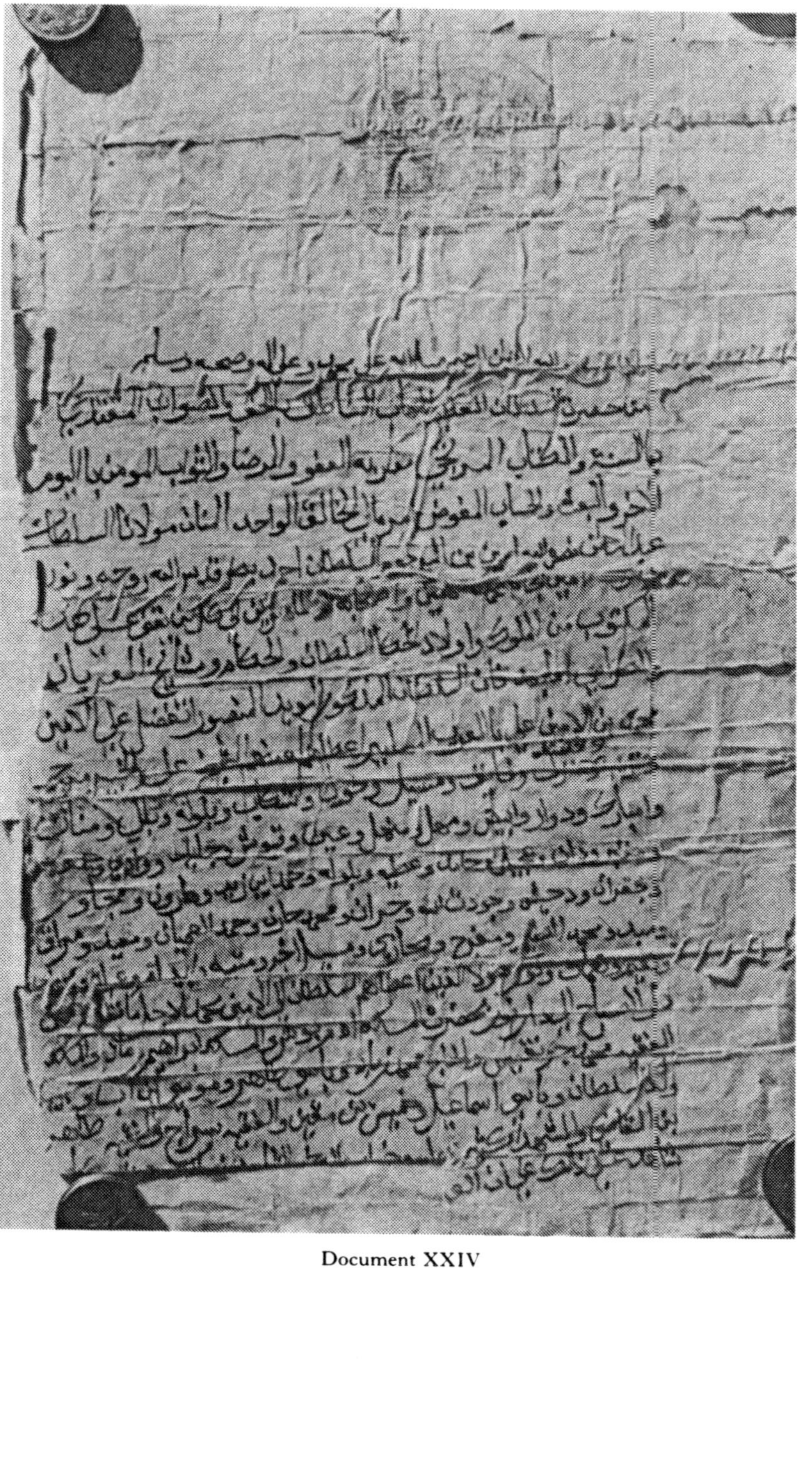

Document XXIV

CONTENTS


Preface and acknowledgements — *page* ix
List and concordance of documents — xiii
Transliteration and abbreviations — xv

**Chapter 1 The Dār Fūr Sultanate**
Introduction — 1
The administration of northern and central Dār Fūr — 4
Taxation and revenue — 6
The law and its administration — 8

**Chapter 2 Estate and privilege**
The growth of the estate system — 12
Immunity — 17
The charitable estate — 18
The procedure — 20

**Chapter 3 Literacy and Chancery**
Official literacy — 22
An official chancery? — 23

**Chapter 4 A Diplomatic Commentary**
Physical description and language — 26
The structure of the charters — 28
(a) seal — 28
(b) *invocatio* — 29
(c) *intitulatio* — 30
(d) *inscriptio* — 32
(e) *expositio* and *dispositio* — 32
(f) final injunctions — 33

**Chapter 5 Translations and Commentary**
Document
**I** The *faqīh* ‘Abdallāh's charter — 35
**II** to **VI** The Jawāmi‘a *fuqarā*’ of Jadīd al-Sayl — 37

**VII** to **XXIII** The Tunjur *fuqarā'* of Khirībān 45
**XXIV** and **XXV** The Masāmīr Arabs 76
**XXVI** to **XXXVII** The land and followers of Nūr al-Dīn b. Yaḥyā 79
**XXXVIII** to **XLI** The Princesses Fāṭima Umm Dirays and Zahrʻa 99
**XLII** to **XLVII** The merchants Muḥammad Kannūna and ʻAlī Bey Ibrāhīm al-Ṭirayfī 106

Sources and bibliography 119
Notes 124
Indices
(a) Titles and honorifics 151
(b) Administrative and legal terms 153
(c) Botanical and topographical terms 157
(d) Personal and place-names 158

## MAPS AND DIAGRAMS

Map 1. The Dār Fūr sultanate 15
Map 2. Northern and central Dār Fūr 16
Diagram 1. The Keira sultans 2
Diagram 2. A typology of documents 24

## PLATES

Document XXIV vi
Document XVI 60
Document XXIII 72
Document XXVIII 83
Document XLV 116

# PREFACE

We present here translations[1] of forty-seven documents chosen from a total now approaching five hundred concerning land and related matters issued by the sultans of Dār Fūr or their officials in the eighteenth and nineteenth centuries. For the most part the documents have survived as family archives preserved by the descendants of those to whom they were originally addressed. In making our selection, we have sought to illustrate the main administrative developments of the period as presented in the whole corpus. Thus the archives of three holy families are given (I to XXIII), the archive of a chief and his patrons (XXIV to XXXVII), five documents (XXXVIII to XLI) concerning two princesses, and finally six (XLII to XLVII) dealing with the land of two merchants. These proportions do not reflect the whole corpus where the papers of the holy families predominate, since they have been the most successful in holding on to both their land and their documents.[2]

The introduction tries to situate the charters and court records within the environment which produced them. Chapter 1 gives a brief summary of the political and administrative history of the Dār Fūr sultanate; chapter 2, again briefly, outlines the principles whereby privileged status, rights in people and landed estates were granted. Chapters 3 and 4 take up the question of literacy and of the existence of a formal chancery and present a brief diplomatic commentary. Since we hope that this volume, together with a companion volume presenting land charters and related documents from the Sinnār sultanate,[3] will stimulate

[1] The texts of the documents translated will be published in *Al-arḍ fī-Dār Fūr*, ed. R. S. O'Fahey and M. I. Abū Salīm, Occasional Paper no. 6, Middle Eastern Section, Department of History, University of Bergen, Norway (1983).

[2] It is for this reason that we are particularly grateful to Professor and Madame J. Tubiana for their kindness in allowing us to publish here translations of the archive of Nūr al-Dīn b. Yaḥyā (XXIV to XXXVII). They hope to republish the documents at a later date with a more detailed local commentary.

[3] *Documents from Eighteenth Century Sinnār*, ed. and transl. M. I. Abū Salīm and J. L. Spaulding, *Fontes Historiae Africanae: series arabica*, vol. II (forthcoming). See also M. I. Abū Salīm, *Al-Funj wa'l-arḍ: Wathā'iq tamlīk* (Khartoum, 1967).

research on this type of documentation (not least in the search for further archives), we have made some comparisons with diplomatic practice in the Islamic heartlands. But if the similarities are often obvious, the means of transmission are usually obscure.

With three exceptions (XXXVIII to XL), all the documents here were found, photographed and transcribed in Dār Fūr. The majority were recovered by O'Fahey in the course of visits in 1969, 1970, 1974 and 1976[1]. Generally, the documents were found as family archives, numbering from two to three to the largest single archive, fifty-eight documents (ranging from *c.* 1720 to 1916) belonging to the Awlād Jābir holy clan of Mellit. Most were found in northern and central Dār Fūr, especially in and around the capital, al-Fāshir. The procedure adopted was to register and photograph the documents in the field (since there was no question of physically collecting them) and then to try and build up an exegesis upon them on the spot. Once their historical significance was understood, their owners were generally very willing to let them be photographed and to give whatever information they had about them. Difficulties of travel and time made systematic search almost impossible; one contact led to another in a haphazard fashion. Nevertheless, it became clear that there are many more documents waiting to be photographed, but that their discovery is likely to be piecemeal, not to say accidental. Their recovery is, however, a matter of urgency since each year a proportion are destroyed by fire, rain or insects and each year the generation of those who have some idea of their meaning grows fewer.[2]

The documents translated here deal with local communities and their affairs; the mainstream of the state's history appears only incidentally. It is precisely because of the range, detail and vividness of the information they offer, on taxation, on the estate system, on relations between the state and the local communities, and even on local topography and flora, that we have thought it worthwhile to publish this selection. We hope also that the present volume will serve as a modest contribution to the comparative study of "feudalism" and related institutions.

Specialists will regret the absence of the texts in the same volume; our defence is that this is a selection not a *regesta*. The translations are as literal as is compatible with comprehensibility; titles, the various taxes and a number of other local terms are given in transliteration

[1] The complete collection is deposited in the Central Records Office, Khartoum, and at the Department of History, University of Bergen.

[2] As one example: in 1974 O'Fahey visited Tarnī, south-west of al-Fāshir, to photograph the documents of the family of the *abu'l-jabbāyyīn* or chief of the sultanate's tax-collectors. For various reasons, they could not then be photographed. By the time of a return visit in 1976, the entire archive had been destroyed by fire.

(usually of the singular form) rather than translated. This admittedly leads to a number of inelegancies, but at least avoids unwarranted certainty as to their meaning. The indices are designed to be a crucial part of the commentary.

A book with several years of gestation gathers many debts. Our greatest is to the owners of the documents themselves, for their hospitality, their quick appreciation of the value of their heritage and their patient help in deciphering them. The generosity of the people of Dār Fūr makes the study of their country a delight. A great debt is owed to the Province administration, in particular to the former Governor Sayyid al-Ṭayyib al-Marḍī, for their willingness to allocate scarce resources to a task that they readily perceived as being of importance to the province. Professor R. H. Pierce of the University of Bergen has given much guidance over legal terminology, while Professor P. M. Holt has been very generous in placing his great knowledge of Sudanese history at our disposal. Finally, but not least, our friend Professor J. O. Hunwick has gone far beyond his duties as editor of the series in which this volume appears in seeing this book into print.

R. S. O'Fahey and M. I. Abū Salīm
*Bergen and Khartoum*
*August 1981*

# DOCUMENTS

Documents referred to by a Latin numeral only appear in the volume. All other documents are cited by their catalogue number in the photographic collection, Department of History, University of Bergen, with other details of their provenance where appropriate. A number of the documents translated here were first published in M. I. Abū Salīm, *Al-Fūr wa'l-arḍ: wathā'iq tamlīk* (Khartoum, 1975); the page references are given below.

| *Number in volume* | *Catalogue number/provenance* |
|---|---|
| I | DF13.3/2; Abū Salīm (1975), 124–5 |
| II | DF126.14/1 |
| III | DF128.14/3; Abū Salīm (1975), 128–30 |
| IV | DF127.14/2 |
| V | DF129.14/4; Abū Salīm (1975), 133–5 |
| VI | DF130.14/5; Abū Salīm (1975), 131–2 |
| VII | DF108.12/16 |
| VIII | DF107.12/15 |
| IX | DF101.12/9 |
| X | DF109.12/17 |
| XI | DF111.12/19 |
| XII | DF112.12/20 |
| XIII | DF100.12/8 |
| XIV | DF103.12/11 |
| XV | DF105.12/13 |
| XVI | DF104.12/12 |
| XVII | DF113.12/21 |
| XVIII | DF96.12/4 |
| XIX | DF110.12/18 |
| XX | DF99.12/7 |
| XXI | DF98.12/6 |
| XXII | DF102.12/10 |
| XXIII | DF106.12/14 |

| | |
|---|---|
| XXIV | Abū Salīm (1975), 111–12 |
| XXV | Abū Salīm (1975), 115–16 |
| XXVI | Abū Salīm (1975), 99–100 |
| XXVII | Abū Salīm (1975), 109–10 |
| XXVIII | Abū Salīm (1975), 117–18 |
| XXIX | Abū Salīm (1975), 105–6 |
| XXX | Abū Salīm (1975), 113–14 |
| XXI | Abū Salīm (1975), 89–91 |
| XXXII | Abū Salīm (1975), 98 |
| XXXIII | Abū Salīm (1975), 104 |
| XXXIV | Abū Salīm (1975), 96–7 |
| XXXV | Abū Salīm (1975), 92–3 |
| XXXVI | Abū Salīm (1975), 101–3 |
| XXXVII | Abū Salīm (1975), 94–5 |

The following three documents were first published in Na'ūm Shuqayr, *Ta'rīkh al-Sūdān al-qadīm wa'l-ḥadīth wa-jughrāfiyatuhu*, 3 vols., Cairo, n.d. [1903], II, pp. 139–41.

| | |
|---|---|
| XXXVIII | Abū Salīm (1975), 136–7 |
| XXXIX | Abū Salīm (1975), 138 |
| XL | Abū Salīm (1975), 139 |

| | |
|---|---|
| XLI | DF211.22/7 |
| XLII | DF205.22/1 |
| XLIII | DF206.22/2 |
| XLIV | DF207.22/3 |
| XLV | DF210.22/6 |
| XLVI | DF209.22/5 |
| XLVII | DF208.22/4 |

# TRANSLITERATION AND ABBREVIATIONS

Arabic or Arabicized words have been transliterated according to the system used by the *Encyclopedia of Islam*, but with the omission of the subscript ligatures and the substitution of "j" for "dj" and "q" for "ḳ". The resultant transliteration gives no indication of the Sudanese vernacular pronunciation; in some instances we have preferred to use "ō" for "ū".

Our spelling of Fur words is based on the only grammar of the language, A. C. Beaton, *A Grammar of the Fur Language*, Sudan Research Unit, University of Khartoum (1970) (mimeograph). The symbol, ɔ, represents the English sound as in "p*o*t", while ŋ represents the sound in "si*ng*ing".

In the translations, square brackets enclose either words or phrases added for the sake of clarity or reconstructions of lacunae in the originals. Half square brackets represent a word or phrase read but not understood, or, in some instances, a conjectural reading. A series of dots marks lacunae that cannot be reconstructed.

AP[1] or [2]: The papers of the Rev. Dr A. J. Arkell (see bibliography)

*BSG*: *Bulletin de la Société de Géographie*

*GAL*: C. Brockelmann, *Geschichte der Arabischen Literatur*, 5 vols. (Leiden, 1937–49)

PA: Province archives, al-Fāshir, etc.

*SNR*: *Sudan Notes and Records*

# 1

# The Dār Fūr sultanate

## Introduction

The Dār Fūr sultanate was an African kingdom and a Muslim state; one polity among many in the Sudanic Belt, the vast zone below the Sahara stretching from the Atlantic Ocean to the Red Sea. It thus lay in that part of Africa that has been exposed for over a thousand years to influences from the Mediterranean and Muslim worlds to the north. Within the Sudanic Belt, Dār Fūr itself lay open to immigration and ideas coming from both West Africa and the Nile valley. The outlines of the sultanate's political history in the eighteenth and nineteenth centuries are reasonably well-known, as are the state's central administrative structures.[1] But its economic and social history is only now beginning to be uncovered both through Arabic documents of the type presented here and through the systematic collection of local oral traditions.

The origins of the Dār Fūr sultanate are obscure; the original nucleus of the state was a Fur kingdom based upon the Marra Mountains of central Dār Fūr and the lands immediately to the west. Its roots may go back to the fifteenth century. The oral traditions of Dār Fūr record a long tradition of state formation in the area; two empires or states, those of the Daju and Tunjur, are said to have preceded that of the Fur. The Marra Mountains were the ancestral home of the Fur, a people with their own complex language and culture and with no obvious linguistic affinities with their neighbours.[2] They rapidly emerged as the dominant power in Dār Fūr ("the land of the Fur") in about the mid-seventeenth century under the leadership of Sulaymān *Sɔlɔŋduŋɔ* (Fur, "of reddish complexion, Arab"), the first historical ruler of the Keira dynasty (ruled *c.* 1650–80).

By about 1700 Sulaymān's successors, Mūsā and Aḥmad Bukr, had moved their *fāshirs* or royal camps down on to the plains west of the mountains and rapidly consolidated their authority over the other peoples of the region, Arabs and non-Arabs, cattle and camel nomads and hoe farmers. The central zone occupied mainly by sedentary

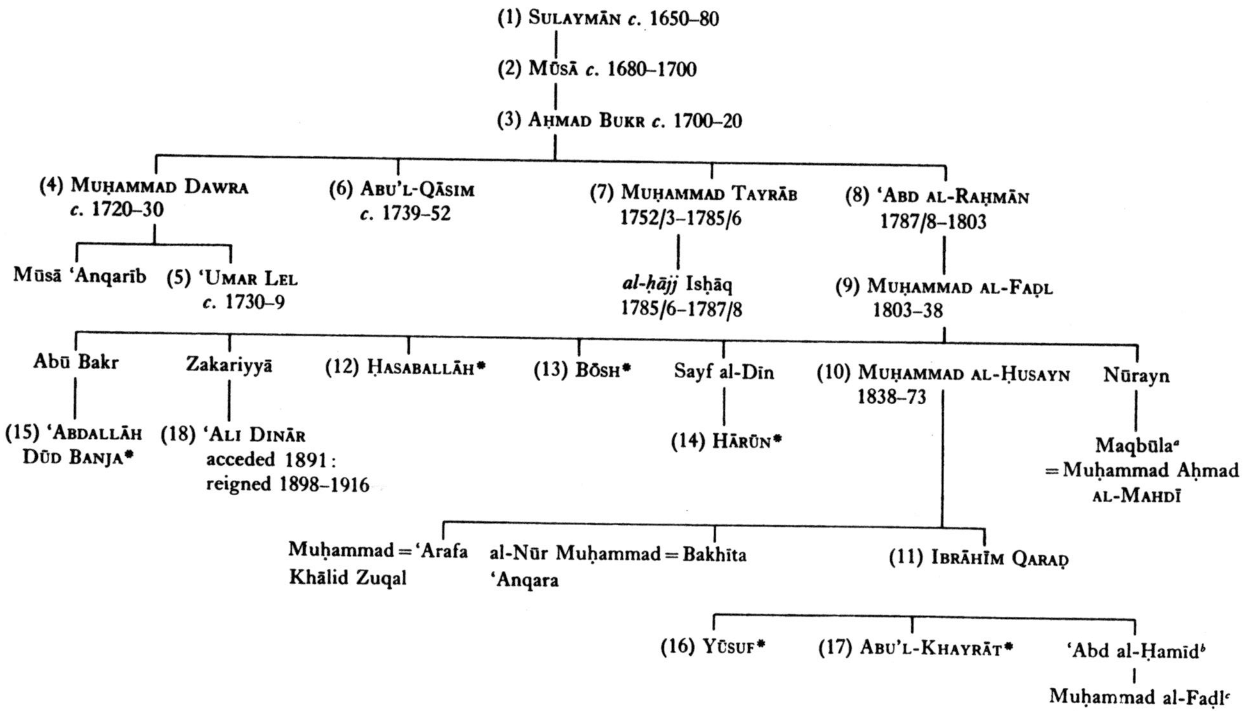


* "Shadow sultans", 1874–98. (*a*) Mother of Sir Sayyid 'Abd al-Raḥman al-Mahdī. (*b*) "Emir of Zalingei", 1929–31. (*c*) "Emir of Zalingei", 1931–7.

Diagram 1. *The Keira sultans*

peoples remained the heartland of the sultanate, although the sultans successfully extended their control over the camel nomads to the north and much less successfully over the cattle nomads, the Baqqāra, in the south.[3] Between 1720 and 1750 a series of wars with Wadai, the neighbouring state to the west, appear to have blocked expansion in that direction, while cultural and commercial ties, which grew throughout the eighteenth century, increasingly drew Dār Fūr into the orbit of the riverain Sudan and, more remotely, Egypt. By about 1750 the sultanate was exporting, on an increasing scale, slaves, camels and other goods to Egypt across the desert along the famous "Forty Days Road", *darb al-arba'īn*.[4] This eastward orientation, which gradually transformed the state from an "African" to an Islamic/Arabic environment, culminated in the conquest in about 1200/1785–86 of Kordofān, a vast area of great commercial importance lying between Dār Fūr and the White Nile. By the end of the eighteenth century, the sultanate embraced a huge area of over 300,000 square miles, ruling a multiplicity of peoples and supplying the major part of Egypt's trade with Africa.

This transformation was the result of a number of internal factors; the employment by the sultans of slaves as soldiers, labourers and bureaucrats, the impact of Islam and Arabic upon local particularisms, and the effacement of the local and lineage chiefs before the authority of a rich and powerful elite of courtiers around the sultan (a process well-documented here in documents XXVI to XXXVII). These trends were symbolized and consolidated by the establishment of a permanent capital, al-Fāshir, to the east of the Fur lands in about 1206/1791–92.[5] However, the subordination of the older chiefly order by the courtiers, generals, merchants and *fuqarā'* or holy men was never total and outside the capital and its immediate vicinity tribal cohesiveness remained strong.

Outside forces soon began to press upon the sultanate; in 1821 Kordofān was lost to a Turco-Egyptian invasion force, a part of the beginning of the progressive occupation of the Sudan by Egypt. Although the sultanate was threatened at intervals by its powerful neighbour,[6] its downfall in 1874 came from a different direction, at the hands of the northern Sudanese trader, al-Zubayr Pasha Raḥma, who had built a trading and slaving empire in the lands south of the sultanate. In a series of skilful campaigns that foreshadowed the military achievements of the Mahdi, al-Zubayr conquered Dār Fūr whose last sultan, Ibrāhīm Qaraḍ (1873–74), died in the final battle at Manawāshī. al-Zubayr was cheated out of his conquests and Dār Fūr was incorporated into the Turco-Egyptian Sudan. However the Keira dynasty's hold on the loyalty of their subjects was tenacious and a line of pretenders, "the shadow sultans" (see diagram 1), held out with their Fur supporters against both the Turco-Egyptians and the Mahdists in

Jabal Marra, in effect a temporal journey back to the days before Sulaymān and imperial splendour. When the Mahdist state was shattered at Kararī in 1898, a grandson of Sultan Muḥammad al-Faḍl, 'Alī Dīnār, hastened from Omdurman back to Dār Fūr, where with the support of the surviving notables of the old regime he was able to revive the sultanate. The British accepted the *fait accompli* and 'Alī Dīnār ruled his state until 1916 when, urged on by Turkish Pan-Islamic propaganda and distrustful of both the French colonial advance in the west and the British in the east, he declared war on the Condominium Government. The British reacted by invading the sultanate, a move they had been planning for some time; 'Alī Dīnār's army was defeated and he himself killed a little after, and Dār Fūr was once again incorporated into the Sudan.

## The administration of northern and central Dār Fūr

Before describing the system of estates and privileges which forms the subject of most of the documents given here, an account of the administrative system in which they were embedded is necessary.[7] As might be expected of a multi-ethnic state which flourished for nearly three hundred years and which was heir to an even older tradition of state formation, the sultanate's administration was complex. Since the documents presented here come from northern and central Dār Fūr, much of it does not concern us; for example, the administrative structure of the Fur lands in the south and west, the heartlands of the state which supplied the sultans with much of their food and manpower, does not appear in these documents.

The centre of the Keira state for the period covered by most of the documents here was al-Fāshir, "the *fāshir*" or royal camp on the Rahad Tandaltī, lying north-east of the Marra Mountains. Before the establishment of al-Fāshir by the end of the eighteenth century, the capital had moved with the sultan. It is difficult to exaggerate the *fāshir's* importance in the life of the state; it was the stage for the sultan's public life, the arena of the elite's conflicts and consumption, and the judicial, administrative and revenue-collecting heart of the state; the latter function is accurately described by the synonym, *bayt al-jibāya* "the house of tribute" (a term which appears in V).[8] The capital and the land around it lay outside the provincial organization, being administered by the *ɔrreŋduluŋ*, "(master of) the door-posts", who acted as the sultan's chamberlain.

The sultanate was divided into four great provinces, the northern province (*dār al-takanāwī* or *dār al-rīḥ*, the latter meaning "the land of the wind"), the eastern (*dār dālī* or *dār al-ṣabāḥ*), the south-eastern (*dār umɔ*) and the south-western (*dār diima*). Their boundaries fluctuated, but the eastern and northern provinces met roughly at al-Fāshir. The eastern province, stretching east and south from the capital, was administered by a great court official (the only province to be so administered), the *āb shaykh dālī* "the father shaykh *dālī*", who issues XXI here.[9] *Dār dālī* was divided, like the other provinces, into a number of district chieftainships or *shartāyas* administered by a *shartay* (pl. *sharātī*), usually an hereditary position within a prominent local family.

The northern province, within whose boundaries the land described by the documents mostly lay (see map on p. 16), had a complex history. Before Sultan ʿAbd al-Raḥmān (1787/8–1803) settled there, Rahad Tandaltī, around which al-Fāshir was to grow, appears to have been the centre for the governor of the north or *takanāwī*.[10] The *takanāwī* appears to have been a very ancient office that probably had its roots in Tunjur times; variants of the title with the significance of the ruler's ritual assistant or *alter ego* are found among several peoples in Dār Fūr.[11] With the establishment of al-Fāshir, the *takanāwīs* moved north to the Kutum region, where by the 1820–30s they appear to have faded into impotence.[12] The title also appears to have been increasingly expropriated as an honorific by some of the northern *shartays*, although the details are unclear.

Its decline can be linked to the rise from about 1800 onwards of a new office, that of *maqdūm* (pl. *maqādīm*). The *maqdūms* functioned outside the old title hierarchy, being commissioners appointed by the sultan for a specific task, to govern a particular area or to lead a campaign, "who in some measure represents the person of the king".[13] The office was not intended to be hereditary or permanent nor was Dār Fūr ever formally divided into provinces ruled by *maqdūms*; the person so appointed could be either a slave or a freeman and upon completion of his assignment he simply reverted to his former rank. However, in northern Dār Fūr the *maqdūms*, probably by default, became hereditary governors of the north. In about 1810 Ḥasan Segere (written as Siqirī in XX) was appointed as *maqdūm*; he came from a family remotely of Arab origin from Jabal Meidob who held the Fur title, *iriŋa* "exalted" (it appears as *iriqā* in XX) and who had owned land in the Wana Hills (north-west of al-Fāshir) since Sultan Aḥmad Bukr's time (1700–20).[14] Ḥasan died in about 1855–56 and was followed by his son, Muḥammad, who was in turn succeeded by Ādam b. Ḥasan.[15] The family survived the Mahdist upheavals; in 1899 ʿAlī Dīnār restored the title and their lands to the family in the person of Muḥammad Sharīf b. Ādam (born 1872–73; died *c.* 1925).[16]

In the sultanate's heyday, the *maqdūms* of the north governed a vast province, whose boundaries extended from Kabkābiyya to Dār Qimr in the west, to Jabal Sī in the south-east and, in the years when Dār Fūr controlled Kordofān (1785–86 to 1821) across northern Kordofān to Jabal Ḥarāza.[17] A mosaic of peoples lived in the province, from the Zaghāwa of the north-west (who appear in XXVI to XXXVII) to the Zayyādiyya, Berti and Meidob in the east.[18] In the southern parts of the province on sandy ridges or patches (Arabic *qōz*) live small farming communities of diverse ethnic origins, exemplified here by the Jawāmi'a immigrants from Kordofān settled at Jadīd al-Sayl (II to VI) and the Tunjur at nearby Khirībān (VII to XXIII). Within the province lay the great trading centre of Kobbei, the southern terminus of the "Forty Days Road", *darb al-arba'īn*, the sultanate's trade link with Egypt (XLII to XLVII).

Under the *takanāwīs* the province was divided into approximately twelve *shartāyas*, each in turn being divided into a number of *dimlijiyyas* administered by a *dimlij* (pl. *damālij*); this system continued under the *maqdūms*.[19] As elsewhere in the sultanate, the *shartays* were the linkmen of the administrative system; they bore the brunt of the centre's demands for revenue and were required to appear regularly at court. In case of war, if the *maqdūm* was ordered to raise a force, the *shartay* would raise one or two men from each village. His judicial powers were limited; if a homicide occurred he would levy a collective fine of cattle from the locality before sending the parties involved before the *qāḍī* or *maqdūm*. From the documents the *shartay* appears, at least in northern Dār Fūr, to have been the subordinate local agent of the central administration.[20]

The *dimlij* and *wakīl* were the lowest ranks in the administrative hierarchy to be listed in the inscriptions of the charters (see below p. 32); the *dimlij* was responsible for two to three villages, the *wakīl* was the village headman.

The *shartays* and *dimlijs* ruled over the settled communities who made up the core of the province. Among the nomads and semi-nomads further north this hierarchy was paralleled by "the maliks of the nomads and their shaykhs, *kursīs* and servants" (XXVI; see also XXIV), which appears appropriately in charters from Dār Zaghāwa. Throughout the sultanate tribal chiefs were usually called *malik* "king", although some bore the title, *sulṭān*. What distinguished "the little sultans" (such as the Sultan of Zaghāwa Kobe or Sultan Muḥammad Shalabī in IX), to use al-Tūnisī's phrase, from other tribal chiefs was the possession of the *naḥās* (literally "copper"), kettle-drums formally granted them by the Keira sultans.[21]

## Taxation and revenue

The main tasks of the hierarchy of chiefs described above were the collection of taxes and the administration of justice. A third duty, the raising of warbands, was no longer pressing in the nineteenth century as war became infrequent and such forces as were needed, for slave raiding or chastising nomads, were provided by the slave bands of the leading notables.[22]

Taxes in kind could hardly have been collected nationally; each local community paid a variety of taxes and levies, of which only a proportion were passed up through the administrative system; most were stored and consumed locally. The centre controlled the distribution of revenues from producers to consumers, from village or nomad encampment to chief, slave communities or warbands – the estate system described below was one facet of this redistributive process. The needs of the court were met by specialized networks whereby, for example, Jabal Marra supplied corn, the royal food; southern Dār Fūr, game.

The charters distinguish between "the lawful ordinances", *al-aḥkām al-shar'iyya*, that is the Islamic taxes *zakāh* and *fiṭr*,[23] and "the customary ways", *al-subul al-'ādiyya*, the many traditional taxes.[24] *Fiṭr* was a poll-tax paid usually at the end of Ramaḍān at the rate of one *midd* of grain (approximately eight litres capacity measure) per head. *Zakāh* or the tithe was the basic state grain and animal tax. It was known colloquially as *umm thalāthīn*, "mother of thirty", since it was usually assessed at a rate of three *midd* in every thirty; thus a field yielding 300 *midd* would pay 30 *midd* or one *umm thalāthīn*, a unit known elsewhere in the Sudan as a *rayka*. In practice, a harvest of less than 300 *midd* was not taxed. What the tax was actually paid in varied from district to district; in Jabal Marra corn was grown for the court although it was rarely eaten locally; in the savannas the more usual grains (*'aysh* in the documents) were millet, either the common millet (*dhurra*) or the bulrush (*dukhn*). Nomads paid in animals or clarified butter.[25]

The *takkiyya* tax, the most burdensome of the customary taxes, seems to have been a land-tax, assessed on fields under cultivation, whereby each household was assigned to pay so many *takkiyyas* or pieces of cloth. Whatever its exact basis, the *takkiyya* was in effect a "money" tax since the *takkiyya* was the most widely used unit of exchange within the sultanate; by comparison other units, rocksalt, hoes, copper rings or chewing tobacco tended to have only a local circulation. Nachtigal who saw some of the tax returns estimated that the tax yielded about 100,000 pieces of cloth annually, while the rate of assessment is indicated by a letter from a *takanāwī* ordering the return to a *faqīh* of eight *takkiyyas* since he had been assessed to pay ten instead of two, the correct rate.[26]

There were many customary taxes; specialized levies such as slaves from some of the peoples of the southern borderlands, rocksalt from parts of Jabal Marra and clarified butter from the cattle-keeping nomads of the south.[27] Communal fines could be imposed for homicide, causing bush fires and the like; hospitality and fodder for the great ones of the state and their animals could be a great burden on local communities.

How onerous this plethora of exactions and dues was may be guessed at from the care with which they are listed in the charters. In many cases their exact meaning remains to be discovered.

The supervision of the collection and storage of the revenues (*jibāya*) throughout the state was the responsibility of the *abu'l-jabbāyyīn* who from the late eighteenth century on came from a Musabbaʿāt clan living around Tarnī, south-west of al-Fāshir. One of the greatest of the state's officials, he controlled an extensive hierarchy of subordinates, the *jabbāyyīn*, who were found in every *shartāya*.[28] "The *jabbāyyīn* of the grain, cotton and seed" as they are called in several charters,[29] directly supervised the collection of the taxes and their storage in clay-lined pits (*maṭmūra*). Only the reckoning (*ṭaliba*) was sent to al-Fāshir. Just how direct this supervision was may be deduced from a letter of Sultan Muḥammad al-Faḍl to the *jabbay* Mūsā reproving him for illegally taxing an exempted community; "But, now, you have measured out their grain and have taken it all despite the fact that they are people of sanctity and dignity (*ahl ḥurma wa-karāma*)".[30]

The *jabbays* did not collect the taxes and other dues from the sultan's estates, of which the greatest was Jabal Marra itself; these were sent directly to al-Fāshir. Neither, of course, did they collect taxes from those who held estates or privileged status from the sultans, although the care which the recipients of sultanic favour took to have their grants confirmed suggests that the reproof quoted above may often have been necessary. Nor did the *jabbays* collect the market and customs tolls, *maks* and *khidma*. These were the responsibility of the *abbo daadiŋa*, a title-holder with extensive estates at Qōz Bayna just south of al-Fāshir, who in this guise was called *malik al-qawwārīn* (or *al-makkāsīn*) and whose officials delivered the tolls to him.[31]

## The law and its administration

In its principles the law and its administration in Dār Fūr differed little from most Muslim lands. Whatever the theoretical obeisance made to the primacy of the Sharīʿa, administered according to the Mālikī school, in practice customary and state law were dominant. Nor were the *qāḍīs* ever the sole administrators of the law, whether Sharīʿa or customary.

The customary law of the Fur people is said to have been codified by the legendary Sultan Daali (who reigned possibly in the late fifteenth century), hence its name, *kitāb* or *qānūn dālī*. Although the code is said to have been written down, no such document has yet been found.[32] The *qānūn dālī* prescribed fines for a range of offences, and indeed fines became the foundation of customary law throughout the sultanate, not just in the Fur lands. Fines, payable in rolls of cloth or animals, were levied for adultery, theft, cursing and the like, while bloodmoney (*diya*) was imposed for homicide or injury. There is no evidence that the Sharī'a punishments were ever imposed, while customary law ensured that women were largely excluded from inheritance arrangements.[33] Few examples of criminal cases (in the western sense) survive among the corpus of court transcripts; one such, however, is illustrative. A slave, jointly-owned by four women, is accused of cutting off the ear of the plaintiff's son; the judge orders the slave's value to be assessed and of his value of eight cows, four are given to the plaintiff as compensation.[34]

A system of justice based upon fines was, of course, very profitable for the ruling elite. The right to collect fines, or to render justice, thus became a valued part of what the sultan granted to those he favoured with privileges or estates; *zinā*, the fine for "fornication", *fisq*, for "adultery", *ḥukm*, the legal fee and others (see Index of administrative and legal terms) would have brought in a steady income to an estate-holder. In practice, it seems that judicial profits tended to be shared between the estate-holders and the *shartays*; the latter never entirely abandoned their judicial prerogatives.[35]

The twelve court transcripts (*sijill*) given here concern land in its various aspects, boundary disputes, trespass and several complex disputes over communal leadership (particularly XIII to XV). Although based upon what may be termed Dār Fūr customary and governmental land law, they are heard and judged according to Sharī'a procedure and principles, with the judges occasionally referring to such lawbooks as the *Mukhtaṣar* of Khalīl b. Isḥāq (died 776/1374) as in XXII, XXXV, XXXVII and XLIII or a commentary on the *Mukhtaṣar* by 'Abd al-Bāqī b. Yūsuf al-Zurqānī (1020–99/1611–88) in XXII.[36]

By combining the evidence of the court transcripts with anthropological investigation it may eventually prove possible to write a general study of customary/Sharī'a land law (or better, the law concerning natural resources) under the sultans.[37] Some of the general principles in regard to land and the estate system cited by the judges are discussed in Chapter 2. As regards court procedure, the transcripts do not appear to present any great divergences from normal Sharī'a practice.[38] What is striking, if not unexpected, is the power of sultanic documents. The Mālikī school is in any event more liberal in regard to the legal acceptance of written evidence than the other law schools. The transcripts make it clear that the production of charters, provided they were accepted as authentic by the judge, was invariably decisive without the need for their authenticity to be established by oath.

We have no evidence that the *qāḍīs* or other officials kept regular court records (*sijill* in its more common meaning), but they may well have done so.[39] The *sijills* themselves follow a logical and natural pattern, their formal elements varying according to the peculiarities of the hearing they describe.[40] They can, however, be misleading in that they are not verbatim records of the hearing, but rather an abbreviated report of what seemed to their writers to be the essential points. As *aide-mémoires*, of considerable legal sophistication, they reasonably omit much that would render them more intelligible to the historian; among the omissions are often the precise nature of the dispute and the relationship of the contending parties to each other. Fortunatelv most of the transcripts give us enough to reconstruct the case, at least at a superficial level. That they are a *post factum* construction of the significant elements is made clear by references in some to the duration of the hearing, or number of hearings, following adjournments to enable the disputants to return with their witnesses.[41]

The administration of justice was the prerogative of the ruling elite, not just of the *qāḍīs*; the latter never had exclusive jurisdiction.[42] Of the twelve hearings, only four are heard by *qāḍīs* (XIII, XIV, XVI and XXII); two are heard by *maqdūms* (XX and XXIII), two by *wazīrs* (XXXV and XLIII) two by other chiefs (XV and XXXI), and finally two by a *faqīh* who appears to have been acting informally for the sultan (XXXIV and XXXVII).[43] One *qāḍī*, *al-ḥājj* 'Izz al-Dīn, who was a renowned holy man of the late eighteenth century, is described in *sijills* of his, other than the two that appear here (XIII and XVI), by such titles as *shaykh al-Islām* and *shaykh al-quḍāt*.[44] His superior status may explain what appears to be a regular judicial entourage in his two transcripts, "The officials Muḥammad Diyā and the gaoler (*al-sajjān*) k.sī."

The sultan naturally stood at the apex of the judicial hierarchy, both directing cases to be heard by specific officials or acting as the final court of appeal. The classical Islamic rôle of the ruler in "the investigation of complaints", *al-naẓar fi'l-maẓālim*, is referred to indirectly in XXXI when the dissatisfied defendant demands that the dispute be referred to the sultan, while XXXVI is a rescript from the sultan enforcing a judgment that had evidently been referred to him.[45] A more informal appeal is made by the judge to the sultan in XXIII, where the former seems to have felt that in a case of trespass while the law found for the defendant, equity favoured the plaintiff and so sought a ruling from the sultan. The latter simply ordered the defendant, a member of the royal clan, to remove himself forthwith. It is difficult to gauge how far the sultan involved himself in the rendering of justice; it probably depended on the nature of the dispute and the rank of the disputants. It may be significant that the only two transcripts of hearings before the sultan so far recovered both concern disputes involving forged charters where the expertise of the sultan's scribes may have been needed.[46] 'Alī Dīnār certainly had no compunction in overturning tribal custom; he hanged adulterers on several occasions and abruptly informs one of his *shartays*,

"Concerning the man caught for the killing...we have forgiven him the bloodprice (*dam*) of the dead man."[47]

The *sijills* give the impression, which is supported by oral sources, that the law was effectively administered under the sultans. One can widen the generalization; during the period covered by the documents given here, the sultanate was efficiently administered in the sense that the orders and demands of the elite reached down and were enforced at the local level; in return their subjects could expect a measure of justice and not too much *ẓulm* "oppression".

# 2

# Estate and privilege

## The growth of the estate system

All the documents here arise, directly or indirectly, from grants made by the sultans of privileged status, landed estates or rights over people to chiefs, holy men, merchants and members of the royal family. The origins of this system and the possible external influences behind it are far from clear. The formulae found in the lawbooks and hearsay from Egypt and elsewhere no doubt helped to provide the legal framework, but local realities dictated the substance. However much garbed in Islamic dress, Dār Fūr "feudalism" was a local phenomenon that grew in step with the elaboration of the centralized state.

The sultanate grew from a tribal kingdom; as it subjugated or assimilated its neighbours beyond the Fur heartlands, the Fur chiefs were slowly transformed into courtiers and administrators. Expansion thus led to a physical concentration of men and resources around the ruler at the capital. In the eighteenth century the court or *fāshir* was mobile, feeding in turn upon different districts in the fertile west and south-west, but the establishment of al-Fāshir east of the mountains as a permanent capital at the end of the century made the need to mobilize resources more acute. The sort of precise bureaucratic allocation and management of resources possible and customary on the banks of the Nile was not feasible in the savannas. To provide for the burgeoning elite, it was necessary that they be able to exploit the countryside and its human resources, but extensively rather than intensively.[1] Another aspect of the same process was internal colonization; in a sparsely-peopled land, a marginal change, a market on the border between nomads and farmers, a chief's settlement, a community of holy men, could create nodal points from which wider socio-economic transformations followed.

Two forms of grant appear early on in the sultanate's history; the grant of limited rights of revenue collection over extensive regions or communities for mainly military and administrative purposes, and the grant of tax-exempt or privileged status (for which *jāh*, "of high status or dignity" was the commonest term). Out of these two forms was to emerge in the nineteenth century a standardized grant of *milk* or allodial rights over smaller precisely-defined districts and their inhabitants. The move from the administrative/military estate to the alienation of land as freehold in the form of a charitable donation (*ṣadaqa wa-hiba*), regardless of the function of the grantee and without a direct return to the state has its parallels elsewhere in the Muslim world.[2]

According to Shuqayr, Sultan Mūsā (*c.* 1680–1700) was the first ruler to grant estates to his chiefs.[3] No documents have yet come to light to support this claim but there are several references to grants by Mūsā's successor, Aḥmad Bukr (*c.* 1700–20) in later charters or court transcripts.[4] The earliest charters so far discovered are two issued by Muḥammad Dawra (*c.* 1720–30), although they are stamped with Bukr's seal; they grant exempted status and land to various Awlād Jābir *fuqarā'* settled among the Zayyādiyya nomads of the north-east. The two charters were either issued while Dawra was *khalīfa* or the nominated heir of his father or during his own reign.[5] It is therefore probable that charters and the rights granted therein began to be issued in about 1700, not long after the sultanate had moved down from the mountains on to the savannas.

Although we cannot trace the earliest stages of its evolution with any confidence, the estate system undoubtedly arose in response to a shift away from a tribal or territorial system of rule to a more centralized form of administration. Put more simply, the clan chief leading his people as a war-band evolved into a warleader commanding the retainers from his estates and ultimately into the courtier whose lands and people served the more peaceful purpose of maintaining himself and his entourage at court.[6]

It is possible, and to some degree necessary, to describe the estate system using the Arabic terminology employed in the documents. But this is misleading if *milk*, *iqṭā'*, *ṣadaqa* and the like are understood solely by reference to their use in the Middle East or in the lawbooks. The estate system in Dār Fūr expressed a patron/client relationship defined by land or community rather than an exploitative system comparable to the irrigation-based systems of the Middle East. In the savannas, by contrast for example to Egypt, land was abundant, people scarce and surpluses marginal, and where people were mobile, they needed to be wooed rather than winnowed by their chiefs.

The sultan was the fount of all favour; a sacred bond between the ruler and his land stands at the base of sacral kingship: "(The sultan) speaks in public of the soil and its productions and of the people as little else than his slaves".[7] This bond was annually acted out in the "First Sowing" rite performed both by the sultan at the capital and by the district chiefs.[8] These beliefs and the more prosaic fact of their exceptional fertility may explain why two Fur districts, Jabal Marra and Dār Fongoro in the far south-west, were royal domain, *rɔ kuuriŋ* in Fur, *ḥākūrat al-sulṭān* in Arabic.[9] Revenues from both districts (especially corn from Jabal Marra and honey from Fongoro) went directly to feed the *fāshir*.[10] Moreover, the sultan held other estates throughout his state, while the sites of former *fāshirs* were apparently also treated as royal domain.[11]

Our knowledge of the military and administrative estate or command is largely secondhand, since no documents (if such were issued) directly describing such estates have survived. al-Tūnisī emphasizes their military purpose;

> The sultan does not give any of these notables a salary or pay, but they all have an assignment (*iqṭā'*) from which they take the revenues (*amwāl*). And with the revenues they take, they buy horses, weapons, coats of mail and clothes which they distribute to the soldiers.[12]

"Revenues" are defined by al-Tūnisī to include the customary taxes, but not the *zakāh* tax on grain or animals.[13] If al-Tūnisī is correct, then by contrast with the charitable estates whose beneficiaries took all the revenues, the holders of the military/administrative estates took only the customary taxes, *al-subul al-'ādiyya*. The estate-holders were expected to maintain their warband from these revenues and to parade with them before the sultan at the annual "Leathering of the Drum" festival so that they could be adjudged "levied", *taḥṣīl*, "that is to say paid and equipped from a portion of the revenues".[14]

These estates seemingly evolved from clan chieftainships, military commands, patron/client relationships and the like. Great Fur clans like the Konyuŋa, whose roots went very far back, came to hold numerous titles and estates.[15] Others had their fortunes laid by the enterprise of newcomers. One example is the *shartayship* of Birged Kajjar to the east of Jabal Marra. An immigrant Arab, Sulaymān b. Aḥmad Jafdāl, won Sultan Tayrāb's favour by his skill in treating sick horses. He was granted an *ḥākūra* in the Birged country; some years later the sultan dismissed one of the Birged *shartays* and gave his lands to Sulaymān. This act may have been prompted by a revolt of the Birged against Tayrāb. Later additions to their estates led to Sulaymān's successors swallowing up three further Birged *shartayships*, to emerge as *shartays* of Birged Kajjar and the dominant power among the Birged people.[16] Similarly, the military prowess of a warrior from Baqirmi, Aḥmad Jurāb al-Fīl who played a crucial part in the fall of the eunuch Muḥammad Kurra in 1804, was rewarded by an estate.[17] In these examples, and elsewhere, what began as a personal grant evolved into district chieftainships.

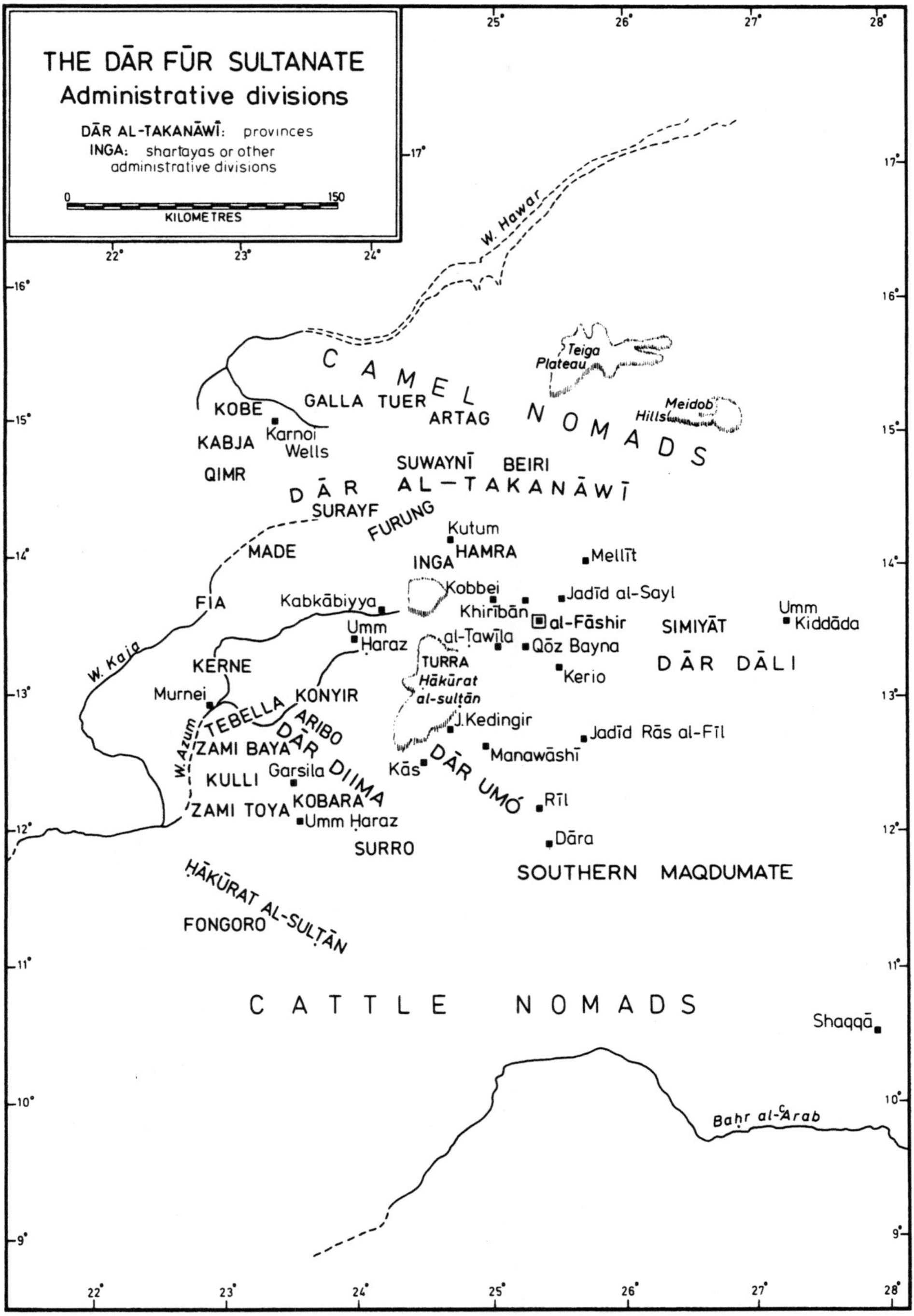


Map 1. The Dār Fūr sultanate.

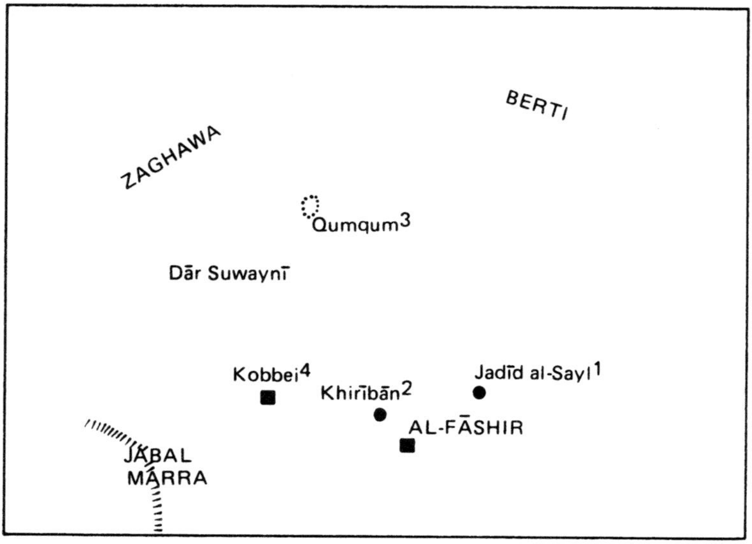


Map 2. The estates: a sketchmap. 1. Jadīd al-Sayl, documents II to VI. 2. Khirībān, documents VII to XXIII. 3. Qumqum, documents XXVI to XXVII. 4. Kobbei, documents XLII to XLVII.

The great officers of state undoubtedly dominated the estate system and their estates generally retained a military character; unfortunately it is only hinted at in those documents we have. Great officials such as the *āb shaykh daali*, head of the slave hierarchy, held estates throughout the sultanate, but only hints as to their scale survive. A Zaghawa *fuqarā'* clan is granted land by Muḥammad al-Faḍl, "in the district of al-Ṭawīla, the house of the Father Shaykh".[18] At nearby Shōba, the Awlād Zaydān *fuqarā'* received charters from three successive *āb shaykhs* within the space of a few years since their land was evidently encompassed by the same great estate.[19] South of al-Ṭawīla, at Ṭarnī, lay the estate of the *abu'l-jabbāyyīn*, head of the tax-collectors.[20] In 1317/1899–1900 'Alī Dīnār restored his ancestral estates to the *maqdūm* of the north, Muḥammad Sharīf Ādam; they numbered seven, covering an extensive region north of al-Fāshir.[21] A glimpse of the estate's military function comes in a report of 1915 that the *abbo daadiŋa* to 'Alī Dīnār, Maḥmūd 'Alī, had two hundred slave troops on his estates at Qōz Bayna (south of al-Fāshir). Moreover, the same sultan granted Maḥmūd the entire Zayyādiyya tribe as an estate.[22] In the nineteenth century it is probable that not only the *maqdūms* but such war chiefs as the *malik saariŋa*, "king of the swordsmen", *abbo daadiŋa* and *malik andaŋa*, "king of the scouts", used their estates primarily to maintain bands of slave troops.

Although the larger administrative estates evidently declined in importance as the state both became less warlike and more centralized (or else, became in effect chieftainships), they never completely disappeared. And while the charitable estate, described below, became the standard form of grant, an informal patron/client relationship between the great title-holders and local beneficiaries often continued. Again we have mainly hints; the Jawāmi'a *fuqarā'* of Jadīd al-Sayl (see II to VI) paid *salamāt*, "presents", to the *abbo daadiŋas* since their land was deemed to fall within the latters' sphere of influence.[23] Patronage was always crucial; *malik* Nūr al-Dīn b. Yaḥyā (see XXVI to XXXVII), evidently a courtier in the entourage of the *wazīr* Ḥāmid b. Aḥmad Sakīn, obtained the estate of Qumqūm "through the mediation of", *bi-wāsiṭa*, the *wazīr* with the sultan (see XXIV). Patronage of a different form appears in IX; the Tunjur Sultan, Muḥammad Shalabī, is given charge of his people in the northern province who are thereby removed from the local administration. Thus he writes to the *takanāwī* emphasizing that his people are not to be taxed.

## Immunity

As a new, powerful and nominally Muslim state, Dār Fūr attracted to it holy men from both east and west. These desirable newcomers were induced to settle in the sultanate by the promise of protection and land. Immunities, exemptions or sanctuaries in various forms are to be found in Sudanic Africa from Mauritania to the Nile valley.[24] And beyond: the commonest term for immunity in Dār Fūr, *jāh* "honour or privilege", was also used in South Arabia to describe the immunities held by the descendants of a holy man who had established a sanctuary, *ḥaram* or *ḥawṭah*. In South Arabia the sanctuary served as a neutral ground for trade and the settlement of disputes, while not only the descendants but also those living under their protection were exempted from customs duties and certain taxes.[25] In Sudanic Africa the emphasis is perhaps more in the immunity of the holy man and his descendants, although the distinction between personal immunity and physical sanctuary is a fine one.[26]

VII, VIII, and X here are examples of a very common form of Dār Fūr charter, wherein the sultan grants the recipients "the privilege of God and His Prophet, and my privilege", *jāh allāh wa-rasūlih wa-jāhī*. Privilege bestowed immunity from taxes and from interference by the chiefs, but does not appear to have directly included any form of rights over land, as the disputes recorded in XXII and XXIII confirm (see discussion below, pp. 69–75). The first dispute also suggests, as does the sequence of charters VII to XI, that immunity was beginning to fall out of fashion by the middle of the nineteenth century, being replaced, like the administrative estate, by the standard "charitable estate". *Jāh* is the commonest term used for immunity, but *ḥurma*, *karāma* (*ahl al-karāma* in IX) and *ḥurr* also appear as synonyms.[27]

It was probably because immunity was essentially a passive right that it began to decline in importance. The trend can also be seen in XXVIII, where Muḥammad al-Faḍl grants the Zaghāwa chief, Nūr al-Dīn b. Yaḥyā, his maternal relatives (that is, the right to collect their taxes); the latter are described as having been given *al-ḥurma wa'l-jāh*.

## The charitable estate

Most of the charters presented here grant (or confirm the grant of) a landed estate, whose boundaries are usually carefully defined, as a "donation and gift", *ṣadaqa wa-hiba*.[28] A smaller number concede rights over groups of people.[29] Thus both forms of grant fall within the classical Islamic theory of *iqṭā'*, either as "the concession of property", *iqṭā' al-tamlīk*, or "the concession of usufruct", *iqṭā' al-istighlāl*. Furthermore, as Kropàček has noted, the estate system in Dār Fūr has analogies with, for example, developments within the Ottoman empire. If the military/administrative estate described above has parallels to the Ottoman *timar*, the charitable estate is perhaps comparable to the *rizqa*.[30] But whatever the wider parallels, by the nineteenth century the sultans were regularly making grants of allodial property regardless of the function or status of the grantee, whether prince or princess, merchant, notable or holy man.

The sultan, as the sovereign owner of the land, alone had the right to alienate land as freehold. Nor was this seemingly simply a theoretical right; thus in XXIX the sultan confirms the gift of an estate to one of his daughters from her husband. And despite the theoretically irrevocable and heritable nature of such grants, the sultan retained his sovereign rights; in V, the estate called "Bayd", which previously had belonged to Sultan Muḥammad Al-Faḍl's mother, is described as having "reverted to the palace", *raja'at li-bayt al-jibāya*, before being regranted to a *faqīh*.

It is not always clear from the charters for charitable estates if they were intended to be heritable, in contrast to the *jāh*-charters which frequently extend immunity to cover the recipient's kin and followers and their descendants. Among the political elite there was probably a considerable "turn-over"; the estate, "Ni'ama", had four owners – two *maliks*, a *maqdūm* and the *ḥabbōba* Umm Būṣa – before being granted by Muḥammad al-Ḥusayn to his son-in-law (XXXVIII). Similarly, in XLIV, Muḥammad Kannūna is granted an estate that had formerly belonged to another merchant, but references to previous owners in the charters are not common. Not surprisingly, the holy men held on to their land more successfully than the political elite since estates and followers were part of the spoils system; as one example, the all-powerful slave Muḥammad Kurra used estates to win support during the crisis in 1803 that led to the accession of Muḥammad al-Faḍl.[31] But all sought to have their grants confirmed by successive sultans, so that the holy families particularly came to acquire long chains of charters.[32] When ʿAlī Dīnār returned to Dār Fūr in October 1898, he must have been besieged by *faqīhs* and others seeking confirmation of their estates to judge by the flood of charters issued shortly thereafter.

What was granted? People and land, and land that was carefully delimited. The size of these estates, the extent of the cultivable land they contained, the number of villages or people, their yield etc., are all questions yet to be answered. Some estates, like that of Nūr al-Dīn b. Yaḥyā at Qumqūm were evidently large (see map 2); others, like the village of Inqirī, granted "with its fields both fallow and cultivated" (see XLV), were probably much smaller. Size also influenced status; the *faqīh* Nuʿmān was given (but not granted) some land within the *malik* Maydōb's estate (XXXV), while Muḥammad b. Madanī was seemingly granted all of his community's land at Kamala Keirei (XI). However, until the estates are mapped out on the ground, their economic range and potential cannot be adequately described. But to judge by the number of boundary disputes that ended up in court, boundaries were jealously defended.[33]

A comprehensive listing of the grantee's rights in his estate is given in V,

> ...as an allodial estate, with full (rights of) possession and his confirmed property...(namely rights of) cultivation, causing to be cultivated, sale, donation, purchase, demolition and clearance.[34]

This sounds like a formula culled from one of the works of *shurūṭ* or compilations of exemplary legal formulae. The significant rights granted were the right to collect the taxes and judicial fines from the people of the estate and immunity from the visitations of the chiefs and tax collectors. Again, the size and status of the estate presumably determined the value of these rights; the grant of a charitable estate over the lands of one's own community, as at Kamala Keirei, no doubt had a less exploitative implication than the grant of the estate "Niʿama" with its fifty slaves (XXXVIII).

XXXVIII suggests the existence of estate slavery, that is slaves tied serf-like to estates, but it is in fact one of the very few such direct references in the entire corpus. Slaves were undoubtedly widely used; the sultans planted slave settlements (known as *ʿabīdiyya*, see XX and XXI) throughout the state and the ruling elite made extensive use of them.[35] But how integral slaves were to the estate system is not yet known. An intermediate serf-like status, distinguished from slavery, is hinted at in another charter; three men quarrelled with their neighbour,

Tōr b. Ḥāfiẓ b. *al-sulṭān* Aḥmad Bukr. Sultan 'Abd al-Raḥmān resolved the dispute by giving the three men to Aḥmad Bukr's grandson;

> They are to serve him in everything he needs service for, service in sowing, service in his households or guardianship over his property. Thus they, together with his slaves, are equally in his service; and their descendants are to serve the descendants of Ḥāfiẓ after him as an inheritance for them.[36]

If land without people was not especially valuable, people were always of value. In particular, nomads were useful both to supply animal products from their own herds and to herd their lord's animals. And since animals were one of the few ways to conserve "capital", the chiefs who were almost by definition the richest in animals needed herdsmen.[37] In XXIV and XXV some fifty Arabs, in XXVI two men and their small brother, and in XL ten men are granted as "nomads and herders", *'urbān wa-ru'āh*. But in no case are these herders described as slaves. This gift of people as servants also appears in XXVII and XXVIII where *malik* Nūr al-Dīn is granted his maternal relatives (*akhwāl*).

## The procedure

The procedure for obtaining an estate was standardized. Both the documents and oral sources suggest that the would-be grantee made his request in person; *ṭalaba minnī ḥākūra* "he asked me for an estate" (V), *ḥadara amāmanā* "he came before us" (I). He would also usually choose the locality, most often one where he or his ancestors had previously settled (as in VII to XI). Or the petitioner could seek new land;

> Sharīf Thābit came and sought for himself an unoccupied district to be given to him as an estate (*iqṭā'*). So our lord Sultan Muḥammad al-Faḍl told Sharīf Thābit to carve out for himself an estate and record its boundaries and present (the description of the estate) to him. So Sharīf Thābit carved out a locality for himself in Marbūṭa district.[38]

Or the petitioner could seek an already-established estate as in V and XLII.

The next and crucial step was the demarcation of the boundaries of the land to be granted. Demarcation, a judicial process, often took place even when an established (*ma'lūm*) estate was granted anew (as in V) or when earlier charters were presented for confirmation (as in III). The grantee went to the chosen area with a commissioner or *muwajjah*. Two commissioners were usually present for the demarcation; the sultan's representative (often of exalted rank; in V he is the *āb shaykh dālī*) and a representative of the local chief who was thus made aware of the grant. And thereby warned in advance. The procedure is described in XLV: the sultan has given the village of Inqirī to the merchant 'Alī b. Ibrāhīm and sends out the *amīn* 'Abdallāh, who is joined by an official, Ibrāhīm, representing the *amīn* 'Abdallāh Kūr (or Kawr). They met at the village and "Called together the people of the boundaries (i.e. the neighbours) and the *khabīr* 'Alī himself". The boundaries of the village and its land are then demarcated and a deposition drawn up, namely XLV. In another deposition it is made clear that the boundaries were established on oath; "Thirteen men were present (for) the testimony and they swore upon the Qur'ān and went around (the land)."[39] The deposition was taken back to the court and the description of the boundary incorporated into the charter.

Boundaries were marked by reference to prominent local features, hills, trees, rocky outcrops, riverbeds, wells and the like. Apparently in south-western Dār Fūr, where estates were small and near to each other, dry-stone walls were often built to delimit estates.[40] The descriptions are detailed enough to make it possible to trace the estates on the ground.

# 3

# Literacy and chancery

## Official literacy

As the sultanate grew and became more centralized, so its administrative system became more literate. But official literacy was not only a function of centralization, it was also the result of Islamization, if only because the bearers of literacy were the *fuqarā'* or holy men.[1] Their imprint is made manifest not least by the numerous Qur'ānic echoes to be found in the documents that follow. By the nineteenth century, routine administrative letters were issued not only by the sultans and the great chiefs but also by the district and local chiefs. Equally letters were exchanged about what would seem to have been comparatively minor matters.[2]

While all that was written was written in Arabic the spoken language of the court was generally Fur. Although the sultans and their courtiers usually knew both languages,[3] Fur was preferred as the spoken language.[4] It would, however, be very difficult to deduce this from the documents themselves, where only a handful of Fur titles and placenames appear in the Arabic script. This functional bilingualism remained until the end of the sultanate; even 'Alī Dīnār, who apparently knew enough Arabic to compose a poem in praise of the Prophet,[5] Dictated his correspondence in Fur which was taken down directly into Arabic.[6] Whatever the spoken language of daily life and administration, be it Fur or one of the other languages current in Dār Fūr, all official correspondence was in Arabic and, unlike West Africa, seemingly no attempt was made to reduce any of the local languages to writing.

In this situation of linguistic complexity, Marc Bloch's warning quoted at the beginning seems appropriate. The use of the language and forms of Arabic diplomatic by the *faqīh*/scribes, however maladroit their employment of these was on occasion, obscures the underlying Fur dimension. This caveat should be remembered in the discussions that follow, and in any criticism of the failure by the *faqīhs* to attain to the "classical" norms.

## An official chancery?

It is an unresolved question if there was in the pre-1874 sultanate a chancery in the accepted sense of an institution or institutions for the reception, issuing, copying, registering and retention of official correspondence. When he restored the sultanate in 1898, ʻAlī Dīnār introduced an efficient chancery run by a body of secretaries under the *faqīh* Abbakr al-Sanūsī; his letters are generally standardized in their writing and format.[7] But ʻAlī Dīnār knew the Mahdist chancery, as is reflected in some of the forms used in his letters. Nothing is known of the fate of the archives of the pre-1874 sultanate – if they existed – although some of the spoils from the occupation of al-Fāshir in 1874 found their way to a museum in Cairo.[8] An argument against the existence of a formal secretariat is the lack of any indication in the documents as to where they were drawn up. However, some tax records were kept at court; when Nachtigal asked in al-Fāshir in 1874 if there were any historical records he might consult, all that he was given, apart from a few royal genealogies, were, "Government documents of which only the part which fixed the *dīwān*, taxes or imposts, for the whole kingdom, presented any interest."[9] This suggests an intermediate stage in the evolution of bureaucratic practice whereby the mechanisms for the issuing of documents with a more or less standard format existed, but not for consistently registering and preserving copies. The onus for preserving the charters and legal judgments lay with the individual or party who benefited from them. It would seem, therefore, that while incoming letters, tax records and the like were kept at court, outgoing correspondence was not copied and stored.[10] However, on some legal judgments issued by deputy judges (*nāʼib sharʻī*) there appear marks of authentication from a senior judge (see XXII); these may indicate that *sijills* were circulated and preserved in more than one copy.[11]

The documents were written by *faqīhs*, but their names are rarely given; here, and this is characteristic of the whole corpus, only the scribe of XXVI and XXVII is named, ʻUbaydallāh ʻUthmān.[12] Cuny describes a Shaykh Ṣalāḥ (or Ṣāliḥ) as "the secretary of the Sultan (Muḥammad al-Ḥusayn)".[13] One informative reference to a *kātib* occurs at the end of a letter from Sultan Muḥammad al-Faḍl to Muḥammad ʻAlī Pasha of Egypt, in reply to a demand from the latter that the sultanate submit to Egypt. The demand is stoutly rejected by the Keira sultan in a letter embellished with appropriate Qurʼānic quotations and written by "the *faqīh* Muḥammad wad ʻAmmārī, a graduate (*mutakharrij*) of al-Azhar and tutor (*mudarris*) to the Sultan Muḥammad al-Faḍl and his sons at al-Fāshir".[14] The unnamed secretaries can often be recognized by their handwriting and associated with particular sultans and seals; VII, a

- 1 From The Sultans
  - internal
    - originating charter, *maktūb*, *wathīqa*, *rasm*
    - confirmatory charters
    - administrative letters, *rasm*
    - letters to *fuqarā'*, e.g. IV
    - letters of appointment, *farmān*
    - letters of commission
    - *sijills*
  - external
    - deeds of property, *ḥujja*
    - letters to foreign powers or persons
    - *laissez-passers* for pilgrims/travellers
- 2 From administrative officials
  - confirmatory charters
  - administrative letters
  - *sijills*
- 3 From *qāḍīs* or their deputies
  - *sijills*
  - related legal documents

Diagram 2. *A typology of documents issued by the sultans and their officials*

charter from 'Abd al-Raḥmān, is written in the same fine hand as two other charters from the same sultan.[15] Similarly, VIII and XVI, both from Muḥammad al-Faḍl, are by the same hand; the writer of these and two other documents[16] left characteristically wide right-hand margins and used the same seal. Less easy to distinguish are the various secretaries who served Muḥammad al-Ḥusayn; IX, X and XLIII were probably written by the same scribe, again with the same seal.[17] This latter appears to suggest that different secretaries had charge of different seals – the typology of the seals is discussed in Chapter 4 – a tantalizing hint that the system was rather more sophisticated than we at present know.[18]

The variety of documents so far discovered reflects the range of activity of the sultan and his officials (see Diagram 2). Some of these activities form the subject of this book, the granting or confirmation of privileges or lands, the rendering of legal judgments. These may be termed the internal activities of the chancery, but evidence survives of external legal and diplomatic activity. Appropriately, since the expansion of the trade between Egypt and Dār Fūr from about 1750 was of crucial importance to the latter, some of the earliest examples are commercial. These were *ḥujaj* (sing. *ḥujja*) or deeds listing the property of merchants who had died in the sultanate which were drawn up and sealed with the sultan's seal before being forwarded to Cairo.[19]

Just as some of the correspondence of medieval Muslim rulers has been preserved in the archives of their European recipients, so some Dār Fūr letters have survived in the same haphazard way. The most celebrated are the letters from 'Abd al-Raḥmān to Bonaparte in Egypt written in late 1798, in which the sultan requests safe passage for his caravans, complains of Mamluk extortion and asks for the restoration of the original customs rates.[20] Others have survived in the travel literature; in one the Pethericks are politely denied leave to visit the sultanate, in another the Austrian Consul in Khartoum is told that Muḥammad al-Ḥusayn knew nothing about the murder in Wadai of the German explorer Eduard Vogel.[21] Naturally the letters that have survived are miscellaneous in their content; thus Muḥammad al-Faḍl writes to a *faqīh* at al-Dabba on the Nile donating to his mosque 60 slaves, 140 head of cattle, 40 horses, 5 camels, 80 *mithqals* of gold and a number of brocaded saddles – an immense *ṣadaqa*, the occasion for which is not unfortunately known.[22] Some of the correspondence between the rulers of Egypt and Dār Fūr has also been preserved;[23] in one letter Muḥammad al-Faḍl greatly offended Muḥammad ʻAlī by omitting to call him "brother", because the latter was not technically an independent ruler.[24]

Dār Fūr's position on the *ṭarīq al-sūdān*, the pilgrim route from West Africa, gave rise to another category of document, the safe-conduct. Thus Muḥammad al-Faḍl issues a safe-conduct for one Muḥammad al-Barnāwī, while Ibrāhīm Qaraḍ issues a very similarly worded document for the traveller Gustav Nachtigal.[25]

Among the internal activities of the chancery not represented in this volume are letters of appointment issued to chiefs and others; Nachtigal records as a very bad omen at the opening of a campaign that,

> the sultan had provided [the *maqdum* ʻAbd al-ʻAzīz] with a firman, commission, with a red seal instead of the customary black one, and had given him a black burnus instead of a red one.[26]

Whether such letters of appointment were regularly given in the pre-1874 Sultanate is uncertain, but several later ones have survived.[27] It is also probable that the sultans on occasion appointed by letter merchants to act as *khabīrs* or caravan leaders, especially as they often carried out diplomatic missions for the former.[28] One less common category was a letter of commission granting permission to make a raid for slaves, *ghazwa* or *salaṭiyya*, in the southern borderlands; al-Tūnisī gives what may be a reasonably authentic example from Muḥammad al-Faḍl.[29]

The existence of a chancery at the court can be deduced rather than described. We know that it existed by reason of the documents that have survived; we can surmise that it was institutionalized because of the latter's conventions and forms, and we can gain a partial idea of its range, membership and functions. Of its inner workings and organization, we know at present very little.

# 4

## A diplomatic commentary

### Physical description and language

The documents were written in black ink on imported handmade paper which came mainly from Italy via Egypt.[1] The sultanate must have consumed paper in considerable quantities; documents were written only on the recto, often with a wide right-hand margin, and the writing is not crabbed in an effort to save paper. In fact Dār Fūr appears to have re-exported paper further west.[2] The documents do not conform to any standard size; the average is perhaps between 25 to 30 by 15 to 20 centimetres.

The range of literary competence, from the perspective of "standard" Arabic, is very broad; II, for example, is stylistically a polished production, while XXXI has several very colloquial passages. A detailed study of the local forms and deviations can only be profitably pursued in conjunction with a study of the different forms of Dār Fūr colloquial Arabic.[3]

Over and above the occasional scribal error, there are certain consistent misspellings, for example the use of "t" for *tā' marbūṭa* as in *ḥaḍra* "presence". Some of these errors of orthography arise from the transfer of speech habits to the written form; thus "s" for "ṣ" or "th", "t" for "th", and "h" for "ḥ". Also common is a tendency to drop the *alif maqṣūra*.

Lexically a number of usages appear in the documents, the most numerous being the topographical and botanical names which are listed in a separate index (see pp. 157–8). Other local words include *shawba* (in VIII and elsewhere) meaning "warband"; *zawl* (in XIX and XLV) "man", and *khalbāṭ* "trouble, confusion" (in XXXII). In the case of titles, some are clearly derived from Fur, e.g. *falqanāwī*, pl. *falāqna*, "royal messenger, herald" from *folgony*; the origins of others are less certain. *Shartay* (or *sharṭay*), pl. *sharāti*, "district chief" is said to come from the Daju *chorte*, which like the Fur for *shartay*, *kiiso*, can mean both "drum" and "chief"; *mayram*, pl. *mayārim*, "princess" may be Kanuri in origin, while *fāshir*, which may be a Tubu word, in the sense of "royal encampment" was widely used outside Dār Fūr (see further, index of titles and honorifics, pp. 151–3).

Among the grammatical and syntactical peculiarities may be mentioned a phrase that appears in a number of the inscriptions (*inscriptiones*) of the charters:

> *ilā ḥaḍrati kulli man taqifu ʻalayhi hadhihi'l-wathīqa...min al-umarā'*...(III),

literally, "To the presence of anyone at whom this document shall stop...from among the *amīrs*...(which we have translated as, "To everyone to whom this document comes"). This reverses the commonly found formula:

> *ilā kulli man yaqif ʻalā hādha'l-maktūb...min* (VII),

"To all who encounter this document...from among."[4] A direct transfer from the colloquial language is the not infrequent use of the definite article as a relative pronoun; thus in XXXI we find *al-sayyidnā* for *alladhi sayyidnā* "which our lord...", *al-makān al-Nuʻmān* "the place which Nuʻmān..." (XXXIV), and *al-yarushshhum* "he who sprinkles on them..." (VIII and elsewhere).[5] There is also a constant uncertainty as to the use of the feminine and masculine forms (and a failure to make them agree); thus in XIII, for example, one finds *tilka'l-arḍ* and *dhalika'l-arḍ* in the same sentence. The scribes also found it difficult to move from direct to indirect speech (see XXXVII). On this latter point, it may be noted that colloquial forms most frequently recur in the reported speeches of the disputants in court, which suggests a measure of direct reporting.[6]

In regard to the writing of the numerals there are also some peculiarities; occasionally dates are written backwards, that is following the direction of the writing, for example in XLV. Three unusual forms that recur are 8 φ and ϒ. The first also appears on several official letters from Borno and Bivar has argued at length that it represents "eight".[7] His arguments, which have been disputed for Borno,[8] seem also to fall down in Dār Fūr. Thus XLII has its seal-date written as ١٢8٣. The charter is clearly dated 1256 and it would seem therefore that 8 must equal "five". This is the most decisive example, but elsewhere it also seems more likely that the figure represents "five" and it has been taken as such in this volume. The second figure is probably "five" as well,[9] but the value of the third figure remains for the moment unresolved.

## The structure of the charters

Structurally the documents may be divided into two general categories, the charters and other administrative letters and the *sijills* (on the latter, see above p. 10). The charters and letters, whether issued by the sultan or his officials, follow the same general format which may, in the terminology of the European medievalists, include some or all of the following elements, namely *sigillum* (seal), *invocatio*, *intitulatio*, *inscriptio*, *expositio*, *dispositio*, *sanctio*, *datum* and *locus*. The following comments are not intended as a complete diplomatic commentary but rather to distinguish some of the main elements; individual idiosyncracies are discussed in the commentary upon the documents. Some comparative comments are made, but it is difficult to venture too far here since so little material has been published from other parts of Sudanic Africa. Indeed, Islamicists have tended to concentrate on Ottoman and Persian practice, where there are substantial archives, to the neglect of the Arabic tradition.[10] To compare Dār Fūr practice directly with the usages of the islamic heartlands risks missing the crucial intermediate step of internal development within the Sudanic Belt.

### (a) *The seal*

All the charters and most of the *sijills* and administrative letters are sealed above the text;[11] a few charters bear the same seal impression twice (e.g. V) and one *sijill* (XLIII) has the same seal impression placed symmetrically in a pyramidal form three times. Three documents, two from a *takanāwī* and one from two *shartays*, in an archive not given here, bear what appear to be camel-brands in place of a seal.[12]

Despite the simplicity of their wording, the seals are of great interest. They were made from copper and inked over to give a white impression on a black background (but see above p. 25). Their quality varies enormously, some are very fine, others crude, reflecting perhaps the difference between home-made and imported seals.[13] Some were imported from Egypt; the young al-Tūnisī on his way to Dār Fūr in 1218/1803 along the desert route met a courier going to Cairo, "to renew [*li-tajdīd*] the seal, with which the sultan's orders were sealed, because there was no one proficient [in making them] there [in Dār Fūr]".[14]

As for the respect in which the sultan's seal was held, Cuny has a revealing story; Muḥammad al-Ḥusayn invited one of the leading Coptic merchants of Asyūṭ, Surian Shinūda, to settle in Dār Fūr,

> Since the protocol of the Fur court did not permit that the imperial seal should be affixed to a decree without it being rigorously enforced, and perhaps because the [sealed] decree should not be given to a foreigner, still less a Christian,[15] the *khabīr* [caravan leader] took the seal itself with him, as a token of the mission with which he had been entrusted, namely to bring back to Dār Fūr a son of the House of Shinūda. The proposal was not accepted.[16]

It is beyond the scope of this introduction to establish a typology of all the sultanic and other seals used in the corpus. The oldest seal is that of Aḥmad Bukr which heads the two charters of Muḥammad Dawra referred to above (p. 13); it is well made and reads simply, "The Sultan Abbakr, son of the Sultan Mūsā". All the later sultans had more than one seal.[17] Their wording is simple, almost invariably giving no more than the sultan's pedigree which never goes back beyond Sulaymān, described in one of Muḥammad al-Ḥusayn's seals as *ṣāḥib al-birr wa'l-iḥsān* "lord of righteousness and beneficence"; thus consigning the shadowy, and probably pagan, Fur kings of Jabal Marra before him to official oblivion. Occasionally, on some of Muḥammad al-Faḍl and Muḥammad al-Ḥusayn's seals, a verse or two from the Qur'ān is given in a panel around the seal's circumference.[18]

The seals usually bear dates which are not necessarily accession dates. Thus Tayrāb's seal, which appears on two charters,[19] bears the date 1172/1758–59 which for other reasons is probably not his accession date. Nor can 1214/1799–1800, which appears on some of ʻAbd al-Raḥmān's charters (see VIII), be his accession date. *Per contra*, 1218/1803–4 on Muḥammad al-Faḍl's seals probably is the date of his accession. The dates on the various seals of Muḥammad al-Ḥusayn produce two confusions; some examples end with the statement, "He acceded to power on Wednesday, 22 Ṣafar al-Khayr 1254", that is 17 May 1838. Since it is known from other sources that he came to power in 1254, this can reasonably be taken as his accession date. However, some examples of the seal, in form otherwise identical, end with the date, 22 Ṣafar al-Khayr 1256; one explanation is that several cuttings of this seal were ordered from Cairo and the year filled in (or altered) when appropriate.

### (b) *The invocatio*

There is considerable variation in the use of the formal diplomatic elements within the documents. This is even more the case with the invocations than with the intitulations and inscriptions, the latter having a greater regularity of form. At first sight, but perhaps misleadingly, their presence or absence, their particular form, reflect simply the idiosyncrasies of the scribes.

Our earliest examples, Muḥammad Dawra's two charters, are consistent; both have the phrase, *al-ḥamd li-llāh waḥdah*, written in the left-hand corner above the seal, recalling very remotely Almohad practice.[20] By contrast, the two documents from Sultan Tayrāb begin directly with the *intitulatio*. All the charters of 'Abd al-Raḥmān begin with an *invocatio*,[21] either elaborate as in II or relatively simple with a *basmala* and *taṣliyya* as in VII and XXIV (but preceded by *bi-barakatih* in XXVI and XXVII), similar to Funj practice of about the same period.[12]

The *invocationes* of Muḥammad al-Faḍl's charters have several distinctive features. Almost all begin with the motto, *mā shā' allāh*, placed below the seal. The *invocatio* itself consists of a *basmala* and *taṣliyya* usually preceded by the phrase, *bi-barakatih* (as in VIII, XXV, XXVIII and XXXVI).[23] In most of these a space equal to two or three lines of text is left between the *invocatio* and the rest of the text. This is vaguely reminiscent of Mamluk and earlier decrees where the space was used for the *'alāma*, the motto or signature of the ruler.[24] But of this there is no hint in our charters.

Muḥammad al-Ḥusayn's documents are consistent in usually not having an *invocatio*; here only I, a charter that also differs in other respects, opens with a *basmala* and *taṣliyya*. With equal consistency 'Alī Dīnār's documents always have an *invocatio* (see VI and XII); but here, as in almost all other aspects of their diplomatic, his documents conform to Mahdist models.[25]

### (c) *Intitulatio*

The *intitulatio* may be divided into the substantive titles and laudatory epithets. Of the titles, the sovereign and earliest one is *sulṭān* which is all that appears in the two charters of Muḥammad Dawra. It may not be too wrong to suggest that *sulṭān* rendered in Arabic *aba kuuri* or *fɔraŋ eri*, "lord of obeisance" or "exalted of the Fur", the Fur titles of the ruler. "Sultan" always remained the sovereign title, in the sense of coming directly before the ruler's name,[26] although construct titles soon appear in Tayrāb's charters, where we find *sulṭān al-muslimīn* and *khalīfat rabb al-'ālamīn* (in DF166.18/26) and *sulṭān al-'arab wa'l-'ajam* (DF173.18/33). "Sultan of the Muslims" is used by virtually all the subsequent sultans as is *khalīfa* in various constructions, all very exalted in their religious implications, the most frequently recurring being *khalīfat rasūl rabb al-'ālamīn* and *khalīfat ummat sayyid al-mursalīn*. What significance these and less theologically-charged titles such as *khādim al-sharīʿa wa'l-dīn* had for those who wrote them is hard to say. It is, however, striking that despite lengthier and far more fulsome laudatory phrases, the charters of Sinnār or Borno rarely make such overweening religious claims.[27]

The *intitulationes* used by ʿAbd al-Raḥmān and his son have certain features in common, among them the listing of laudatory epithets when the sultan is named after the *ammā baʿd*; the commonest listing is *al-mabrūr al-mu'ayyad al-manṣūr al-sulṭān al-madhkūr*.[28] The scribes of both rulers were evidently receptive to outside influences; in some of ʿAbd al-Raḥmān's charters Ottoman (and earlier) titles appear, such as *sulṭān al-barrayn wa'l-baḥrayn*, "Sultan of the Two Lands (i.e. Europe and Asia) and the Two Seas (i.e. the Black and the Mediterranean Seas)", and *khādim al-ḥaramayn al-sharīfayn*, "Guardian of the Two Noble Sanctuaries (i.e. Mecca and Medina)", both somewhat inappropriate for the ruler of a kingdom in the middle of Africa.[29] The phrase, *al-sulṭān ibn al-sulṭān*, which appears in II, also recalls Ottoman practice.[30] ʿAbd al-Raḥmān's scribes may have borrowed these directly since he is said to have sent rich presents to the Ottoman Sultan, who replied bestowing upon him the *laqab*, *al-rashīd*, which appears in XXVI and XXVII here and is frequently used of him by later rulers.[31] The use of two titles, *khāqān* "sovereign" (*al-khāqān al-akram* in XVII and XXIX) and *qahramān* "steward" (in XXVIII),[32] which appear only in charters of Muḥammad al-Faḍl, may be a further Ottoman echo.

But how variable these constructions were, may be seen by comparing the exceedingly elaborate *intitulatio* that introduces Muḥammad al-Faḍl's letter of defiance to Muḥammad ʿAlī Pasha with the simplicity of, "From the Sultan of Fur", *min sulṭān fūr*, in a letter accompanying sumptuous presents to a *faqīh* near Dongola.[33] The titles and epithets of Muḥammad al-Ḥusayn, however, do appear to have a certain regularity of form, ranging from the simple as in X to the elaborate in III and V. One puzzle is the appearance in some[34] but not all of his letters of the *laqab*, *al-mahdī*; for a ruler as devout as Muḥammad al-Ḥusayn this must have had some significance, but nothing is known about its use from Dār Fūr sources.

One of the most significant historically of Islamic titles, denoting classically leadership of the Muslim community, *amīr al-mu'minīn* "Commander of the Faithful", first appears in Muḥammad al-Faḍl's charters (XXIX, XXXII, XXXV and XXXVII). By Muḥammad al-Ḥusayn and ʿAlī Dīnār it is almost invariably used, appearing just before the final "sultan" that defined the name. From the examples of its use in the western and central Sudanic Belt brought together by Murray Last, it would appear to have long been used in the area, but largely without any recognition of its classical implications.[35] To Last's examples one may add not only Dār Fūr but also Wadai; two very late sultanic letters from the latter begin, *min amīr al-mu'minīn sayyidinā al-sulṭān*...[36] However, it seems not to have been used in Sinnār.

### (d) *Inscriptio*

If the titles used by the sultans strive to situate them in a Muslim context, the *inscriptiones* are more directly informed by Dār Fūr realities. As with the other diplomatic elements, they show an increasing elaboration over time; the inscription in one of Muḥammad Dawra's charters reads simply, "(To) all the governors and leading notables", *jamīʿ al-ḥukkām wa-wulāt al-umūr*.[37] By 'Abd al-Raḥmān's time the *inscriptio* had grown into a list of titles defining the main groups who, within the state, were "the lords of the state and holders of power", *asyād al-dawla wa-aṣḥāb al-ṣawla*. But there is also a seemingly less flattering description; "And all the oppressors who trample upon the rights of the Muslims".[38] From its position within the *inscriptio*, it does appear to be in apposition to the preceding title-holders. The only parallel phrasing known to the present writers comes from a charter (of uncertain date) copied into the West African Chronicle, *Ta'rīkh al-fattāsh*, where the *inscriptio* opens, "Let every oppressor and miscreant from among our personal forces, the men of our army, our high-handed officials...withold his oppression from them...", in effect combining the *inscriptio* with the *sanctio* (on the latter, see below p. 33).[39]

Within the *inscriptio* the titles are carefully and systematically grouped together, royal titles ("sons of the sultan(s)", *mayram* and *ḥabbōba*), central and provincial administrative titles (*wazīr*, *maqdūm*, *malik*, *shartay* and *dimlij*), and the tax officials (*jabbay*, *makkās* and *qawwār*). Moreover, the ranking of these groups appears to have varied from charter to charter; thus the royal titles tended to sink down over time in the listings (compare VII, VIII and X). In charters concerning nomads, the nomad chiefs (*malik*, *kursī* and *shaykh*) are included (see XXIV, XXV, XXVI and XXXIX), although they are not specifically named in those charters granting land. This precision of usage is confirmed by a charter from Kordofan whose *inscriptio* includes "the shaykhs and chiefs of Kordofān".[40]

### (e) *Expositio and dispositio*

The organization of the elements within the body (*ṣadr*) of the charter (*maktūb*, *kitāb*, *jawāb*, *rasm*, or occasionally *wathīqa*) is far from rigid; essentially there was an *expositio* or narration and a *dispositio*, defining the charter's purpose, although not necessarily in this order. The wording is stereotyped, brief and to the point, markedly so by comparison with the Funj charters. Whatever the structure of a particular charter, the sequence of events is usually clear; the request for a grant or the presentation of an earlier charter (or charters) in the case of a confirmation, occasionally the demarcation of the estate again and the issuance of the charter.

Originating charters, that is, those that initially grant land, privilege or people, begin their *expositio* abruptly; there is little trace of the *arenga* of many European and classical Islamic charters. Occasionally general principles are enunciated, notably in I, a charter suffused by a religious spirit absent in the others, and less explicitly in, for example, V,

> Since we have relinquished this to him that he may seek support therein in his affairs, both religious and mundane. And in this we hope for a reward from God on the Day of Resurrection and Return, and God is a surety for what we say.[41]

The confirmatory charters usually begin with a brief exposition of the circumstances of their being issued; the initiative came from the recipient who presented his charter or charters at court for confirmation, or made a request for the grant to be confirmed. The earlier charters were examined (*naẓara*) to see whether they were authentic (*ṣaḥīḥ*, *ṣawāb*). This was no formality; in a court hearing of 1271/1854–55 before Muḥammad al-Ḥusayn, the sultan nullifies a forged charter,

> We found it to be a forgery (*muzawwar*) both in its handwriting and seal; so we have rendered it null and void and have expunged it from the court (*al-majlis*).[42]

Following this judgment, the sultan issued a brief decree (rather than a charter) confirming the authenticity of the charters belonging to the successful litigants (DF102.13/5).

In the *dispositio*, the sultan gave or assigned the grant (*a'ṭā*, *aqṭa'a*) or confirmed (*tammama*, *atmama*, *amḍā*) the earlier charters. As we have seen, in some instances a detailed description of the estate's boundaries is given. The *dispositio* often ends with a statement of the legal nature of the grant (*iqṭā'*, *hiba*, *ṣadaqa*).

### (f) *Final injunctions*

The *sanctio* cannot always be easily disentangled from the *dispositio*; the most common introduction to the former is, "Let none interfere", *lā aḥad yata'arraḍ*. These prohibitions were especially directed towards the tax officials, who are often specifically named. Despite the fierceness of some of the sanctions, for example in VIII, the tax officials appear occasionally to have ignored them (see above, p. 8), where the sultan reproves a *jabbay*). However, the general expectation of obedience may explain the brevity of the sanctions when compared to the elaborate but probably less effectual threats found in the later Funj charters.

There is little regularity in the dating of the charters or court transcripts; some are fully dated, some by the year only, many are undated. None give any *locus* or indication of where they had been drawn up.

# 5

## Translations and commentary

### I: The *faqīh* 'Abdallāh's charter

The first charter[1] presented here eloquently describes one aspect of the relationship between the sultans and the *fuqarā'*, the material rewards granted by the former in return for spiritual services by the latter. Here Sultan Muḥammad al-Ḥusayn issues a charter for the *faqīh* 'Abdallāh b. Abu'l-Ḥasan, confirming an earlier grant of land to the *faqīh* by Muḥammad al-Faḍl. The *faqīh* had been granted the land for teaching the sultan's sons the Qur'ān.

There is another example of such a grant; a *faqīh* Muḥammad of the Mīma people, a small Arabized tribe living to the south-east of al-Fāshir, taught the children of 'Abd al-Raḥmān, who granted him an estate at Simayn near Wadā'a, the centre of the Mīma.[2]

The charter's form differs markedly from others issued by the same sultan, but there is no reason to doubt its authenticity. Among the differences are the presence of an *invocatio*, a *basmala* and *ḥamdala*, where Muḥammad al-Ḥusayn's charters usually open directly with the *intitulatio, min ḥadra*. . . , and the generally humble tone of the *intitulatio*. Similarly, the religious feeling in the quotation from Muḥammad al-Faḍl's charter contrasts with the usual tone of his charters.

## I

*seal* . . .

In the name of God, the Compassionate, the Merciful: praise be to God, and blessing and peace be upon the Messenger of God and his family, with peace.

Thereafter: says the lowly slave, who confesses his sin and

shortcoming and seeks the forgiveness of his Lord, the Omnipotent; scion of the pious ones and offspring of the good [and] pure, the Commander of the Faithful and Sultan of the Muslims, Sultan Ḥusayn, son of the late Sultan Muḥammad al-Faḍl.

The *faqīh* 'Abdallāh, son of the *faqīh* Abu'l-Ḥasan, came before us and showed us an order from our father, the late Sultan Muḥammad al-Faḍl. We examined it and found therein a statement which said:

> The *faqīh* 'Abdallāh, son of the *faqīh* Abu'l-Ḥasan, has shown kindness by teaching my sons the Qur'ān and this is the most meritorious act of kindness, for as the Most High God said, "What should be the reward for kindness if not kindness"?[3] Therefore, we sought for something [to reward] his kindness, so I considered the land and found that it endures until the end of time and found it the most worthy and suitable form of recompense. So I assigned him a piece of land and made it an endowment[4] for him, as a gift and donation for himself and his descendants. None are to dispute with them concerning it until the end of time, and I have marked the boundaries for them.

Then I looked at the order of our father and found it a most suitable proceeding. We confirmed and ratified for him the gift of our father, Sultan Muḥammad al-Faḍl, as a gift and donation, that he should take [literally, "eat"] the *fiṭr*, *zakāh*, *ḥāmil* and the customary taxes.

The boundaries run along [the land of] the Isirr[a] [people][5] by the thicket and the rocks of the [cultivable] land [*ḥajar al-ṭīn*], and in the middle of the rocks and east of the depression; and cross the floodbed going east at Khayr Khanaqa, and run by [the land of] the Awlād Dardūq through the marshy ground to the north of the hill and south of 'Āīsh m.l.f.ḥ., and by the rock in the middle of the sand patch and the middle of Umm Habīlāt [i.e. "the mother of the *habīl* trees"], and east of Umm Qarqaf, and east of the rounded rock below the sand patch, and north; and [the boundaries] run with [the land of] the Awlād Khamīs and Bilāl at the white rocks, and descend to the rocky outcrop; and run with [the land of] the people of Jadīd at al-Sayl[6] between the marshy ground and the sand patch until they reach between Karās and the fields of the *imām* Sa'd al-Dīn[7] and by the *sayyāl* and *ḥijlij al-na'sh* trees;[8] and they descend at the riverbed and reach the deserted cultivations and south between the rocks; and they descend by the al-Fāshir road to the thicket.

This we have given him, for as the Most High God said, "This is Our gift and He makes abundant and withholds as He wishes."[9]

In [Dhu'l-] ḥijja...

## II to VI: The Jawāmi'a fuqarā' of Jadīd al-Sayl[1]

Twelve miles north of al-Fāshir along the modern lorry track to Millīṭ (Mellit) lies the settlement of Jadid al-Sayl, the "new" village by the "floodbed" (*al-sayl*) that brings rain water down to al-Fāshir via the Ḥallūf water course. The present village, built around the mosque, lies just east of Jabal Jadīd.

Various holy clans have been settled in the district since the early eighteenth century; most claim to have come from the Jawāmi'a people of central Kordofān and their clan names, Awlād Jāmi', A. Mūrunj, A. Sulaymān, Ja'afiriyya and Ghanamiyya, are also to be found among the Kordofān Jawāmi'a.[2] The history of these clans has yet to be investigated and indeed only a few of their documents have yet been located and photographed, but it is clear that Jadīd was an important religious settlement comparable to the Fallāta community at Kerio[3] or the Borno (Kanuri) centre at Manawāshī.

Browne described the settlement in about 1794,

> It is a town of *Fukkara*, who are reported to be so little famous for hospitality, that they will hardly furnish to a traveller water to allay his thirst. In this town are many houses, and some of them belong to merchants who derive their origin from the eastward.[4]

The district has always been important because of its strategic location on the northern approach to al-Fāshir and its constant water. It was between Jadīd and Ḥallūf that Mūsā 'Anqarīb defeated his father, Sultan Muḥammad Dawra, in civil war about 1720, and nearby at Selei in 1916 that the battle of Biringia between 'Alī Dīnār and the British led to the final annexation of Dār Fūr to the Sudan.[5]

A fine red brick mosque stands at Jadīd al-Sayl. One tradition has it that an earlier mosque was built by Sultan 'Umar Lel, who is also said to have first established a village there.[6] However, document II implies that at least one group of *fuqarā'* had settled there by the reign of Muḥammad Dawra, 'Umar Lel's predecessor. The charter is incomplete, but III may confirm that the original grant by Dawra was given to endow a mosque. The present mosque is ascribed locally to

Sultan ʻAbd al-Raḥmān; it is a square structure built of large red bricks with several rows of pillars, in which is buried the famous *qāḍī* ʻIzz al-Dīn.[7]

Since little is known of the district's history, any exegesis must be based on the charters. They illustrate, however, a sultanic policy of encouraging the building of mosques and the settlement of *fuqarā*ʼ around the capital. Mosques still stand at al-Firsh, Jadīd Rās al-Fīl, Kerio (but now covered by sand), Manawāshī, Azagarfa/Arāri and at the now-deserted commercial centre of Kobbei. At Azagarfa, for example, *al-ḥājj* ʻAbd al-Nūrayn, also from Kordofān, is said to have built the mosque there with the assistance of Muḥammad al-Faḍl.[8]

The first two charters, II and III, both confirm a grant of land at Qiraywud al-Zarāf, west of Jadīd al-Sayl. The sequence of events is complex and may be set out thus,

(a) Sultan Muḥammad Dawra grants Qiraywud al-Zarāf to the *faqīh* Muḥammad ʻIzz al-Dīn as "a donation, benefice and endowment", *taṣaddaqa wa-ḥabbasa wa-waqqafa*.

(b) The endowment is ratified by sultan ʻUmar Lel,

(c) and by Sultan Abu'l-Qāsim,

(d) and by Sultan Muḥammad Tayrāb.

Neither the original nor the three confirmatory charters have survived, but that they once existed in written form is confirmed by III, where "shaykh Musallim presented their charters (*kutub*) to (Sultan Muḥammad al-Faḍl)".

(e) The endowment is confirmed for Muḥammad ʻIzz al-Dīn's sons by Sultan ʻAbd al-Raḥmān; this is II.

(f) Some years later Musallim b. Muḥammad ʻIzz al-Dīn presents the earlier charters to Muḥammad al-Faḍl, who sends out a commissioner to demarcate the boundaries which may have been under dispute. The endowment is confirmed in a charter issued on 2 Dhu'l-ḥijja 1221/10 February 1807 where it is described as "a perpetual endowment so that they can make use of its land tax (*kharāj*) for the mosque". A précis or extract from this charter is given in III.

(g) The *imām* Ibrāhīm b. Saʻd al-Dīn, "master of the mosque at al-Jadīd", whose relationship to Muḥammad ʻIzz al-Dīn is unknown, presents Muḥammad al-Faḍl's charter to Sultan Muḥammad al-Ḥusayn, who confirms it in III.

Thus II and III appear to be the lone survivors of at least seven charters issued. On grounds of style and calligraphy II is the most impressive charter so far discovered. It was perhaps not written by one of the sultan's regular secretaries; it may be compared with VII which bears the same seal. No other document from ʻAbd al-Raḥmān begins similarly or has an *invocatio* beginning with a *ḥamdala*, and the only one that has a similarly elaborate rhyming *intitulatio* is the charter transcribed in al-Tūnisī's book (1965), 68–9/50–1) and which may have been drafted by the author's father. Also noteworthy is the phrase, *dārunā al-fūrāwiyya* "our Fur land" which appears nowhere else.

# II

*seal* Sultan ʿAbd al-Raḥmān, son of Sultan Aḥmad Bukr, son of Sultan Mūsā: the year 1214.[9]

Surely, in truth, our refuge is in God.

Praise be to God, the True; praise Him: may the blessings of God be upon our Lord Muḥammad, His Prophet and Servant, his companions and his family after him.

From the pre-eminent among his peers and the luminary of his contemporaries, who has been singled out from among them by successive favours and boundless virtues, as the sun [is singled out] at noontime and the moon among the shining stars. Our lord [the sultan, son of the sultan], the glorious Sultan ʿAbd al-Raḥmān, may God render him victorious over all his enemies and support him. Amen.

To all who encounter this charter; *maliks*, *amīrs*...of the state, *wazīrs*, *qāḍīs* and the generality of the Muslims.

Sultan Muḥammad donated, gave as a benefice [*ḥabbasa*] and endowed the land of Qiraywud al-Zarāf to the *faqīh* Muḥammad ʿIzz al-Dīn and his descendants. Then Sultan ʿUmar implemented this and ratified it; then Sultan Abu'l-Qāsim implemented this and ratified it; Sultan Muḥammad Tayrāb then implemented this.

Now I, inasmuch as God, the Benefactor, has made me ruler in the kingdom of my father, have confirmed this benefice [*ḥubs*] uninterrupted endowment and present donation for the purpose of obtaining the approbation of the most high God, with [the hope of] succour in obedience to the most high God. Let none of the people of our Fur land meddle with the sons of Muḥammad ʿIzz al-Dīn and their descendants. I have confirmed this with all its boundaries.

These [run] from al-Muḥayr and to the hillocks of al-Wayka [Qiraywud al-Wayka] and to m.d.bā; and to the rain pool of al-Sharāk and by the water course of al-Sharāk to the two *tabaldī* trees, and to the *tabaldī* tree of the fields of Abū Hajūra; and to the fallen *tabaldī* in the direction of the new path to the hillocks at the rain pool of the ʿ*arad* tree, which is called Abū Dawra rain pool; and to the *tabaldī* tree of the fields of the sand patch and by

Muḥammad Kādūk's fields which are in the lands of Tūm k.m.r.j.; and to the *tabaldī* tree of Umm Qad that ends by the boundary [of the land] of the *faqīh* Muḥammad Gharbāwī's sons which is called the land of al-Ḥimyar.

This is an uninterrupted endowment. Whosoever interferes with it disobeys...despises the authority of the dominion, because of [his] obstinacy, violence and retribution will fall upon him....

## III

*seal* ...

From the presence of the mighty, glorious, mighty,[10] respected and venerated sultan, whose renown is spread abroad in all creation, scion of the most noble, offspring of the most outstandingly praiseworthy, the Commander of the Faithful, our lord and master Sultan Muḥammad al-Ḥusayn al-Mahdī, son of Sultan Muḥammad al-Faḍl, may the mercy of God be upon him wherever he is, Amen.

To the presence of everyone to whom this charter comes and [who] examine its truthful contents, namely, *amīrs*, *wazīrs*, *maliks*, sons of the sultans, [*mayrams*], *ḥabbōbas*, [*qāḍīs*], *jabbays*, *shartays*, *dimlijs*, *wakīls* and all the servants among the people of this state in positions of authority and power.

Thereafter: we have the honour to inform you that the *imām*, *faqīh* Ibrāhīm, son of the *faqīh*, *imām* Sa'd-al-Dīn, owner of the mosque of al-Jadīd, presented a charter to me from my father, the late Sultan Muḥammad al-Faḍl, [which said] that he had looked at a charter from his [lit., "my"] grandfather,[11] Sultan (Muḥammad] Dawra, (who took over power after Sultan Aḥmad Bukr...[and granted])[12] the land of Qiraywud al-Zarāf to the *faqīh* Muḥammad 'Izz al-Dīn and his descendants in perpetuity. Then his son, Sultan 'Umar, endorsed this and maintained it. Then Sultan Abu'l-Qāsim, Sultan Muḥammad Tayrāb and Sultan 'Abd al-Raḥmān implemented, maintained and preserved it in its established form. Then his [Muḥammad 'Izz al-Dīn's] son, shaykh Musallim, presented their charters to him [Muḥammad al-Faḍl], and he sent 'Amāra, the *malik* Ibrāhīm walad Wīr's nephew,[13] to go round and delimit it with all the landmarks of its boundaries so that it should not be obliterated. So he went and delimited it for them. Then [Muḥammad al-Faḍl] assigned and confirmed everything that 'Amāra had delimited:[14]

From al-Muḥayr and to the hillocks of al-Wayka [Qiraywud al-Wayka] and m.d.bā rain pool, from the direction of the north and west – the part which the water covers – and to al-Sharāk rain pool and to al-Sharāk riverbed and the land of Tūm k.m.r.j., ending at the boundary of [the land of] the *faqīh* Muḥammad Gharbāwī's sons at the land of al-Ḥimyar, as a perpetual endowment so that they can use its land tax for the mosque.

None are to appear and interfere with them there, none of the officials, *amīrs*, *maliks*, governors, subjects, soldiers, and especially the *jabbays*, both their official ['*āmil*] and their chief and their assistants, the servants of the shield,[15] the *bannā*',[16] the senior *qāḍī* of the Law and his deputies, and the generality of the Muslims. Whosoever interferes with the *faqīh* Muḥammad 'Izz al-Dīn's descendants within the boundaries of the aforementioned land, which the commissioner 'Amāra has surveyed, and whosoever trespasses upon their property and dispute with them in what God has granted to him for the triumph of His Law and the *sunna* of His Prophet, because of [his] obstinacy violence and retribution will fall upon him such as he has never seen [fall] on anyone before.

I said this, and its reliance is upon God, its committal and recourse are unto Him, and He is sufficient for it; how good a Keeper is He![17] Amen.

This was on the second day of dhu'l-ḥijja 1221, the year, one thousand, two hundred and twenty-one of the *ḥijra*.[18]

Then I, Sultan Muḥammad al-Ḥusayn, examined this charter and found it authentic and have thus confirmed the bequest and the charter of endowment [*waqfiyya*] for the land of Qiraywud al-Zarāf with its boundaries, marked and referred to in this charter for the *imām*, *faqīh* Ibrāhīm and his partners.

Let none interfere with them, none of those to whom we have referred in the body of this our charter. I have relinquished to them the *zakāh* and *fiṭr*, namely the ordinances of the Law, and I have exempted them from the customary taxes, namely *dam*, great and small, *fisq*, *hāmil*, *nār* and *quwwār*. None are to interfere in this; we have left this as a help for them for the sake of religion and the world and in this we hope for a reward from God on the Day of Resurrection and Return.

This was written in the year 126(0).[19]

IV arises from a fundamental service the *fuqarā'* were expected to perform for the sultans, the offering of intercessory prayers (*du'ā'*)[20] or complete recitations (*khatma*) of the Qur'ān to safeguard the state.[21] That the sultan's request here was prompted by an actual threat to the state is suggested by another letter in which Sultan Ibrāhīm Qaraḍ makes an identical request to the Awlād Jābir *fuqarā'*, a request that can only have been in response to the threat of invasion by al-Zubayr in 1873–74.[22] IV could also have been written in response to al-Zubayr's first moves against the sultanate.[23]

## IV

*seal* . . .

From the Commander of the Faithful, Sultan Muḥammad al-Ḥusayn, the victorious through the (Most High) God. Amen

To the *faqīh* Sa'd al-Dīn: you and your brothers and sons and all the *fuqarā'* who offer up prayers – [all] your relatives, and I exclude none of you – fullest greetings from me to you.

Thereafter: by this I inform you that we charge you [with the task] of making on our behalf a thousand recitations of the noble Qur'ān and of donating them to us in accordance with our design [of gaining] victory over the enemy and security for the country. Strengthen your determination [to undertake] it; perform the recitations with sincere intent and pure speech.

Let none of you disobey the *faqīh* Sa'd al-Dīn; follow in his path; devote yourself to this service for me so that you bring it to a conclusion. Reject disobedience and (perform) this act of seeking refuge [in God], concerning which we have informed you. "It is God alone Whose Help can avail."[24]

## V

The *faqīh* 'Izz al-Dīn asks for and is granted the estate, "Bayd", formerly held by the mother of Sultan Muḥammad al-Faḍl, Umm Būṣa.

*seal*[25] . . .

[From the presence of the Sultan of the Muslims and the Caliph of the] Lord of the Messengers, the servant of the Law and

Religion, he who trusts in the Lord of the Universe, our [lord and master Sultan Muḥammad al-Ḥusayn] al-Mahdī, may God be gracious to him in the two abodes through the influence of the lord of men and jinns, Amen.

To the presence of everyone to whom this charter comes and [who] examine its truthful contents, namely, *amīrs*, *wazīrs*, *maliks*, sons of the sultans, *mayrams*, *ḥabbōbas*, *qāḍīs*, *jabbays*, *shartays*, *dimlijs* and others from among the people of this state in positions of authority and power.

Thereafter: we have the honour to inform you that the *faqīh* 'Izz al-Dīn has requested of me the estate called "Bayd", which formerly belonged to the *ḥabbōba īya* Umm Būṣa, the mother of our late lord.[26] After her death it reverted to the House of Tribute [*bayt al-jibāya*]. I accepted his request and responded to it; I gave and assigned it to him as a gift and donation. I sent Ḥusayn, an official [*maqām*] from the *malik* Murād's entourage, and also the *āb shaykh* Raḥma, to take possession of it. [They all went] together to this aforesaid piece of land and delimited it and its boundaries in every [direction...from the direction] of the east, between [the land of] the *ḥabbōba* and the Habābīn,[27] the big demarcated sandy depression [*fardal*] which borders...the *tunṭub*[28] tree, and to the *hijlīj* tree and *nabaq* tree which are in the torrent bed, and the stony outcrops which...the Habābīn; and from the direction of the north [the boundary runs] alongside [the land of] "the son of the sultan" the *faqīh* [Ḥasab al-Karīm's sons],[29] the date palm[30] and the *hijlīj* tree which is on the side of the riverbed, and to the *siriḥ* tree which is between...from the sand patch and marked to the *habīl* tree and to the big *ḥarāz* tree which is in the riverbed...from the west by the edge of [the land of] the *faqīh* Ḥasab al-Karīm's sons at the trunk of the big *nabaq* tree by the *siriḥ* tree...the trunk of the *hijlīj* tree and to the *habīl* tree and to the *hijlīj* tree which has three branches, and to the trunk of the *habīl* tree which is on the edge of the riverbed, and across the water course, and marked to the *tunṭub* tree, and marked to the twin *hijlīj* trees which are at the head of the sand patch of the *ḥaskanīṭ* bushes, and to the *mukhīṭ* tree and to the *hijlīj* tree which is in the marshy ground [*al-naqa'a*], and to the *hijlīj* tree which is in the water course of the '*arad* tree, and ending beside [the land of] the sons of "the son of the sultan" *faqīh* Ḥasab al-Karīm: and from the direction of the south [running with the land of] the *faqīh* Sijill at the *hijlīj* trees which [stand] in a row at the head of the sand-patch, and to the '*arad* tree which is in the bed of the water course, and runs along the bed of the water course and to the short *tabaldī* tree which is by the bank of the water course; [then the boundary] crosses the water course and runs to the twin *hijlīj* trees and the *hijlīj* tree which is on the side of the high sand-patch, and to the fallen *tabaldī* tree whose location is well known. And the boundary was marked at the bent *sayyāl* tree which is at the pool...

This land, which is defined by these boundaries and surrounded by them, [is the land of] the *faqīh* 'Izz al-Dīn as an allodial concession with full possession and as his confirmed property...to be cultivated, causing to be cultivated...sale, benefit, purchase, demolition, clearance [of land]...[31] Let none of those to whom we have referred in the body of our charter dispute with him there. We have relinquished to him the *zakāh* and *fiṭr*, by which I mean [the Sharī'a taxes] and have forgiven him the customary taxes, namely *dam*, great and small, *fisq*, *hāmil*, *nār* and *quwwār*. Let none approach him in his estate for any of the customary dues, and let none of the *jabbays* or other officials approach him. I have forbidden them to lay their hands upon the *faqīh* 'Izz al-Dīn's estate, since we have relinquished this to him that he may seek support therein for his affairs, both religious and mundane. And in this we hope for a reward from God on the Day of Resurrection and Return, and God is a surety for what we say.

This was written in the year 1263.[32]

## VI

The *faqīh* Jiddaw walad Bukhārī seeks a charter from 'Alī Dīnār to confirm a charter of Muḥammad al-Ḥusayn dated 1260/1844–45; it is not clear if this latter is III here.

*seal* ...

In the name of God, the Compassionate, the Merciful: praise be to God, the Noble Ruler, and blessings and peace upon our lord Muḥammad and his family.

Thereafter: from the most mighty Sultan and most noble Caliph, to whom all nations are submissive and to whom the Arabs and barbarians bow their necks, the Commander of the Faithful, who trusts in his Sublime Lord and hopes for His abundant forgiveness, son of the most noble and offspring of the pure and good, Sultan 'Alī Dīnār, son of Sultan Zakariyyā,[33] son of the late Sultan Muḥammad al-Faḍl.

To all who encounter this decree and witness its contents below the seal, from among the holders of authority, *amīrs*, *wazīrs*, *maliks*, *shartays*, *dimlijs*, sons of the sultans, *mayrams*, *ḥabbōbas*, *jabbays*, *qawwārs*, *makkās*-s and all the officials, all the people of the state, and the holders of authority and power: may God be a guide to them and be pleased with them. Amen.

Thereafter: greetings to you, and may the fullness of mercy and blessings be upon you. We hereby inform you, our beloved (servants),[34] that on the third day of the blessed month of Sha'bān of the year 1316,[35] Jiddaw walad Bukhārī, of the Jawāmi'a *fuqarā'* living at the said[36] Jadīd al-Sayl, presented to us a paper (bearing) a charter and seal of our father,[37] the late Sultan Muḥammad al-Ḥusayn al-Mahdī, the victorious through the Most High God – may God have mercy on him and grant him Paradise as a repose in the hereafter – (which was) dated 1260[38] and which conferred therein upon his grandfathers, from the grants and benevolences of our late father, lands in the district of Labadī and Shabāb whose boundaries are referred to in the letter which he presented to us.

We read it and – since, as you are aware, I am from their worthy offspring and progeny and have succeeded to the government of all Dār Fūr – have confirmed the order concerning the lands referred to as a grant to Jiddaw Bukhārī. I have issued to him this, an order in his hands, to keep with the order of my father, the late Sultan Muḥammad al-Ḥusayn al-Mahdī, the victorious through the Most High God – may the mercy of God be upon him – in order that no one oppose or dispute with him in these lands. Whosoever interferes with him will have no one to blame but himself.

Greetings to whosoever follows the right course and dreads the consequences of evil. Amen, and greetings. 4 Sha'bān 1316.[39]

---

## VII to XXIII: The Tunjur fuqarā' of Khirībān[1]

---

Dār Fūr tradition is unanimous that a Tunjur dynasty were at one time rulers of a vast empire that embraced not only Dār Fūr but also Wadai in what is now Eastern Chad. Their origins, and the date, nature and extent of their dominion are shrouded in mystery; all that seems certain is that their empire was superseded in Dār Fūr first by the Keira Fur dynasty, who may indeed have been related to them, and, a little later, in Wadai by a line of rulers from the Maba people. The scale and number of the ruins associated with the Tunjur may confirm what the traditions imply, that they were the true "founding fathers" of state formation in the region.[2]

A number of the leading families of the Keira Sultanate claimed Tunjur descent, among them the *takanāwīs* of the north and the powerful family of Ibrāhīm w. Ramād, one of whose sons appears as judge in XV here. Under the Keira Sultans, the Tunjur (of whom others are settled as far west as Nigeria) lived in scattered communities throughout central Dār Fūr; their chief, one of those tribal rulers entitled to be called "sultan" had his centre at Jabal Ḥurayz, south-west of al-Fāshir.[3] It was from Jabal Ḥurayz that 'Abdallāh Maṭlūq, from the ruling Kirātī clan, is said to have moved north to Kamala Kīrī in Khirībān district (north-west of al-Fāshir) in the reign of either Sultan Mūsā or Aḥmad Bukr, probably towards the end of the seventeenth century. There he settled and opened up land for cultivation (*iḥyā'* "reviving" from the legal phrase *iḥyā al-mawāt*), later receiving a charter of privilege (*jāh*) from Sultan Muḥammad Tayrāb.[4]

'Abdallāh's sons prospered and multiplied at Kamala Kīrī and, despite the recurrent family squabbles that found their way to court, reinforced their hold over the land by obtaining from successive sultans charters confirming their rights there. The fifteen documents presented here open with a sequence of charters, typical of a number of such sequences held by other *fuqarā'* families; the first, VII, is a confirmatory charter issued by 'Abd al-Raḥmān for Badawī b. 'Abdallāh Maṭlūq, the second, VIII, a further confirmation from Muḥammad al-Faḍl in 1221/1806–7.

The community evidently still preserved its links with their ruler in Jabal Ḥurayz for in IX the Tunjur Sultan writes to the governor of the north, the *takanāwī*, within whose jurisdiction Khirībān lay to say that Muḥammad al-Faḍl had placed the various communities of his own Kirātī clan in the north under his direct authority. Being numbered among these "people of sanctity" (*ahl al-karāma*), the Kamala Kīrī community were not to be taxed by the *takanāwī* or his officials.[5] Here we have a glimpse of the higher level of "administrative estate" (see introduction, pp. 12–17), whereby the great notables were granted authority or *ḥukm* over whole communities, a level rarely seen in the archives of the *fuqarā'*.

The privilege was again confirmed for Madanī, Badawī's brother, in X, issued by Muḥammad al-Ḥusayn in 1841. However, in the following year in XI, issued by the same sultan, the land at Kamala Kīrī, held until then collectively by 'Abdallāh Maṭlūq's descendants, was delimited and granted as an "estate" (*iqṭā'*) to Muḥammad and his father, Madanī. This grant arose because Muḥammad complained personally to the sultan over ill-treatment and trespass by some royal slaves (see XX and XXI). What this signified for the other members of the community is not clear; presumably it did not mean that they lost their land, rather that the personal grant took precedence over the collective privilege (meaning, in practice, that Muḥammad was effectively head of the community). So at least the judge ruled when, some twenty years later, this conflict between estate and privilege was tested in court in a case which forms the subject of XXII.[6]

The sixth and final charter given here, XII, was issued by ʻAlī Dīnār for Muḥammad b. Muḥammadayn and confirms the privilege, making no reference to his father's estate.

## VII

A confirmatory charter issued by Sultan ʻAbd al-Raḥmān for the *faqīh* Badawī b. ʻAbdallāh Maṭlūq.

*seal* Sultan ʻAbd al-Raḥmān, son of sultan Aḥmad Bukr. The year 1214.[7]

In the name of God, the Compassionate, the Merciful: may the blessings and peace of God be upon Muḥammad and his family.

From the presence of the most noble lord, who shows preference for the best of his servants and notables, Sultan of the Muslims and Caliph of the Prophet of the Lord of the Universe, who trusts in [God], the Creator, [the Benefactor; our lord Sultan ʻAbd al-Raḥmān,] may God render him victorious, Amen; son of the late Sultan Aḥmad Bukr.

To everyone to whom this document comes, the *maliks*, sons of the sultan, *mayrams*, *falqanāwīs*, *korays* and other officials, the lords of the state and holders of power.

Thereafter: the said, divinely-assisted, divinely-approved and victorious sultan has confirmed for the *faqīh* Badawī his old and known privilege, the privilege of his father, the *faqīh* ʻAbdallāh Maṭlūq. He has presented to us a charter of Sultan Muḥammad Tayrāb in which he granted to the *faqīh* ʻAbdallāh the privilege of God and His Prophet. We have confirmed for his son, the *faqīh* Badawī, the privilege of his father.

[There is] not [due] from them *dam*, *fisq*, *hāmil*, *nār*, *quwwār* or the *jibāya* of the bread and cotton; they are free from all the customary taxes.

This is my letter to all who are oppressive and tyrannical. Beware, beware of disobedience and obstinacy.

12[8]

## VIII

A confirmatory charter issued by Sultan Muḥammad al-Faḍl for the *faqīh* Badawī b. 'Abdallāh al-Tunjurāwī.

*seal*[9] ...Sultan Muḥammad al-Faḍl, son of Sultan 'Abd al-Raḥmān al-Rashīd, son of the late Sultan Aḥmad Bukr, son of Mūsā, son of Sulaymān.
Muḥammad al-Mā...12...

What God Wills.

With blessings: in the name of God, the Compassionate, the Merciful; may the prayers of God be upon him after whom there is no prophet.[10]

From the presence of the Sultan of the Muslims and the Caliph of the Community of the Lord of the Prophets, servitor of the Law and Religion, who trusts in God, the Exalted, the One, the Incomparable, the Just, the Enduring; our lord and majesty, Sultan Muḥammad al-Faḍl...may God render him victorious, Amen; son of the late Sultan 'Abd al-Raḥmān al-Rashīd...

...To everyone to whom this decree comes...*shartays*, *dimlijs*, *jabbays* of the grain and cotton, *makkās*-s, *qawwārs*, and all the oppressors who trample upon the rights of the Muslims.

Thereafter: the *faqīh* Badawī b. *al-faqīh* 'Abdallāh al-Tunjurāwī has presented to us a charter of my uncle, the late Sultan Muḥammad Tayrāb, concerning their old and known privilege. I read it, found it to be authentic and have confirmed his old and known privilege for him.

No one is to interfere with him in his property, fields, *dam*, *fisq* and *hāmil*. None of the mighty, the *maliks*, sons of the sultan, *mayrams*, nor the *jabbays*, *maliks*, and sons of the warband[11] are to interfere with them, because their privilege is an old one from the time of my grandfathers and fathers. I, likewise, have confirmed their former old privilege. Let no one interfere with them.

Those who sprinkle them with cold water, shall I splash with blood, and this herein is a warning to you. Whomsoever the warning reaches, no excuse will save him. This is my letter and seal for all who read and ponder it.

It was written...the year 1221.[12]

# IX

A letter from Sultan Muḥammad Shalabī to the *takanāwī* Yaḥyā b. Muḥammad.

*seal* Sultan Shalabī, son of Sultan b.l.mī. The year 1241[13]

We seek help through Him:[14] we pray and seek peace from His Prophet, the veracious, the trustworthy.

From the sultan who keeps in mind His Lord's mercy [and is] grateful, our lord[15] Sultan Muḥammad Shalabī, may God cause him to rest in peace,[16] Amen; son of the late Sultan 'Umar b.l.mī, may God prolong his days, Amen.[17]

To the possessor of splendour, power and rank, who reposes his trust in the (One, the Judge),[18] the *āb takanāwī* Yaḥyā, son of the late *āb takanāwī* Muḥammad.

Thereafter: I hereby inform you about the Tunjur. Our lord, the blessed, upright and victorious Sultan Muḥammad al-Faḍl – may God prolong his days – has placed me in charge of all my people who live in the lands of the *takanāwīs*,[19] *shartays*, *dimlijs* and all the soldiery, and has barred from them the *jabbays*, the mighty, the *maliks*, the people who take [the taxes]. Therefore, do not take [anything][20] from my community, the Tunjur Kirātī, (namely) the descendants of the *faqīh* 'Abd al-Raḥmān, Ḥammād's descendants, 'Abd al-Fattāḥ's descendants and the descendants of 'Uthmān.

After you receive your letter, O Father of the land [where] these aforesaid people are living, [namely] at Kafōt and Khirībān in your land... to them. We shall keep them within your jurisdiction.[21]

Let no one oppress them, neither one of the mighty, nor the servants [of the state, nor] the *jabbays*, [nor] all the oppressors. You, personally, are to restrain them. Let no one draw near to them. Thus have we informed you that they are people of sanctity (*ahl al-karāma*).

# X

A confirmatory charter issued by Sultan Muḥammad al-Ḥusayn for shaykh Madanī, brother of the *faqīh* Badawī.

*seal* The property of the Commander of the Faithful, Sultan Muḥammad Ḥusayn, son of

Sultan Muḥammad al-Faḍl, son of Sultan 'Abd al-Raḥmān al-Rashīd, son of Sultan Aḥmad Bukr, son of Sultan Mūsā, son of Sultan Sulaymān: the year 1256.[22]

From the presence of [he who] watches over [his] servants, [who] guards the lands, [who] forbids wrongdoing and evil, the Commander of the Faithful, Sultan Muḥammad al-Ḥusayn, victorious through the Most High God, Amen.

To all who encounter this decree, the *amīrs*, *wazīrs*, *maliks*, *shartays*, *dimlijs*, sons of the sultan, *mayrams*, *ḥabbōbas*, *jabbays* of the grain, cotton and seed, all the people of the state and holders of power, the oppressors who trample upon the rights of the Muslims.

Thereafter: shaykh Madanī presented to me a charter of my late father. I read that it promulgated for his brother, Badawī b. *al-faqīh* 'Abdallāh al-Tunjurāwī, a confirmation of the contents of a charter[23] of Sultan Muḥammad Tayrāb which established[24] their old and known privilege.

I found it to be authentic and have confirmed that no one is to interfere with them in their property, fields [and their rights to] *dam*, *fisq* and *hāmil*. Let none of the mighty, the *maliks*, sons of the sultan, *jabbays*, sons of the warband, interfere with them, since [they have] a privilege of God and His Prophet. [There is] not [due] from them either *zakāh* or *fiṭra*.

Whosoever sprinkles them with water, shall I splash with blood. This is my letter and decree to whomsoever receives it.

It was written in the month of Ramaḍān, the twenty-fourth (day) having elapsed, 24, in the year 1257.[25]

## XI

A charter issued by Sultan Muḥammad al-Ḥusayn granting an estate to the *faqīh* Muḥammad and his father at Kamalā Kīrī.[26]

*seal*[27]

From the Commander of the Faithful, Sultan Muḥammad al-Ḥusayn, victorious through the Most High God, Amen.

To all who encounter this decree, the *amīrs*, *wazīrs*, *maliks*, *shartays*, *dimlijs*, sons of the sultans, *mayrams*, *ḥabbōbas*, *jabbays*, *qawwārs* and *makkās*-s, all the people of the state, the oppressors who trample upon the rights of the Muslims.

Thereafter: I have shown favour to and have granted the *faqīh* Muḥammad the land of his grandfather, ‘Abdallāh, [being] their cultivations.[28] I sent them to the *maqdūm* Ḥasan, and he dispatched from his entourage the Shaykh Amīn al-Katakāwī.[29] They went to this land, Kamalā Kīrī, in the *shartay* Muḥammad n.l.mū’s district; and the *faqīh* Muḥammad and his father, Madanī w. ‘Abdallāh Maṭlūq, had with them eight men who swore upon the Book of God [as to] the boundary of their land.

The boundary[30] begins on the eastern side with [the land of] the *faqīh* Ḥabīb’s people, [namely] the *mayram* Khādimallāh’s sons, at [the] riverbed; [then] it runs by Umm Rajī field, and to the channel of the riverbed,[31] [that is] the boundary with Dabirtū; and to the tomb which is there [at] the white [*al-h.s.l.mās*],[32] and it runs to the white hillocks and to the waterhole of Tūrā [or Tawrā],[33] and to [the land of] the *faqīh* Wadā‘a’s sons, [that is] the boundary at *faqīh* ‘Uthmān Jundī’s fields. Then [the boundary] runs to the Azbāba hillocks, [that is] the boundary with the Fallāt[a] of *faqīh* ‘Izz al-Dīn, and to the fields of r.kh., and to [the land of] the *falqanāwī* sh.q.r. Then it runs to Jabal sh.q.r al-kabīr, and to Jabal al-Samū‘; then it runs to the Kalwa riverbed, and to Jabal Umm ‘Arīf, and to the floodbed of an *inḍirāb* tree; then it runs to Jabal Sarāya and ‘Arā; then it runs to Jabal Martabū, and to the Maqābil hillocks, and to the fields of Ma‘qūq; and the boundary comes back to the riverbed with [the land of] the *mayram* Khādimallah’s people. These are the boundaries of the said land which *al-ḥājj* Amīn, Shaykh of the Takārīr,[29] demarcated – the land of Kamalā Kīrī.

I have granted to *faqīh* Muḥammad and his father, Madanī, as an estate for them and their descendants after them, as a confirmed property and [with] full possession, and I have relinquished to them all its revenues, both Sharī‘a and customary, namely, *zakāh*, *fiṭra*, *dam* and *fisq*.

Let no one interfere with their land at the said locality, and let this not be changed by any sultan after me.

The witnesses present [were] the *faqīh* Musallim, *faqīh* Muḥammad, *faqīh* Khabīr, shaykh Abū Bakr, *faqīh* Muḥammad Daqīsān, *faqīh* Dhiyāb, *faqih* Jamīlallāh, and *faqīh* Muḥammad Ḥumaydī. These witnesses were present accompanying the commissioner, *al-ḥājj* shaykh Amīn.

It was written in the month of God, Dhu’l-Qa‘da, 25, in the year 1258.[34]

# XII

A confirmatory charter issued by Sultan 'Alī Dīnār for Muḥammad b. Muḥammadayn b. Madanī.

*seal* Sultan 'Alī Dīnār, son of Sultan Zakariyyā, son of Sultan Muḥammad al-Faḍl, son of Sultan 'Abd al-Raḥmān al-Rashīd, son of Sultan Bukr...

In the name of God, the Compassionate, the Merciful: praise be to God, the Ruler, the Noble; and blessing be upon our lord Muḥammad and his family, and peace.

Thereafter: from the servant of his Lord, the Commander of the Faithful and Sultan of the Muslims, who trusts in God, Lord of Creation; firm upholder of the Muḥammadan Law, staunch in the religion of Islam in all the western regions, our lord and master Sultan 'Alī Dīnār, son of Sultan Zakariyyā – may the Lord of Creation protect him from all misfortune and calamity – offspring of the most lofty star and elevated mountain, the late Muḥammad al-Faḍl – may God render him victorious; inexorable time has removed him and ⌜*wa'l-m.k.d.*⌝.[35] Amen.

To all who encounter this decree and witness its contents under the seal, *amīrs*, *wazīrs*, the lords of power and the people of the state, namely the *maliks*, *shartays*, *dimlijs*, sons of the sultans, *mayrams*, *ḥabbōbas*, *jabbays*, *qawwārs*, *makkās*-s, *kōrays*, and all (the oppressors who trample upon the rights of Muslims...to inform you about all...) to protect you against the evil of complete loss,[36] amen; that the bearer of this our decree is Muḥammad b. Muḥammadayn, son of the said *faqīh* Madanī. We found that he possessed noble decrees[37] issued by our fathers and grandfathers, the former authorities, namely the late Sultans Aḥmad Bukr,[38] Tayrāb,[39] 'Abd al-Raḥmān al-Rashīd,[40] Muḥammad al-Faḍl,[41] and our father Sultan Muḥammad al-Ḥusayn,[42] victorious through God, who honoured and granted thereby to the aforementioned *faqīh* Madanī a position of authority over[43] the district of Kamalā Kīrī by a declaration.[44] Therefore no one, besides himself, was to interfere with them, neither in their [rights to] *dam*, nor in their properties, nor in their *fisq*, *hāmila*, *zakāh*, neither in their small [affairs] or their great. They have become privileged of God and His Prophet; they are honoured [and] venerated.

Therefore we have confirmed for them their ancient privilege [which had] been proclaimed by the aforesaid lawful decrees. We have promulgated this our order for them as a token[45] [of our forebears], May God make them rest in peace,[46] and we have included their dwelling and livestock in the two lands (?), so that they are protected against enmity and trespass. Whomsoever this warning reaches, will be able to give no excuse as a plea.[47] Greetings to whomsoever follows the right way. Greetings.

1318 2 Ṣafar the Good.[48]

XIII, XIV and XV are three instalments in a land dispute between two branches of the Tunjur clan, the Awlād 'Abd al-Raḥmān, over the ownership of some land at Yawma in Khirībān district. The quarrel evidently had a long history, being maintained over nearly three generations, from about 1770 until after 1840. From the five occasions when the dispute reached the courts, we have only the following three transcripts. The first two hearings, before the *qāḍī* Sa'īd and the *khalīfa al-ḥājj* Isḥāq,[49] resulted in each party obtaining a judgment (*ḥukm*) in its favour. In XIII the famous judge, *al-ḥājj* 'Izz al-Dīn of Jadīd al-Sayl to the east of Khirībān (see above II to VI), refers the contradictory judgments to the *faqīh* 'Abd al-Raḥmān Kākama. Kākama pronounces both invalid, hears the evidence of the witnesses and sends the parties back to the *qāḍī* for judgment. The latter rules that the evidence (*bayyina*) of ownership (*milk*) presented by the plaintiffs, the descendants of 'Abdallāh Maṭlūq, in the form of witnesses of long memory was stronger than the evidence for actual prescriptive possession (*ḥiyāza* or *ḥawz*, see below p. 136, no. 58) produced by the party of Muḥammad Nartaq. The judge then sends out a commissioner to re-assign the land and to administer an oath enforcing his settlement of the dispute.

But the party of Muḥammad Nartaq remained dissatisfied and a number of years later, in 1249/1833–34, they brought the case before 'Izz al-Dīn's son, Muḥammad al-Ḥārith who had succeeded his father as judge in the district. Now the plaintiffs, they alleged, possibly unwisely, that the judge's father had not given them justice. In XIV, Muḥammad al-Ḥārith emphatically confirms his father's judgment and specifically forbids Muḥammad Nartaq's party to raise the case again.

Despite this prohibition, Muḥammad Nartaq's party led by his son brought their dispute before the *malik* 'Abdallāh b. Ibrāhīm Ramād,[50] (XV) perhaps hoping that another judge would prove more sympathetic to their cause. But their hopes were in vain; the *malik* merely reads the two earlier judgments, consults the '*ulamā*' and confirms the previous rulings.

The three transcripts both illustrate the litigious enthusiasms of the *fuqarā*' and the variety of judges (three *qāḍīs*, a sultan's son and a *malik*) available to them. They also underline the importance of holding on to successful judgments, for, in effect, XIV is a confirmation of XIII and XV of both XIII and XIV.

## XIII

Transcript of a hearing before the *qāḍī al-ḥājj* 'Izz al-Dīn.

*seal* ... 'Izz al-Dīn b. *al-ḥājj* Mūsa: the year 1187.[51]

The reason for the document[52] [is as follows]. Thereafter: it has been established by a lawful judgment before the *qāḍī al-ḥājj* 'Izz al-Dīn, in a case between *faqīh* Aḥmad [acting] for himself and representing Daḥm, 'Abd al-Ṣādiq, Muḥammad Dashāsh, Badawī, Muḥammad and 'Uthmān [and Muḥammad Nartaq's party].

*Plea by the plaintiff*[53]

Then the *faqīh* Aḥmad made his plea that they had taken their opponent, Muḥammad, to court before the *qāḍī* Sa'īd: "the said *qāḍī* gave judgment to me over [my] land and this is the document of the judgment".

*Plea by the defendant*

Then Muḥammad Nartaq, for himself and representing Ḥasan with his authorization, replied and said, "similarly we took this party to court before the *khalīfa al-ḥājj* Isḥāq; and he gave judgment to us over our land. This is the document of the *khalīfa's* judgment."

*First intervention by the judge*

Then the aforesaid judge examined [the case and] referred them to the learned *faqīh* 'Abd al-Raḥmān Kākama that he might examine these judgments from the legal point of view, to confirm what the Law approved and to annul what was found to be defective. Thereupon the learned *faqīh* 'Abd al-Raḥmān examined the documents, annulled them and sent the judgment for appeal. Both [parties then] made their pleas in his court.

*Further plea by the plaintiff*

Aḥmad made his plea that this land was cultivated [land[54]] of his fathers and the fathers of those he represented.[55] They had opened it up from Sultan Aḥmad Bukr's time as their property and had occupied and had full disposal of it until Sultan 'Abd al-Raḥmān's time.

*Further plea by the defendant*

Muḥammad Nartaq replied that this land was their fathers'; they had occupied it from Sultan Muḥammad's time, being in occupation until the said time.[56]

*Submission of evidence*

The learned *faqīh* 'Abd al-Raḥmān queried everything [said] by the two litigants [ruling] that each must come with evidence[57] in support of his claim. Then the *faqīh* Aḥmad came with three men. They gave testimony on behalf of *faqīh* Ahmad and those he represented to [rights of] property and possession[58] from Sultan Bukr's time. There was a witness to property and possession from Sultan 'Umar's time; there was a witness to possession only from Sultan Muḥammad's time,[59] and a witness testified to possession only[60] from Sultan Bukr's time. Aḥmad's testimony was thus concluded, and the *faqīh* Aḥmad's testimony was legally valid.

Afterwards the *faqīh* Muḥammad Nartaq's testimony was three [men]; they testified to possession only from Sultan Muḥammad's time.[61]

*The case is referred back to the judge*

When the testimony was concluded, the *faqīh* 'Abd al-Raḥmān wrote to us in his own hand, referring the case to us in order that the Law might deliver judgment. Thereupon the judicial official examined the stipulations of the School [of Law][62] and found that the testimony to property [rights] was stronger than possession, and that legal validity was stronger than that which lacked legal validity.

*The taking of the oath*

Therefore we ordered *faqīh* Aḥmad and those he represented to swear upon their testimony[63] and establish their right to their fathers' cultivations.

Then Muḥammad and his associate said, "I shall bring the *faqīh* Idrīs Sanbal's Book,[64] and every owner of a cultivation, and his witness, shall swear upon this Book".

The judge then authorized this and sent the *faqīh* Aḥmad...[65] to them to be present at the site of the land. The witnesses and the parties to the dispute were to take the oath and the witnesses were to assign to each person his father's cultivation.

Thereupon the *faqīh* Muḥammad brought the Book and the rest of his partners were at the land and delegated to him their proxy.[66] The partners included Khamīs, 'Uthmān, 'Arībī, ['Uraybī], 'Ubayd, Khiḍr, Idrīs, 'Alwa, Ibrāhīm, Bukr, Ismā'īl, 'Uthmān, 'Abd al-Raḥmān, Ḥasan, Khalīl, Ādūm[a], Sulaymān, Muḥammad, 'Isā, Isḥāq and Hārūn.

The parties to the dispute stood up and bore witness to the swearing of pardon by the *faqīh* Muḥammad and his party of associates by an oath.[67]

The testimony designated for each person from *faqīh* Aḥmad's party his father's cultivation; [and the settlement] to which they bore witness was reported to us by the commissioner. He presented this to us in their presence, and its authentication.

*The judgement*

Then we awarded judgment to the *faqīh* Aḥmad by dismissing the complaint of *faqīh* Muḥammad Nartaq and those of his partners who were with him. The land has been established as the property of the *faqīh* Aḥmad and those of his partners who were with him, each of the partners [having] his father's cultivation.

*The witnesses*

Present and witnessing this were the *faqīh* Ismā'īl, the *faqīh* Sharaf, and the officials Muḥammad Dī [or Day] and the *sajjān* k.s.ī.[68] And God is the best of witnesses.

## XIV

Transcript of a hearing before the *qāḍī* Muḥammad al-Ḥārith.[69]

*seal* the *qāḍī* Muḥammad Ḥārith b. *al-qāḍī al-ḥājj* 'Izz al-Dīn. The year...

The reason [for writing this document is] the registration of an orthodox lawful judgment, free from error and corruption, before our lord, luminary of the Muslim notables, *qāḍī* Muḥammad al-Ḥārith,

*Plea by the plaintiff*[70]

Wherein Muḥammad Shinā in his own cause and representing Jāmi', Maḥmūd, 'Aribi [or 'Uraybī], Isḥāq, Muḥammad Yarwa and Aḥmad Jaraf with their authorization made his plea concerning the land. It was opened up by their[71] grandfather in Sultan Aḥmad Bukr's time. None of their relatives had troubled them there. They had inherited it from testator to inheritor until Sultan 'Abd al-Raḥmān's time, when Aḥmad disputed with them over it before the Shaykh al-Islām,[72] our lord and master, our father *qāḍī al-ḥājj* 'Izz al-Dīn, the just judge; but he did not give them justice. Now he wanted justice from this court of law. Thus [his plea] was concluded.

Then we questioned him further, but he admitted that he was without proof [of his claim].[73]

*Plea by the defendant*

Then Madanī, in his own cause, replied with the avowal that indeed they had both earlier taken their case before the *shaykh al-islām*, with Aḥmad as proxy representing 'Uthmān, Badawī and Muḥammad Kūn [or Kawn] with their authorization.[74] [Aḥmad] made the plea just as it is recorded in the text of the record of the hearing; Muḥammad Nartaqī had been their representative. He further replied that Aḥmad [had said] that this was the land cultivated [by] their grandfather, 'Abd al-Raḥmān,[75] in Sultan Aḥmad Bukr's time and that no one had troubled them there until Muḥammad Nartaqī began a dispute with them over it. When their pleas were completed, he [*qāḍī* 'Izz al-Dīn] had summoned both of the litigants [to produce] evidence, since their claims contradicted each other. Then he instructed the *'ālim, faqīh* 'Abd al-Raḥmān Kawma,[76] that they should each bring their evidence...[77] three men. Aḥmad's evidence testified to [his rights] of property, possession and free disposal, and Muḥammad Nartaqī's evidence testified to possession only.

Then the Law set them both aside,[78] but weighed and compared Aḥmad's evidence with the stipulations of the Law. "Then the Judge of the Judges of Islam[79] decided upon it and gave judgment to us over our land. Here is his judgment."

*The judgment*

Then Madanī produced his judgment. I examined it for its legal admissibility for us, found it to be correct and therefore approved it according as the Law had approved it. Then I took counsel with the *fuqahā'*, the people of the [Mālikī] School, and we asked some additional questions of Muḥammad Shinā. Thus the lawsuit was concluded.

Then I gave judgment against him by dismissing his claim and denying him the right of appeal. I have given judgment to Madanī over his land and have confirmed and ratified my father's judgment.

*The witnesses*

I had as witnesses to the judgment a gathering, namely, *al-ḥājj* Makkī, *faqīh* al-Khurashī, *faqīh* Khalīl, Ṭāhir, *faqīh* Madanī, *faqīh al-ḥājj* Ismā'īl, *al-ḥājj* 'Abdallāh Ibrāhīm and others too numerous to mention for fear of prolonging [the list].

Written in the year 1249.[80]

## XV

Transcript of a hearing before *al-ḥājj* 'Abdallāh b. Ramād.

*seal* Property of the *abū*, *malik* 'Abdallāh b. *al-malik* Ibrāhīm b. Ramād: the year 1255.[81]

The reason for recording the words[82] and of their being committed to writing before the[83] judge and the one so authorized *malik*, *amīn*, *al-ḥājj* 'Abdallāh Ramād, acting for the Commander of the faithful, [arises from a dispute] which occurred between *faqīh* 'Alī, representing his partners, namely, Muḥammad Shin[a], *faqīh* 'Abdallāh, another 'Abdallāh, Muḥammad, and also another Muḥammad, Abū Bakr, Sabīl, 'Uthmān Qandūla, and *faqīh* Madanī b. 'Abdallāh Maṭlūq.

Thereafter: both were present before the aforesaid judge, amenable and obedient to the Law [and] to its implementation. The *'ulamā'* were also present on behalf of them both before him. He summoned the plaintiff among them [to make] his plea.

*Plea by the plaintiff*

Thereupon the said *faqīh* 'Alī, representing his partners referred to above with their authorization, made his plea. They had land [which] had been brought into cultivation by their grandfathers in Sultan Aḥmad Bukr's time, and this was the land of Yawma, which they had disposed of and possessed until it passed to their fathers. "Then in Sultan 'Abd al-Raḥmān al-Rashīd's time the brothers of this *faqīh* Madanī with Aḥmad as their representative disputed with us before *faqīh* 'Abd al-Raḥmān Kākam[a]; he gave judgment to us over our land, but referred us to *qāḍī al-ḥājj* 'Izz al-Dīn.[84] Then the *qāḍī* seized our document and transferred ownership of the land to Aḥmad and those he represented; and from then until now we have not met with justice. We now demand justice from *faqīh* Madanī."

Then we questioned him further but he did not present anything else that we noted.[85]

*Plea by the defendant*

Then the said *faqīh* Madanī replied...cultivations...Sultan Aḥmad Bukr and no one caused them any trouble, "until (the land) came to us except that...[in the time of] Sultan 'Abd al-Raḥmān, Muḥammad, the father of 'Alī here, representing his brothers and partners began a dispute with us. We took our dispute before *qāḍī al-ḥājj* 'Izz al-Dīn; the Law decided between us and he gave judgment to Aḥmad, our representative, and to those he represented over their land. He dismissed the complaint of Muḥammad, 'Alī's father, and of those he represented. After that they did not dispute with us until *qāḍī al-ḥājj* 'Izz al-Dīn died and was succeeded by his son, *qāḍī* Muḥammad al-Ḥārith. Then they took their complaint to him and disputed with us before him. Muḥammad Shin[a], as their representative, disputed with me and I, *faqīh* Madanī, was my partners' representative. The Law decided between us and *qāḍī* Muḥammad al-Ḥārith gave judgment to us over our land just as his late father had adjudged to us. We then took possession of our land, referred to above. This is his judgment and his father's judgment.

We have a question for *faqīh* 'Alī: "Did, or did not, your father go to court with Ahmad before *qāḍī al-ḥājj* 'Izz al-Dīn, and your brother Muḥammad Shin[a] with *faqīh* Madanī before *qāḍī* Muḥammad al-Ḥārith?"

*Acknowledgment by the plaintiff*

He ['Alī] admitted the lawsuits but claimed that justice had not been done.[86]

*The judgment*

When their affair had been thus concluded, I took counsel with the '*ulamā*' and they instructed us[87] to examine the *qāḍīs*' judgments. So we asked *faqīh* Madanī to produce the judgments. He produced both judgments; we read and examined them and found that they had correctly dismissed the claim of Muḥammad, 'Alī's father, and of those he represented and the claim of Muḥammad [Shinā] and those he represented. No appeal against them was lawful nor could anyone re-examine [the rulings].

When the affair had been thus concluded, I confirmed the *qāḍīs*' judgments since no appeal or re-examination [of them] is permitted. I have dismissed the complaint of 'Alī and those he represents over the land of Yawma, just as his father's complaint was dismissed before, and I have given judgment to *faqīh* Madanī and those he represents over their land at Yawma, just as *qāḍī al-ḥājj* 'Izz al-Dīn and his son, *qāḍī* Muḥammad al-Ḥārith, adjudged, and I have confirmed both judgments. I have dismissed *faqīh* 'Alī and those he represents [who are] referred to in the body of the document.

Document XVI

*The witnesses*

I had as witnesses thereunto: *qāḍī* Abū Bakr, *faqīh* 'Abd al-Manān, Jāmūs, *faqīh* Khalīl, *faqīh* Ḥasan, *bāsī* Nūr al-Dīn, 'Abd al-Mājid, Isḥāq, 'Izz al-Dīn, Ḥabīb, Muḥammad w. *al-faqīh* walad Bishāra, his brother *faqīh* Aḥmad, and Ādam w. 'Awaḍallāh.

Among the court transcripts of the Tunjur and Fallāta (Fulani) *fuqarā'* of the Khirībān region are several dealing with disputes with two "sons of the sultans", 'Aqrab (whose father is unknown) and Muḥammad Hūd, a son of Muḥammad al-Faḍl (see below XXIII).[88] Both were a serious nuisance to the holy men, pushing their way in and trespassing on the latters' lands.

In XVI, dated 1220/1805–6, 'Aqrab (living up to his name "Scorpion") claims that he had been granted land at Khirībān by Sultan 'Abd al-Raḥmān; his "charter" turns out to be about another matter entirely (perhaps he was illiterate) and the judge issues an injunction restraining him from Badawī b. 'Abdallāh Matlūq's land. Ten years later, in 1230/1815, 'Aqrab was also successfully sued by the Fallāta holy men for trespass.[89] In neither case, and in contrast to the judge's handling of Muḥammad Hūd in XXIII, does 'Aqrab's royal status seem to have weighed much with the court.

In XVII Sultan Muḥammad al-Faḍl writes to *al-ḥājj* Wāday (or Wādī) informing him that Badawī and his brothers are coming (from court, having presented a petition to the sultan?) to demarcate their land. What is left over is to be given to 'Aqrab. Wāday in turn writes, in XVIII, to Abū Ḥasan who had evidently supervised an earlier demarcation of the Kamala Keirei estate. It is possible that 'Aqrab had kept up the dispute and that the sultan was trying both to pacify him and to protect the holy men.

# XVI

Transcript of a hearing before *qāḍī al-ḥājj* 'Izz al-Dīn.

*seal* . . .

The reason for the document [arises] from a judgment by the one so authorized, *qāḍī al-ḥājj* 'Izz al-Dīn, [in a dispute] that arose between Badawī and "the son of the sultan" 'Aqrab.[90]

*Plea by the plaintiff*

Badawī, for himself and representing his community, made his plea, "We have land in the vicinity of the locality called Khirībān which was opened up by our grandfathers.[91] They bequeathed it to our fathers, and we inherited it from our fathers. It has never ceased to be our property, and we have possessed and owned it from Sultan Aḥmad Bukr's time until now. Recently 'Aqrab, 'the son of the sultan', began to encroach upon our land, and I repeatedly raised our complaint with him, but he has not submitted to the Law".

*Plea by the defendant*

Then the said 'Aqrab was questioned; he replied, saying, "This is the locality that Sultan 'Abd al-Raḥmān granted me and [here is] my charter for it".

*Examination by the judge*

When we read the document, we found [it concerned] a dispute between him and *al-ḥājj* Zarrūq. But this community (of Badawī), their land is far from *al-ḥājj* Zarrūq's land.

*Injunction by the judge*

So we restrained him from their land; but he did not restrain himself and afterwards encroached upon their land. Therefore we sent word to him that he should submit to the Law and if he had a claim to the land of this community he should make a claim. Then *faqīh* 'Abdallāh al-Ṭayyib went out to him. A gathering of Muslims were present and he said to ['Aqrab], "If you have a claim to the land of Badawī's people, go to the Law, but [now] restrain [yourself] and remove [yourself] from their land". Thereafter *faqīh* 'Abdallāh came and informed us of this.

*The judgment*

We have given judgment to Badawī and his community over their land; we have dismissed 'Aqrab's dispute with them and have prohibited him from raising the claim again.

*The witnesses*

Among our witnesses to this were, *faqīh* Aḥmad Majdhūb, *faqīh* Bilayla [or Balīla], *faqīh* Yūsuf Hadī, *faqīh* 'Abd al-Bārī Muḥammad Jurāb, Sanbal, 'Isāwī w. b.r.n., Ādam r.t.f.l. [or r.t.gh.l.], *malik* Fazārī, *malik* Sharaf, the officials Diyya and the *sajjān* k.s.ī,[92] *faqīh* Ādūma, *faqīh* Badawī, Muḥammad t.sh.ī., and a gathering too numerous to record here for fear of prolonging [the list].

With the date: Wednesday, the year one thousand, two hundred and twenty[93] from the Emigration of the Prophet, which is held in blessed memory with prayers and blessings.

## XVII

A letter from Sultan Muḥammad al-Faḍl to *al-ḥājj* Wādī (or Wāday) concerning the demarcation of land between Badawī and ʻAqrab, possibly following on from XVI.

*seal*[94] . . .

In the name of God, the Compassionate, the Merciful.[95]

From the presence of the supreme sultan, the most generous sovereign, who unfurls the banner of justice, the very patient; our lord and august one Sultan Muḥammad al-Faḍl, the victorious, whom God renders victorious, Amen; son of the late Sultan ʻAbd al-Raḥmān al-Rashīd, may God cause him to rest in peace. Amen.

To our servant, *al-ḥājj* Wādī; fullest greetings to you.

Thereafter: concerning the *faqīh* Badawī's coming to you; upon his arrival, he will present witnesses of long standing,[96] who know the boundaries of their ancestral cultivations, recorded in the sultanic charters. They are to swear upon the Book of Almighty God and to demarcate what is [described] in the previous and subjoined charters. You are to transfer the remaining land left over to the ownership of "the son of the sultan" ʻAqrab.

We have hereby informed you, so be not negligent.

The area of this land is called Kamal[a] Kīrī and the *falqanāwī*, the bearer of [this] letter, is our servant the venerable Sanbal.[97]

After shaykh Badawī and his brothers have come and the testimony has been sworn and they have demarcated the boundary of their cultivations which [are described] in the sultanic charters, [ʻAqrab] is to hand over their cultivations to them.[98] You are then to transfer the remainder to the ownership of "the son of the sultan" ʻAqrab.

Greetings.

## XVIII

A letter from *al-ḥājj* Wādī (or Wāday) to *bāsī* Abū Ḥasan: this may be connected with the previous letter.

*seal* The property of *al-ḥājj* Wādī the year 1217.[99]

Praise be to God alone.

From the respected *faqīh al-ḥājj* Wādī, may God preserve his agents[100] and the Muslims. Amen.

To bāsī \Abū Ḥasan/,[101] from me a thousand greetings.

Thereafter: concerning the venerable Badawī w. ʻAbdallāh Maṭlūq, living at Khirībān. Previously you were commissioner[102] when he was before us in a case over that place, which you demarcated for him. The Law now requires you inasmuch as you were then the commissioner.[102]

Therefore, when my letter reaches you please come to us to show us his boundaries, which have been written down for him in our lord's charter. This is my letter to you, brother, and let there be no remissness from you.

And fullest greetings.

The Tunjur holy men were also involved in an acrimonious dispute with their neighbour to the south, the Fulani holy man, Kabbāsh and his kin. In XIX the sultan writes forcefully to the *takanāwī* ordering him to investigate an affray between the Awlād Kabbāsh and the Awlād Maṭlūq. The complicated land dispute that no doubt led to the violence is heard before the *maqdūm* of northern Dār Fūr in XX.

## XIX

A letter from Sultan Muḥammad al-Ḥusayn to the *takanāwī* Muḥammad.

*seal* . . .

From the Commander of the Faithful, our lord and master Sultan Muḥammad al-Ḥusayn al-Mahdī, victorious through the Most High God, Amen.

To the *takanāwī* Muḥammad.

Thereafter: I hereby inform you that *faqīh* Muḥammad has complained to us[103] that Aḥmad b. *al-faqih* Kabbāsh, Saʻd and

'Abd al-Raḥmān deliberately and aggressively surrounded and attacked them [Muḥammad's people] on their estate, and wounded and inflicted great evil upon them, seizing four donkeys and six waterskins[104] from them. This is an affair of the utmost evil.

Immediately my letter reaches you with [the] *falqanāwī* al-Jabbay, send a person [*zōl*] from your entourage to go with him, so that they can investigate the place where they quarrelled,[105] find the culprit among them, return what they took to its rightful [owner], restrain them and keep them away from *faqīh* Muḥammad's estate; and escort Aḥmad, Sa'd and 'Abd al-Raḥmān to our presence, so that the *falqanāwī* can inform us about the culprit among them.

Thus have we informed you.

Greetings, a thousand, thousand, thousand times.

## XX

A judgment delivered by the *maqdūm* Ḥasan Segere in a dispute between the *faqīhs* Kabbāsh and Muḥamad b. Madanī.

*seal* *Iriqā*[106] the *malik* Ḥasan Siqirī. The year 12 ɸ . . .[107]

It has been recorded and established in a lawful judgment enacted by the one so-authorized as the judge in this [case], the *amīn*, *maqdūm* Ḥasan Siqirī, sitting as judge [by appointment from] the Commander of the Faithful, Sultan Muḥammad Ḥusayn, in a lawsuit between *faqīh* Kabbāsh and *faqīh* Muḥammad, representing his father Madanī with his authorization.

*Plea by the plaintiff*

First the *faqīh* Kabbāsh made his plea, "I have land in the district of the *shartay* n.j.l.mū, which Sultan Muḥammad Tayrāb had granted to the *imām al-ḥājj* 'Abd al-Ghanī.[108] [The latter] presented it to my father, *faqīh* 'Abd al-Salām, who possessed and made use of it freely until he died, having bequeathed it to us. We possess and make use of it [now]; our land is called Kurqā Khayrbān [being] the cultivations (*iḥyā'*) of the sons of Darash, [whose] boundaries have been demarcated. Muḥammad has fields [which were] opened up to cultivation by his grandfather and bequeathed to him. Then they committed a transgression in entering my land. So our lord Sultan Muḥammad al-Ḥusayn appointed the *faqīh* Abū Bakr as judge for us and we took our dispute with him [before the judge], who awarded judgment in my favour over my land and rejected [Muḥammad's] claim. Here is my [document of] the judgment."

Thus his plea was concluded after examination, but proof [for his plea] was lacking.

*Plea by the defendant*

Then the defendant Muḥammad, representing his father Madanī with his authorization, made his reply. "Our fields are cultivations opened up by my grandfather, 'Abdallāh, in Sultan Mūsā's time and he possessed and made use of his cultivations until Sultan Muḥammad Tayrāb's time [when the sultan] wrote for my grandfather 'Abdallāh his [right of] privilege and ratified his fields for him as his possesion by means of a charter from him. He possessed and made use of them until he bequeathed them to my father, Madanī. Neither the *faqīh* Kabbāsh nor anyone else has troubled us at our fields,[109] until the slaves (*al-'abīdī*), [namely] the people of the *jabbay's* household, whose leader was called s.n.f.tā,[110] acted unjustly towards us. So I took my complaint to our lord the Comander of the Faithful Sultan Muḥammad al-Ḥusayn; he examined my charters and arranged for me with his servant,[111] the *amīn maqdūm* Ḥasan, that [Ḥasan] should send out from his entourage a man to go with me and demarcate my boundary with the proof against the slaves and prevent them [from trespassing on my land].

Therefore [Ḥasan] sent out *al-ḥājj* Amīn, Shaykh of the Takārīr, [who] went to the land's locality. I summoned my witnesses for him, who were the people [living along] my boundaries, and he administered the oath upon the Book of God to them. They walked around the fields, east, west, north and south; and he granted me ownership of it and forbade the slaves [to enter] my [land].

Then *al-ḥājj* Amīn wrote down the boundaries of my fields for me and went before the *maqdūm* and informed him about it. And the *maqdūm* conveyed [Amīn's report] to our lord and told him about it. Then [the sultan] awarded judgment in our favour over the boundaries of the fields and ratified it for us.[112]

As for the *faqīh* Kabbāsh – between me and him are some demarcated lands[113] [belonging to] the Fūlānī *faqīhs*, [that is] the *faqīh* Jalāla's people, and to the *faqīhs*, [that is] the *faqīh* Wadā'a's sons;[114] these are my boundaries. I have not overstepped the boundary of my cultivation. Rather, it was he who trespassed upon us; for this reason we are [now] impoverished. The court hearing that he mentions – before the *faqīh* Abū Bakr. This is correct, but I did not get justice. My land is mine,"

Thus [his plea] was concluded after examination, but [further] proof [for his plea] was lacking.

*The judge's examination*

Thereupon I recorded the affair of them both and the pleas lacked any other proof. We examined the documents in the presence of a number of the *'ulamā'* and found the charter of our lord[115] to be just as Muḥammad claimed. We questioned Kabbāsh as to the truth [of the affair]: he said [that it was true] except that [Muḥammad] had increased the boundary of his own fields [by encroaching on Kabbāsh's]. We examined the *faqīh* Abū Bakr's document and found that the fields [under dispute] had been reserved [for] Muḥammad by his lord[116] and that there was no proof for the *faqīh* Kabbāsh in any way. [Abū Bakr] said in his written judgment that every claim that was incompatible with customary usage and denied by custom, was to be rejected.

*The opinion of the 'ulamā*

When the case had reached this stage, I took counsel with the *'ulamā'*. They agreed among themselves as to the validity of Muḥammad's charter, [namely] that he was the owner of the cultivations, that he had in his possession charters, that the former [sultans] had ratified [his cultivations] for him as his possession, and that his cultivations preceded the estate carved out by the *faqīh* Kabbāsh because [their opening up] occurred in our lord Sultan Mūsā's time while [those of] Kabbāsh had been carved out in our lord Sultan Tayrāb's time, [that is] the cultivations belonging to the sons of Darash.

Furthermore, [the *'ulamā'* agreed] that Muḥammad had nothing to do but to take the oath as Madanī's representative that he had not extended the boundaries of his fields: [that is that the land] he could make use of and [which] he possessed and owned were his cultivations (*iḥyā'*).

*The 'ulamā'*

This was recorded in the presence of a number of *'ulamā'*; the *faqīh* Muḥammad Sālim, the *imām* Muḥammad al-Miṣrī,[117] the *faqīh* Sa'd, the *faqīh* Najjār (or Bukhārī), the *imām* Sulaymān Jubayr, *al-ḥājj* Muḥammad 'Abdallāh, the *naqīb* Barakāt and the *faqīh* Aḥmad Ṣāliḥ.

*The judgment*

When this became obvious to him, *faqīh* Kabbāsh fled from the court and defied the Law. Therefore, I administered the oath to

Muḥammad Madanī as [his father's] representative. I awarded judgment to him for his fields with their boundaries as demarcated in our lord Sultan Muḥammad Ḥusayn's charter, in accordance as the Law has awarded judgment through his having brought them under cultivation (*bi-iḥyā'ih*). I have dismissed the *faqīh* Kabbāsh's claim and have denied him [the right of] appeal following this [judgment].

*The witnesses*

Our witnesses to our judgment [were] the *faqīh* Hadī, Sirāj, the *faqīh* Makkī, *al-ḥājj* Muḥammad, the *faqīh* 'Abd al-Raḥmān, the *faqīh* Fakhr al-Dīn, the *faqīh* Maḥmūd, Nūr Wīr, the *faqīh* Amīn, the *faqīh* Aḥmad Ṣāliḥ and a gathering too numerous to be recorded here for fear of prolonging [the list]. And God is the best of Witnesses.

The year 1261 of the Emigration of the Prophet.[118]

In XX the defendant, Muḥammad b. Madanī, explains how he and his father came to obtain the land of Kamala Kīrī as their own estate. Some of their land had been seized by a gang of slaves under one s.n.f.tā (in XXI s.n.f.tī) belonging to the household of the chief of the tax-collectors. The slaves, *al-'abīdī*, were thus from one of the many *'abīdiyya* settlements planted by the sultans and their chiefs throughout their state.[119] Muḥammad complained to the sultan who sent him to the *maqdūm* Ḥasan to have his land legally demarcated before granting it to him as a charitable estate (the charter being XI; see further XXII below). We have thus a vivid example of one reason why holy men and others sought personal grants of charitable estate, protection from the slaves of the great.

In XXI the *āb shaykh dālī*, as head of the hierarchy of slave officials, writes on the sultan's behalf to warn off s.n.f.tī from Muhammad's land.

## XXI

A letter from the *malik* Raḥm to the *malik* s.n.f.tī.

*seal* The *malik* Raḥm, Servant of the Sultan. The year 1254.[120]

From the palm of our lord the sultan, the *abū shaykh dālī* Raḥm, may God show him benevolence, Amen.

To the *malik* s.n.f.tī.

Thereafter: the Shaykh Madan(ī) has taken his complaint before our lord, the Commander of the Faithful and the solace of the Muslims, my lord Sultan Muḥammad Ḥusayn al-Mahdī, may God grant him aid, Amen, that he has been ill-treated by you in that you have seized his land.

However, he has a charter from our lord, the late Sultan Muḥammad al-Faḍl, may God have mercy upon him, Amen, [showing] that he has a demarcated boundary [which] the *falqanāwī* Mītī had previously demarcated for him.

Our lord has referred him to me [and] has instructed me to convey to you that you should keep away from their land, the boundary of which [is given] in our lord's charter [and which] the commissioner Mītī has delimited.

Withdraw from it and relinquish it as [laid down] in the charter of our lord the sultan. And if you have taken from them any of their possessions, return it to them.

XXII records a hearing of a dispute among the descendants of 'Abdallah Maṭlūq. One group led by Ādam demands the community's original charter of privileges (*al-ajwāh*) and land. The motive for the demand is obscure, but it may be connected with a dispute over the leadership of the community. Physical ownership of the charters may have been essential to a claim to leadership of the community and hence to the right to dispose of the community's land, or the name(s) of the original grantee(s) may have been in dispute.[121] However, once it is established that all the parties were entitled to participate in the privilege, the defendant Muḥammadayn b. Madanī, upstages the plaintiffs by producing his family's charter of estate or *iqṭā*', that is, XI above.

The judge rules that Ādam and his party had only rights of *iḥyā*, that is *iḥyā' al-mawāt*, namely the right to clear and settle virgin land. In other words, privilege conferred no direct rights over land. Since Muḥammadayn held the land as *iqṭā*', the judge rules in his favour, citing Khalīl's *Mukhtaṣar* on the right of the ruler to grant *iqṭā*' in territory not conquered by force.[122]

## XXII

A hearing before the judge Ḥammād.

And our lord the *qāḍī*
has found it correct
(*ṣaḥḥahu*).[123]

*seal* [illegible]

It has been established, set down and recorded in a legal judgment enacted by the one so-authorized and the judge (*al-ḥākim*) in this matter, the *qāḍī* Ḥammād, acting for his uncle, the *shaykh al-quḍāt*, our master Isḥāq, in [a dispute which] arose between two men, of sound mind, mature age and free from any legal impediments [which would lead] to the nullification of the judgment, – Ādam [acting] for himself and representing his associates, upon their authorization, Muḥammad Rīl, Muḥammad, another Ādam and Aḥmad.[124]

*Plea by the plaintiff*

First Ādam made his plea and said, "I have been ill-treated by Muḥammadayn; I sought from him the charter of privileges (*al-ajwāh*) and the land brought into cultivation by our grandfathers, [namely] Sultan Abu'l-Qāsim's charter and Sultan Tayrāb's charter." Thus his plea was concluded after examination [by the judge].

*Plea by the defendant*

We summoned the defendant, who was Muḥammadayn, [to make] his reply. He said, "I have Sultan Tayrāb's charter; I shall bring it." Thus his plea was concluded after examination [by the judge].

*Examination by the judge*

Thereupon, having understood both their pleas, we enjoined Muḥammadayn to fetch the charter. He was given a postponement and was bound by [the oath of swearing to divorce] his wife to fetch the charter. And within the agreed time, Muḥammadayn brought our lord Tayrāb's charter. We examined it and found [it to be] a charter of privilege (*maktūb jāh*)[125] for their grandfathers and [for] the cultivation of their land. Similarly, Ādam brought a document that [concerned] their grandfathers; they had taken a dispute among themselves over the land before the *qāḍī* 'Izz al-Dīn – concerning the land of Kamāl Kīrī, the cultivations of their grandfathers – and they had had judgment given to them over it.[126] "And Muḥammadayn is one of us in the privilege and the cultivations."[127]

We then examined Muḥammadayn: he said, "No! The land of Kamāl Kīrī is an estate (*iqṭā'*) belonging to me, since our lord Sultan Muḥammad al-Ḥusayn assigned it to my brother, Muḥammad, and my father, Madan(ī) and it is now my possession." We then asked for the charter for the estate and he presented to us our lord Muḥammad al-Ḥusayn's charter. We examined it and found it [to be] an allodial concession (*iqṭā' nājiz*), whereby our lord had favoured and given to the *faqīh* Muḥammad the land of his grandfather, 'Abdallāh, and had sent them to the *maqdūm* Ḥasan. He sent out from his entourage the shaykh Amīn al-Katakāwī. *They went to this*[128] land of Kamāl Kīrī in *shartay* Muḥammad n.l.mū's district; and the *faqīh* Muḥammad and his father, Madan(ī) walad 'Abdallāh Maṭlūq, had with them eight men, who took the oath upon the Book of God concerning the boundary of their land.

> The boundary begins on the eastern side with [the land of] *faqīh* Ḥabīb's people, [namely] the *mayram* Khadimallāh's sons, at the riverbed; [then] it runs by Umm Rajī field and to the channel of the riverbed [that is] the boundary with Dabirtū; and to the tomb which is there [at] the white ⌜*al-h.s.l.mās*⌝,[129] and it runs to the white hillocks, and to the waterhole of Tūrā[130] [or Tawrā], and to [the land of] the *faqīh* Wadā'a's sons, [that is] the boundary at the *faqīh* 'Uthmān Jundī's fields. Then [the boundary] runs to the Azbāba hillocks, [that is] the boundary with the Fallāt(a) of *faqīh* 'Izz al-Dīn, and to the fields of r.khī,[131] and to [the land of] the *falqanāwī* sh.q.r.. Then it runs to Jabal sh.q.r al-kabīr and to Jabal al-Samū'; then it runs to the Kalwa riverbed, and to Jabal Umm 'Arīf, and to the *sayyal inḍirāb* tree; then it runs to Jabal Sarāya and 'Arā; and to Jabal Martabū and to the Maqābil hillocks, and to the fields of Ma'tūq;[132] and the boundary comes back to the riverbed with [the land of] the *mayram* Khādimallāh's sons. These are the boundaries of the said land which *al-ḥājj* Amīn, shaykh of the Takārīr, demarcated – the land of Kamāl Kīrī.

Our lord Sultan Muḥammad al-Ḥusayn has given to *faqīh* Muḥammad and his father, Madan(ī), an estate, to them and their descendants after them as a confirmed property and [with] full possession;[133]

and I have relinquished to them all its revenues, both Sharīʿa and customary, namely *zakāh*, *fiṭra*, *dam* and *fisq*. Let no one interfere with their land at the same locality, and let not this be changed by any sultan after me.

Both their pleas [were set forth] in this manner. We took counsel with the *ʿulamā*'; they agreed with our opinion. We examined the

Document XXIII

Book of God and found that Ādam was claimant (*mudda'i*) to [the right of] cultivation (*al-iḥyā'*) and Muḥammadayn was claimant to the estate (*al-iqṭā'*). [However, rights of] estate take precedence over [rights of] cultivation: as the Author (*al-muṣannif*) says,

> Cultivated land [in the territory conquered] by force may not be assigned as a concession. But cultivated land [in territory not conquered] by force may be so assigned by the *imām*, 'Abd al-Bāqī.[134]

*The judgment*

Following this, we rejected the suit of Ādam and his above-mentioned associates; we have given judgment to *faqīh* Muḥammadayn over his land and have confirmed for him our lord Sultan Muḥammad al-Ḥusayn's charter.

*The witnesses*

Among the witnesses to our judgment were the *faqīh* Aḥmad Zarrūq, the *faqīh* Jamīl, the *faqīh* Ibrāhīm, the *faqīh* Ḥasan, the *faqīh* Aḥmad and the *malik* Muḥammad, and a large gathering of commoners and notables.

The year 128(0).[135]

Our last document from Khirībān, XXIII, raises a similar legal point to XXII. The plaintiff, Muḥammadayn, sues Muḥammad Hūd, a son of Sultan Muḥammad al-Faḍl, for serious trespass. 'Aqrab (in XVI and XVII) and Hud[136] provide two examples of the exploitation by members of the royal clan of the weakness of the central authority in the later years of Muḥammad al-Ḥusayn's long reign,

> He (Muḥammad al-Ḥusayn) also provided *hawakir* on an excessive scale for the numerous members of the royal family, who had previously lived on the prince's own income, arbitrarily tearing away these estates from their earlier associations.[137]

The case is presented legally in terms of a conflict between *iqṭā'* and *jāh*-rights; the judge evidently felt that the former were stronger than the latter – an interpretation supported by XXII – although he does not explicitly say so.[138] However, the judge must have felt uncertain since he refers the case to the sultan for a decision. But the sultan decides against his brother, a decision that suggests that Nachtigal's comment is perhaps overdrawn.

One considerable puzzle is why Muḥammadayn did not produce his own family *iqṭā'* charter, XI, in court to counter Hūd's claim.

## XXIII

A record of a hearing before the *maqdūm* Raḥm.

*seal* (illegible)

The reason for the document and the necessity of recording a judgment from the one so-authorized, the deputy (*nā'ib*) of the Commander of the Faithful, the *amīn*, *maqdūm*, *malik* Raḥm [arises] from a case between the son of the Commander of the Faithful, the *faqīh* Muḥammad Hūd, and the *faqīh* Muḥammadayn [acting] for himself and representing his brothers, the descendants of his grandfather, 'Abdallāh Maṭlūq, upon their authorization.

I brought together the witnesses and summoned the plaintiff among them [to come forward].

*Plea by the plaintiff*

The *faqīh* Muḥammadayn made his plea, saying in his plea, "We have [a piece of] land called Kamāl Kīrī, the cultivated land (*iḥyā'*) of our grandfather, the aforementioned 'Abdallāh. He opened it up to cultivation and made use of it over a period [of time]. Then, in the time of our lord the late Muḥammad Tayrāb he asked [the sultan] for [the right of] privilege and [for the land] as an estate (*al-iqṭā'*). [The sultan] granted the privilege and an estate[139] to him from the boundary of his cultivations. ['Abdallāh] owned it and made use of it until he died; he bequeathed it to his sons, our grandfathers; and they inherited it from him; and our fathers similarly inherited it from their fathers, and we similarly inherited it from them. And now the son of our lord, *faqīh* Muḥammad Hūd, has attacked and seized our villages and farms – everything. He has left us nothing. Because of this I demand justice from him in this court; these are our charters [which provide] full proof for us." Thus [his plea] was concluded, after examination [by the judge] when he said, "[This is] my case."

*Plea by the defendant*

Then we summoned the disputant, *faqīh* Hūd, for his statement of rebuttal and he replied with a disavowal, saying, "I did not know that they had the land I had taken and, in truth, the locality which he is claiming is my land. My father, the late Sultan Muḥammad al-Faḍl, assigned it to me while he was alive and I occupied and made use of it. After his death, my brother [Sultan

Muḥammad al-Ḥusayn] – [may his] life [be] long[140] – who is still with us, confirmed it for me. These are my documents [which provide] full proof for me."

*Examination*

Thus both their pleas were established in our mind, together with those acquainted [with the facts] (*al-'ārifīn*). We ordered them to present their charters and both of them showed them to us. We examined them together with those who were acquainted [with the facts]: we scrutinized them both and found that *faqīh* Muḥammadayn's charter which is ascribed to our lord the late Tayrāb was [a grant of] privilege [for their persons] and for [their] fields, but not as an estate (*bi'l-iqṭā'*), and *faqīh* Muḥammad Hūd's charter was an allodial concession. Then, when the contents of their charters had been examined by us, together with those acquainted [with the facts], I referred the case to my lord – [may his] life [be] long – [and] described the matter to him together with the charters. And he looked at them and instructed me that *faqīh* Muḥammad Hūd was to be banned from their villages and farms.

*The judgment*

Then I summoned [Hūd] and informed him of what my lord had said; he obeyed and left their villages and farms, in the presence of a gathering of Muslims. Thus I authorized this after consultation with those acquainted [with the facts] and they agreed with our opinion.

I have given judgment for *faqīh* Muḥammadayn over his village with his brothers and all their farms, after his [Hūd's] withdrawal from them both [i.e. the farms and the village]. I rejected his suite once more; no appeal will be heard from him following this [hearing].

*The witnesses*

Among those present and witnesses to this [were] the *faqīh* 'Abd Ṣāliḥ, *faqīh* Aḥmad, *faqīh* Fakhr al-Dīn,[141] his father *faqīh* Muḥammad Sālim, *faqīh* 'Abd al-'Āl, Ṣāliḥ, Muḥammad Nīl [or Nayl] and a numerous gathering: God is the Best of witnesses.

It was written in 1289.[142]

## XXIV and XXV: The Masāmīr Arabs[1]

In XXIV Sultan 'Abd al-Raḥmān grants a group of fifty-one Arab nomads, whose names are carefully listed, to the *amīn* Muḥammad Dokkumi b. 'Alī Jāmi'.[2] The nomads are described as having been brought back from *dār al-ṣabāḥ*, "the land of the east", which probably means in this context Kordofān, an interpretation supported by what is known of the *amīn*'s career.[3]

The *amīn's* father, 'Alī b. Jāmi', had accompanied Tayrāb as his *wazīr* on the expedition to Kordofān in 1200/1785–86. During the succession crisis at Bāra caused by Tayrāb's death, 'Alī is said to have committed suicide following his failure because of the treachery of the slave eunuch, Muḥammad Kurra, to carry out Tayrāb's dying wish that his son succeed him.[4] Muḥammad Dokkumi succeeded his father as *wazīr* to the new sultan, 'Abd al-Raḥmān, who later sent him back to Kordofān to arrest Kurra, whom the sultan suspected was trying to make himself independent in the new province. The *amīn* returned again to Kordofān which he governed for a number of years before being recalled and, according to Nachtigal, imprisoned in Jabal Marra by the sultan in order that Kurra, now restored to favour, might have a free hand to ensure the succession of the young and unpopular Muḥammad al-Faḍl.[5]

There were thus several occasions on which the *amīn* could have brought the Masāmīr (or Misāmīr), described in XXV as the descendants of Sallām al-Musmārī, back from Kordofān. The nomads were probably a section of the Zayyādiyya who were (and are) found in both Kordofān and Dār Fūr.[6] XXIV does not specify the obligations of the nomads towards their lord (neither does XXV), simply stating that they had been given to the *amīn*.

In XXV Muḥammad al-Faḍl grants the same nomads, now reduced to forty-seven names, to his *wazīr*, Hāmid b. Aḥmad Sakīn, a descendant of Sultan Ahmad Bukr.[7] In the same document he appoints Qurayb as their shaykh.

# XXIV

*seal* Sultan ʿAbd al-Raḥmān, son of Sultan Aḥmad Bukr, son of Sultan Mūsā. The year 1214.[8]

In the name of God, the Compassionate, the Merciful: may the blessing and peace of God be upon Muḥammad, his family and companions.[9]

From the presence of the supreme and venerable sultan, endowed with justice and righteousness, who follows the Sunna and the Book, who hopes for the pardon, approval and reward of his Lord, who believes in the Last Day, the Resurrection and the Accounting, who entrusts his affairs to the Creator, the One, the Benefactor: our lord Sultan ʿAbd al-Raḥmān, may God render him victorious, Amen; son of the late Sultan Aḥmad Bukr, may God sanctify his spirit and illumine his tomb, Amen, through the influence of Muḥammad the Faithful and his sagacious companions.

To all who encounter this charter, namely the *maliks*, sons of the sultan.[10] officials, shaykhs of the nomads and *kursīs*.

Thereafter: the aforesaid mighty and victorious sultan has granted to the *amīn* Muḥammad b. *al-amīn* ʿAlī the Masāmīr Arabs (or nomads) [and] has given him them, namely, Shaykh ʿAlī, *khabīr* m.r.jī,[11] Tayrāb, Faḍl, Manzil, Fāīq, m.sīl, h.w.l., Shikāb, Bulawla,[12] Balilī,[12] Manān, Ambarāk, Duwwār, Ubayḍ, m.h.l., m.n.h.l., ʿAyn, Qabūsh, Jāīd,[12] Wādī,[12] Jumʿa, ⌜Munīr⌝, Dānī, ʿUjayl, Ḥāmid, ʿAtiyya, Balūla, Ḥamad Abī Zayd, Hārūn, Mujāwwir, Jiʿrān, Duhaysh, Jawdatallah, Hirān, Muḥammad Hārin, Ḥamad "the blind",[13] m.ʿ.d., Mirāq, m.b.d., Muḥammad al-Ṭayr, Mufriḥ, Majāzi, ⌜another⌝ m.s.l., m.tiyya, Aydām, ⌜ʿIyyād, Muḥammad⌝, Naʿīm, Nuʿmān, and Nūl.[14] These are those whom the sultan has given to *amīn* Muḥammad because he has brought them from *dār al-ṣabāḥ* to Dār Fūr.

[Given] in the presence of the *malik* Ādam Bōsh, *malik* Ibrāhīm,[15] *malik faqīh* Muḥammad Junqīs,[16] *al-ḥājj* Muḥammad Ziyād, *bāsī* Ṭāhir,[17] Mūsā b. Ab(o), Ḥabīb "son of the sultan",[18] *bāsī* Ismāʿīl, Khamīs b. Maʿīn, *faqīh* Sirāj,[19] *faqīh* Ṭāhir b. al-*qāḍī*, and numerous witnesses...witness to this as to [its contents]...

## XXV

*seal* Sultan Muḥammad al-Faḍl, son of Sultan ʻAbd al-Raḥmān al-Rashīd, son of Sultan Aḥmad Bukr, son of Sultan Mūsā, son of Sultan Sulaymān. The year 1218.[20]

With blessings. In the name of God, the Compassionate, the Merciful: may the blessing and peace of God be upon our lord Muḥammad and his family.

From the presence of the mighty and glorious sultan, sovereign of the halters of the freemen, chosen of distinguished lineage, Sultan of the Muslims and Caliph of the community of the Lord of the Messengers, servitor of the Law and Religion, who trusts in the Most High God, the One, the Incomparable, the Just, the Patient; our lord and majesty, the triumphant and indefatigable sultan, Sultan Muḥammad al-Faḍl, the victorious, may the Most High God strengthen him, prolong his life and give victory to his armies, Amen; son of the late Sultan ʻAbd al-Raḥman al-Rashīd, may God sanctify his noble soul and illumine his exalted tomb. Amen.

To all who encounter this charter, namely, the *maliks*, sons of the sultan, officials, shaykhs of the nomads, *kursīs* and servants.

Thereafter: the aforesaid divinely-approved, divinely-assisted, felicitous and victorious sultan has granted to the *wazīr*, *amīn*, *faqīh* Ḥāmid "son of the sultan" the Masāmīr Arabs, who had previously been given by his late father, Sultan ʻAbd al-Raḥmān al-Rashīd, to *amīn* Muḥammad ʻAlī Jāmiʻ. [Ḥāmid] presented their charter to us. Now I, the aforesaid sultan, have confirmed [the grant of] the Masāmīr Arabs to *amīn*, *faqīh* Ḥāmid.

They are Shaykh ʻAlī, *khabīr* m.r.jī, Manzil, m.sīl, ḥ.w.l., Shikāb, Bulawla, b.l.,[21] Manān, Anbarāk,[22] Duwwār, Ubayḍ, m.h.l., m.n.h.l., ʻAyn, Qabūsh, Jāīd, Wādī, Jumʻa, Munīr, Dān(ī), ʻUjayl, Ḥāmid, ʻAṭiyya, Balūla, Ḥamad Abū Zayd, Hārūn, Mujāwwir, Jiʻrān, Duhaysh, Jawdatallāh, Hīrān, Ḥamad "the blind", m.ʻ.id, Mirāq, m.b.d., Muḥammad al-Ṭayr, Mufriḥ, Majāzī, another m.sīl., m.tiyya, Aydām, ʻIyyād, Muḥammad, Naʻīm, Nuʻmān and Nūl.[23]

These aforesaid [men] are the descendants of Sallām al-Musmārī; formerly their shaykh was ʻAlī.[24] Now [Ḥāmid] has presented his charter to us. Thereupon I, the aforesaid sultan, have confirmed the shaykhship and the aforementioned men upon

Shaykh Qurayb. They and their descendants are subject to Shaykh Qurayb; and they and their descendants are under the authority of[25] *amīn, wazīr, faqīh* Ḥāmid. They have been established as his and his descendants' Arabs (or nomads).

Let none dispute with him concerning his aforementioned nomads. Beware, beware of disobedience and interference. Greetings.

Written in the year 1221.[26]

## XXVI to XXXVII: The land and followers of Nūr al-Dīn b. Yaḥyā

Taken together, the following twelve documents give a vivid picture of the land, followers and quarrels of a middle-ranking Dār Fūr chief, *bāsī* Nūr al-Dīn b. *al-malik* Yaḥyā.[1] Nūr al-Dīn appears to have been a member of the Kaitiŋa ruling family, hereditary rulers of the *shartāya* of Dār Suwaynī, a large open area north-west of Kutum. The Kaitiŋa, who trace their descent to one Ibrāhīm Kaiti, are regarded genealogically as part Tunjur and part Zaghawa or part Fur and part Zaghawa and their *shartaya* had and has a mixed population of Zaghawa, Tunjur and Fur.[2] Nūr al-Dīn's brother, *malik* Maydōb b. Yaḥyā (XXXIV), was *shartay* of Suwaynī,[3] being apparently succeeded in about 1828 by his son, Muḥammad Rīl (XXXI and XXXII), who was in turn succeeded by his brother, Ṭāhir (XXXIII). Nūr al-Dīn was probably also a Zaghāwī on his mother's side (XXVII and XXVIII) and evidently a follower of the *wazīrs* Muḥammad Dokkumi and Ḥāmid b. Aḥmad Sakīn, since it was through the latter's mediation (*bi-wāsiṭa*) that he obtained the estate of Qum Qūm or Qumqūm (Gumgum) (XXXIV).

Collectively, the documents portray a courtier (*mulāzim* in XXXII) who flourished between 1800 and 1840, rich enough in livestock to bring herders back from Kordofān (XXVI); powerful enough at court (*khidma* in XXXII) to act as patron of his maternal kin (XXVII and XXVIII) and influential enough to acquire a vast expanse of *qōz*, Gumgum, as an estate within which he undoubtedly pastured his herds.[4] Of his service to the state, XXVI implies that he took part in one of the Kordofān campaigns, while in the one document from the Dor Archive not published here, he acts as the sultan's agent (*ra'īs min al-sulṭān*) in the settlement of some affairs in Dār Marārīt on the western marches of the sultanate.[5]

In XXVI, Nūr al-Dīn is granted three nomads, two men and their small brother, whom he had brought back from Kordofān to be "herdsmen for his camels". The charter in fact enacts two things, the grant to Nūr al-Dīn and an exemption from all taxes to the nomads so that they can serve their lord. It is worth noting the numerical range of these grants of herders; in XXIV and XXV some fifty herders are granted to the *wazīrs*, here a modest three, while in XL the *mayram* Zahra, still a baby, receives ten to serve her.

XXVII and XXVIII are originating and confirmatory charters which describe yet another variation in the granting of rights in people. In the first, Sultan 'Abd al-Raḥmān confirms a grant to Nūr al-Dīn made by his brother, *malik* Maydōb, of the people of the village of Kawra (or Kōra), who are apparently Nūr al-Dīn's maternal relatives. The meaning of the grant is spelled out clearly in the disposition of XXVIII, where the sultan exempts (*ḥurma, jāh*) the relatives from the tax-collector in order that they might pay (*qābilū*) their taxes, both *zakāh*, *fiṭra* and the customary taxes, to their relative and patron. Presumably this was regarded as an act of favour by both sides.

In XXIX Muḥammad al-Faḍl assigns the *qōz* of Qumqum to Nūr al-Dīn as an estate, a grant which is confirmed by Muḥammad al-Ḥusayn in XXX, a charter that is exceptionally explicit in its provisions.

## XXVI

Sultan 'Abd al-Raḥmān grants three nomads to Nūr al-Dīn.

*seal* Sultan 'Abd al-Raḥmān, son of Sultan Aḥmad Bukr, son of Sultan Mūsā, son of Sultan Sulaymān. The year 1202.[6]

With blessings. In the name of God, the Compassionate, the Merciful: may the blessing and peace of God be upon our lord Muḥammad and his family.

From the presence of the mighty and generous sultan, sovereign of the halters of the freeman, Sultan of the Muslims and Caliph of the Messenger of the Lord of the Universe, who protects the land of the [Islamic] religion, who trusts in the Most High God, the Praiseworthy, the Glorious, servitor of the Law and Religion, our lord to whom victory and aid are given, Sultan 'Abd al-Raḥmān al-Rashīd, may the Most High God strengthen him and grant him victory, Amen, through the influence of the noble prophet.

To all who encounter this charter, namely, the leading notables, *maliks*, soldiers and troops,[7] *shartays*, *dimlijs*, sons of the sultan, *mayrams*, *maliks* of the nomads and their shaykhs, *kursīs* and servants, all the officials and all the people of the sultan's state.

Thereafter: the aforesaid divinely-approved, divinely-assisted and victorious Sultan 'Abd al-Raḥman al-Rashīd, may God aid him with victory, Amen, has granted and given to Nūr al-Dīn b. *al-malik* Yaḥyā as herdsmen for his camels [some men] whom he brought [back] with him from "the land of the east",[8] [namely] the sons of Ṣāliḥ al-Jābirī, namely, 'Ujayna, Ghadīr and their small brother. The sultan has exempted the three men, the aforementioned Arabs, the sons of Ṣāliḥ al-Jābirī, with a complete exemption from all the customary taxes and service (*khidma*), and has given them to Nūr al-Dīn. They have been established as nomads for him (*ṣārū 'urbān lahu*) and his descendants to make full use of them.

Let none of the *maliks*, shaykhs, *kursīs* and servants interfere with him. Whosoever interferes with him, exposes himself to ruin.

The witnesses present at the council[9] were *bāsī* Bukr, *bāsī* Na'ma, *malik* 'Isāwī, *faqīh* Mālikī,[10] 'Abdallāh al-Naw, *al-ḥājj* 'Alī b. *al-amīn* Muḥammad, Fāris b. *al-malik* Ibrāhīm Ramād and Tāj(ā), and the writer of the document (lit., "letters") was 'Ubaydallāh 'Uthmān.

## XXVII[11]

Sultan 'Abd al-Raḥmān grants Nūr al-Dīn his maternal kin.

*seal* (illegible)

With blessings. In the name of God, the Compassionate, the Merciful: may the blessing [and peace of God be upon our lord Muḥammad and his family].

From the presence of the cynosure of the eminent...who tramples beneath his mount...the flags and banners, he whose deeds are pleasing to God...he whose Lord is his best companion and whose words are pleasing, [sultan of the Arabs] and non-Arabs, master of the sword and pen...upon the Most High God, the Praiseworthy, the Glorious...[our lord] to whom victory and aid are given, Sultan ['Abd al-Raḥmān al-Rashīd]...[12]

To all who encounter this charter...soldiers and troops, *shartays*, *dimlijs*...*mayrams*, *falqanāwīs*...lords of the state[13] and masters...of the sultan's state.

Thereafter: the divinely approved and victorious [Sultan] 'Abd al-Raḥmān al-Rashīd, may God aid him [with victory, Amen], has granted and given to Nūr al-Dīn his Zaqāwa maternal relatives[14]...in Kawrā [or Kōrā] village who before...his maternal relatives, the people of Kawrā village...*zinā*, *ḥāmil*, *quwwār*, *zakāh*, *fiṭra* and all...

Thus the aforesaid sultan has now granted and confirmed the gift of [the *malik*] Maydōb, [namely] all his maternal relatives, the people of Kawrā village...m.r.mī and his sons, Abō and his sons...Nasīr [or Nusayr] and his brothers, the sons of Bātī, Ādā and [his] sons, the sons of Faḍl, the sons of Yūsuf Ḥāmid and his sons;[15] that is all his maternal kin living at Kawrā village. All their customary taxes, of the aforesaid people and their village Kawrā, are to be paid to Nūr al-Dīn, His brother, the *malik* Maydōb, has granted him his maternal kin and Kawrā village and I have confirmed [the gift] to him of Kawrā village with all its customary taxes.

Let none of the people of my kingdom of the Arabs and the Blacks[16] interfere with him; let none dispute with him. This is a grant[17] of the sultan to his slave,[18] Nur al-Dīn, of the earlier gift. [There is] no claim upon him and his descendants until the Day of Resurrection and Raising to Life. Let none interfere with him.

[Given] in the presence of [both] notables and commoners, namely, *faqīh* Mālikī al-Fūtāwī, *malik* Mūsā b. *walad al-sulṭān* Muḥammad Rīz,[19] *malik* Ibrāhīm Tītī [or Taytī], *amīn* Sa'īd Taw, *malik* Ādam b. *al-malik* Ibrāhīm Ramād, Tājā, *faqīh* 'Abdallāh al-Naw, *al-ḥājj* Bashīr, *faqīh* Taka; and the witnesses were so numerous that it is not possible to record them [all]. And God is the Best of Witnesses.

The writer of this document [literally, "these letters"] was 'Ubaydallāh 'Uthmān Muḥammad Shaykh, secretary to the Grand *imām*.[20]

Written in the year 1216.[21]

## XXVIII

Sultan Muḥammad al-Faḍl confirms the grant to Nūr al-Dīn of his maternal kin.

*seal* Sultan Muḥammad al-Faḍl, son of Sultan 'Abd al-Raḥmān al-Rashīd, son of Sultan Aḥmad Bukr, son of Sultan Mūsā, son of Sultan Sulaymān. The year 1218.[22]

With blessings. In the name of God, the Compassionate, the Merciful: may the blessing and peace of God be upon our lord Muḥammad and his family.[23]

Document XXVIII

From the presence of the mighty sultan, most generous steward (*qahramān*), most magnificent coadjutor, who unfurls the banner of justice over the heads of the peoples, Sultan of the Muslims and Caliph of the community of the Lord of the Messengers, servitor of the Law and Religion, who holds fast to the Most High God, the One, Incomparable, Just and Patient, our lord and majesty, the sultan, son of the sultan, Sultan Muḥammad al-Faḍl, the victorious, may God aid him with victory, Amen, son of the late Sultan 'Abd al-Raḥmān al-Rashīd, may God sanctify his spirit, Amen.

To all who encounter this decree, namely, the people of the state and holders of authority, the *wazīrs*, *maliks*, *shartays*, *dimlijs*, sons of the sultan, *mayrams*, *ḥabbōbas*, *falqanāwīs*, *korays*, *jabbays* of the grain, cotton and seed, *qawwārs*, *makkās*-s and all the officials and all the people of the sultan's state.

Thereafter: the aforesaid divinely-approved, divinely-assisted and victorious sultan has granted and given Nūr al-Dīn b. *al-malik* Yaḥyā and has confirmed for him the inviolability of his maternal relatives (*ḥurmat akhwālihi*), the sons of d.r.fī, who had already been granted to Nūr al-Dīn by his late father, Sultan 'Abd al-Raḥmān al-Rashīd, may the clouds of the Most High God's mercy be upon him, Amen. Now [Nūr al-Dīn] has presented his charter to us and we have confirmed upon Nūr al-Dīn his aforesaid maternal relatives, namely, the sons of m.r.m.,[24] the sons of Baḥrī, the sons of d.r.fī, the sons of Bātī, the sons of b.q.t., the sons of Naṣīr [or Nuṣayr],[25] the sons of Dābō, the sons of Faḍl, the sons of Ādī,[26] the sons of Yūsuf, the sons of s.nō, their brothers and descendants and all their people and neighbours[27] and whoever is with them.

The sultan has forgiven them completely all their customary taxes and their *zakāh*, *fiṭra*, *hāmil*, *dam* and *fisq*. The sultan has granted them to Nūr al-Dīn b. *al-malik* Yaḥyā as his servants (*khuddāmahu*). They are to give all their customary taxes and their *zakāh* and *fiṭra* to Nūr al-Dīn. Thereby [the sultan] has given them inviolability and privilege; they and their descendants have become privileged of God and His Prophet and privileged of the aforesaid sultan.

Let no *malik*, *shartay*, *dimlij*, son of the sultan, *mayram*, *ḥabbōba* or *jabbay* of the grain interfere with them and let not their thong and rope [cast upon the ground] be removed.[28] Whosoever sprinkles them (*al-yarushshhum*) with cold water, I shall splash with blood. Beware, beware of disobedience and interference.

Written in the year 1225.[29]

# XXIX

Sultan Muḥammad al-Faḍl grants Qumqūm as an estate to the *bāsī* Nūr al-Dīn.

*seal* (illegible)

In the name of God, the Compassionate, the Merciful.[30]

From the supreme sultan and most generous sovereign (*khāqān*), who unfurls the banner of justice, our lord Sultan Muḥammad al-Faḍl, the victorious, may God grant him victory, Amen; son of the late Sultan ʻAbd al-Raḥmān al-Rashīd, may God grant him rest. Amen.

To all those who encounter this decree, namely, the *maliks*, *shartays*, *dimlijs*, sons of the sultan, *mayrams*, *jabbays*, *falqanāwīs*, *qāḍīs*, *kōrays* and the other notables of the state and holders of power.

Thereafter: the said Commander of the Faithful, Sultan Muḥammad al-Faḍl (may God aid him with victory, Amen) has assigned the land in *shartay* Muḥammad Rīl's district called Qum Qūm, which has been delimited by the commissioner from our (i.e. the sultan's) entourage Bishāra, the commissioner of *takanāwī* Muḥammad Kaykā and the official of the *shartay*[31] called Sōmfatā. The [land] has been assigned to our follower, *bāsī* Nūr al-Dīn, as a gift and donation for the sake of God the Noble, for the Day whereon neither wealth nor children will avail, save unto him who comes to God with a secure heart;[32] a lawful allodial concession [with] complete posession with all its revenues, *zakāh*, *fiṭra*, *dam*, *fisq*, *hāmil* and the other customary taxes.

Its boundaries begin from the direction of the east, from [the land of] the ʻ*abīdiyya*,[33] and run to the "flowing water-hole" where there is a rock; and they run to the Ramla riverbed between *malik* Tītī's [land] and [that] of *malik* Maydōb.

[The boundary] from the direction of the south is the thorn enclosure (*zarība*) of the Mānṣar Abū Ādam, and runs to the second[34] thorn enclosure, and comes to the twin *hijlīj* trees, and runs by[35] the Rafīda riverbed there [at] the twin *sallam* trees, and runs to "the burial grounds" (*al-turab*), and runs by[35] the deserted land (*bōbāya*) of Jumʻa, and runs by[35] the household (*bayt*) of Ḥāmid Muḥammad Kamar Daw to the *hijlīj* tree, crossing Qumqūm path. [The boundary] runs across to the muddy land[36] and *ṭundub* trees which are in the dune (*al-fi'l-dabba*), and runs to "the rocks of the lion", and descends to Muḥammad Abū Isḥāq's thorn enclosure, and runs to al-'Ajūz waterpool, and joins Tūwār (Tuer) path, and runs to the edge of the village of the Awlād Diyāt (or Dayyāt), and follows the Awlād Rashdān path.

And north [the boundary] runs to the field of Jamal, and goes to the *ḥashāb* trees and the boundary to [the land of] the *fuqarā'*, the Awlād Rashdān, and runs by the Qumqūm waterholes (*thammād*), and runs by al-Filfil waterpool, and descends by "the fissure of the lion" (*bi-qadd al-asad*), and to the water-holes of al-Tuwānis,[37] and runs to al-Tuwānis Rock, and runs to Imām Rock,[38] and the boundary rejoins [the land of] the *'abīdiyya* and turns (i.e. joins) with them. This concludes the boundaries which the commissioners demarcated.

They presented [a report] on these boundaries to us which we examined. We found it to be correct and have confirmed his land for *bāsī* Nūr al-Dīn. This land has been established as his property and of his descendants after him.

Let none dispute with him, let none interfere with him, none of the officials and servants. He has disposal of it in the same fashion as something of which an owner disposes as his property, with all its revenues, *zakāh*, *fiṭra* and all the other customary taxes, a lawful allodial concession [with] complete possession, a gift and donation for him and his descendants after him.

"And he who alters it after he has heard it, the sin thereof shall surely lie on those who alter it. Surely God is All-Hearing, All-Knowing."[39]

This is my letter and seal for him who knows it. Beware, beware of disobedience and obstinacy; the disobedient will bring censure upon only himself.

Written in the year 1238.[40]

Furthermore, You, *malik* Muḥammad Rīl, Keep away from this land and its customary taxes; Do not approach it for anything. Keep back from it; disobedience by you will bring censure upon yourself.

Written in the year 1238.[40]

# XXX

Sultan Muḥammad al-Ḥusayn confirms the grant of the estate of Qumqūm to *bāsī* Nūr al-Dīn.

*seal* (illegible)

From the presence of him through whom God illumines the lands, gives relief to [His] servants and sweeps away oppression and evil, the Commander of the Faithful, Sultan Muḥammad al-Ḥusayn, the victorious through the Most High God, Amen.

To everyone to whom this decree shall come, namely, the notables, the *amīrs*, *wazīrs*, *maliks*, *shartays*, *dimlijs*, sons of the sultans, *mayrams*, *falqanāwīs*, *qāḍīs*, *kōrays*, *jabbays*, *qawwārs*, *makkās*-s, and all those oppressors who trample upon the Muslims.[41]

Thereafter: my father, the late Sultan Muḥammad al-Faḍl, granted and assigned to his servant (*li-khādimihi*),[42] *bāsī* Nūr al-Dīn, land in the *shartay's* district called Qum Qūm.[43] He dispatched to him the commissioner Bishār(a) from his entourage, the commissioner of the *takanāwī* Muḥammad Kayk(a), and an official of the *shartay*, Sōmfatā. They assigned possession of it to him, from east, west, south and north.

(There follows the description of the boundaries as given in XXIX.)

The commissioner presented [a report] on these aforesaid boundaries and my father examined it and confirmed it for *bāsī* Nūr al-Dīn. It has been established as an allodial concession [with] complete possession for him, a gift and donation to him and his descendants after him; and [the sultan] forgave[44] him all its revenues, *zakāh*, *fiṭra* and all suchlike customary taxes. He thereby forgave him.

[Nūr al-Dīn] presented to me the charter of my father, the late Sultan Muḥammad al-Faḍl; I read [it] and confirmed this aforesaid land, which these boundaries enclose, to *bāsī* Nūr al-Dīn as a donation and gift and have forgiven him all that pertains to it of customary judicial taxes,[45] *dam*, *fisq*, *hāmil*, *nār*, *quwwār*, and similarly the Sharī'a [taxes], *zakāh* and *fiṭra*, which accrue from it and its inhabitants.[46] [I have confirmed these privileges] to him and his descendants after him.

Let none of those to whom we have referred [above] interfere or dispute with him. Whosoever interferes with him, exposes himself to ruin. This is my letter and decree to all both notable and commoner.

This was [written] on the night of the eleventh [day] to have elapsed in the month of Ramaḍān.

Despite the specific warning to him appended to the end of XXIX, *shartay* (or *malik*) Muḥammad Rīl appears to have been reluctant to accept his uncle Nūr al-Dīn's rights at Qum Qum. In XXXI, a court hearing before a senior chief of the region, he alleges that Nūr al-Dīn has been taking taxes from villages beyond the three that fall within his estate; the dispute is referred to the sultan. XXXII is a sarcastic letter from Sultan Muḥammad al-Faḍl to Rīl, which may have been written in response to the appeal made in XXXI; if Rīl is taking the taxes rightfully due to Nūr al-Dīn, "Then of what benefit is the estate?" A similarly sarcastic vein runs through XXXIII, addressed by Sultan Muḥammad al-Ḥusayn to *shartay* Ṭāhir, brother and successor to Rīl; XXXIII is, in fact, even stronger since in it the sultan threatens to dismiss the *shartay*, a prerogative the sultans rarely made use of.

All three documents vividly illustrate the dynamics of the supra-tribal state, the tensions that arose between the local chiefs and those of their kinsmen who used their position at the centre to gain power back home.

## XXXI[47]

A dispute between *malik* Muḥammad Rīl and his uncle, Nūr al-Dīn, heard before the *qirqīḍ* Ibrāhīm Khalīl Ramaḍān.

*seal* The *qirqīḍ*[48] Khalīl, son of the *malik* Ramaḍān.

In the name of God, the Compassionate, the Merciful; may the blessings of God be upon him after whom there is (no)[49] prophet.[50]

A sultanic document[51] [issued] by the *qirqīḍ* Ibrāhīm[52] Khalīl Ramaḍān, acting for the *āb takanāwī* Yaḥyā,[53] concerning [a dispute] between *malik* Muḥammad Rīl and his uncle, *bāsī* Nūr al-Dīn; with the authorization of our lord the sultan – [may his] life [be] long – our aforesaid lord Sultan Muḥammad al-Faḍl, may God render (him)[54] victorious through the influence of the lord (of the messengers)[55] ⌜al-ʿAdnānī⌝.[56]

[The *takanāwī*] sent[57] the *falqanāwī* to them to bring them before the *āb* [*takanāwī*]. The *āb* referred them to us that they might explain their affair. We asked them to begin their case.

*Plea by the plaintiff*[58]

*Bāsī* Nūr al-Dīn's plea was, "I have some land [which] our lord had assigned to me called Qumqūm. He sent a man as commissioner [who] demarcated [it] for me and made over the land and its three villages to me.[59] This [man] here, the *falqanāwī* of my lord Yaḥyā,[60] ⌜pointed out the dividing line opposite [the land of] the *shartay*[61] [which] reaches out from my land and its villages."⌝[62]

We asked[63] the plaintiff,[64] "Have you any further claim?" He said, "No, my speech is ended".

*Plea by the defendant*

We asked[63] *malik* Muḥammad Rīl to make a reply. He replied, saying, "In truth, the land to which you[65] are referring does have with it three villages.[66] [But] you have seized many villages – about ten – and the people's property. As for your possession[s],[67] which you have laid hold of,[68] they are illegal."

[The] *bāsī* said, "No! They are not illegal. Let us send [the dispute] for referral to our lord."[69]

*Examination by the judge*

Therefore we instructed the *falqanāwī* to take [their dispute] to our lord. But *malik* Muḥammad said, "You, *falqanāwī*, Wait a moment so that we, I and my father,[70] can try and reach an understanding.[71] If he agrees with me, Good! If he doesn't agree with me, take [our dispute] for referral [to the sultan]". At that point they reached an agreement between themselves, were content and stopped the dispute and the investigation going on between them. *Malik* Muḥammad confirmed for him [Nūr al-Dīn] the estate which our lord[72] had given him together with its boundaries.

(The description that follows is the same as in XXIX and XXX, with some errors.)

...this concludes the boundaries of the aforesaid land which the commissioners demarcated. They presented [a report] on these boundaries to our lord. Our lord examined [it] and confirmed [them] for *bāsī* Nūr al-Dīn.

[Nūr al-Dīn] presented [the charter to me]. We ratified and confirmed for him his land[73] as his property [and that of] his descendants after him.[74]

Let none dispute with him, let none interfere with him, none of the officials and servants. He has disposal of it in the same

fashion as something (of which an owner disposes)[75] as his property, with all its revenues, *zakāh*, *fiṭra* and the other customary taxes, a lawful[76] allodial concession [with] complete possession, a gift and donation[77] for him and his descendants after him.
"And he who alters it after he has heard it, the sin thereof shall surely lie on those who alter it. Surely God is All-Hearing, All-Knowing." [And] All-Seeing.[78]
The document was written in 1243.[79]

## XXXII

Sultan Muḥammad al-Faḍl writes to *shartay* Muḥammad Rīl.

*seal* Sultan Muḥammad al-Faḍl, son of Sultan 'Abd al-Raḥmān al-Rashīd, son of Sultan Aḥmad Bukr, son of Sultan Mūsā, son of Sultan Sulaymān. The year 1218.[80]

From the presence of the Commander of the Faithful Muḥammad al-Faḍl,[81] may the Most High God make him prosper, Amen.[82]

To the *shartāya*[83] Muḥammad Rīl.

Thereafter, your uncle, Nūr al-Dīn, has brought his complaint [to us] that you have siezed "the dirt of the estate",[84] which I had assigned to him there. If the matter is as he states, then of what benefit is the estate? Indeed, I gave it to him in order that he might make use of all the taxes which accrue from it because he is our follower at the court.[85]

After what has gone before,[86] you know all this; so now take your hand[s] from the boundary of his estate. Neither you nor your agents are to interfere in anything at all that arises therein, whether great or small. I have relinquished [lit. forgiven] it to him. Likewise, I warn the sons of *al-ḥājj* 'Umar against any aggression towards him.[87] Tell them to stay within their boundaries, which the Law has given them, and to stop their arrogance and intrigue.[88] Beware, beware of disobedience.

# XXXIII

Sultan Muḥammad al-Ḥusayn writes to *shartay* Ṭāhir.

*seal* (illegible)

From the Commander of the Faithful, Sultan Muḥammad al-Ḥusayn, victorious through the Most High God, Amen.

To the *shartāya* Ṭāhir

Thereafter: the occasion of the letter to you [arises] from your uncle, *bāsī* Nūr al-Dīn's villages, which my father assigned to him and whose customary dues and Shari'a taxes [lit. "dirts"] he relinquished to him. Earlier, a warning was given to your brother, *malik* Muḥammad Rīl, about this,[89] and now you have laid your hand[s] upon them. Stop, withdraw your hand[s] from it [them]. If these villages are worth more [to you] than the whole district [you administer], then let us know [and] we shall find [another person] who will serve [us] as [well as] you and who will obey our command and prohibition.

If you have taken anything from the aforesaid villages, return it to them in its entirety. If your uncle returns to us as a complainant, then choose of the two possibilities[90] the one which will be better for you. This is my last word. We have confirmed his old [estate] for him and have added to it for him.

Beware, Do not disturb it. Greetings.

The last four documents concerning Nūr al-Dīn's affairs illustrate once more the variety of conflicts that could arise over land. In XXXIV, the plaintiff, 'Alī Tōm and his associates, attempt unsuccessfully to claim that their land was not part of Qumqūm. Their persistence is such that Nūr al-Dīn has finally to bring sworn testimony to prove that their land lay within his estate.

In XXXV and XXXVI, Nūr al-Dīn, acting for his brother *malik* Maydōb, successfully rebuts the attempts of a determined *faqīh*, *al-ḥājj* 'Umar, to take some land from the *shartay*. The history of the land under dispute, b.nāb.n., is complicated, although clearly laid out in XXXV. The case is first heard before the *wazīr* Yūsuf b. Fiṭr, later to be promoted to *āb shaykh*. But despite a clear ruling against him, *al-ḥājj* 'Umar appeals to Sultan Muḥammad al-Faḍl, who with equal firmness confirms in XXXVI his *wazīr*'s judgment and forbids that the matter be raised again.

But *al-ḥājj* 'Umar's son, Abū Bakr, tries in XXXVII to revive the claim twenty years later in Sha'bān 1245/January–February 1830. By this time, *malik* Maydōb appears to have been dead and the disputed land now seems to have fallen within Nūr al-Dīn's estate, presumably at Qumqūm. But Abū Bakr had no case and Nūr al-Dīn had only to produce XXXV to win judgment.

## XXXIV

A dispute between 'Alī Tōm and *bāsī* Nūr al-Dīn heard before 'Ubaydallāh Muḥammad al-Sanūsī Abū'l-Ḥasan.

*seal* (illegible)

And thereafter:[91] it has been established in a lawful judgment [given] before the court of the Commander of the Faithful,[92] Sultan Muḥammad al-Faḍl, [by] 'Ubaydallāh Muḥammad al-Sanūsī Abū'l-Ḥasan in a case between 'Alī Tōm and *bāsī* Nūr al-Dīn Yaḥyā.

*Plea by the plaintiff*

First 'Alī, for himself and for those he represented upon [their] authorization and ⌜*bi-ḥawk wa-dir'*⌝[93] made his plea, "Our lord the sultan asigned to [the] *bāsī* [the] land of Qumqūm. He occupies it but has been hostile towards us in our place. Our lord gave him no [more] than the three villages [which] his brother, the *malik* Maydōb, had given him. Our lord confirmed for him his brother's gift, the three villages. He occupies [them] but has trespassed onto our cultivations (*iḥyā'*)".[94] He concluded [his plea].

*Plea by the defendant*

The defendant, [the] *bāsī*, replied, "I sought from the sultan through the mediation of (*bi-wāsiṭa*) the *wazīr*, *faqīh* Ḥāmid, the land called Qumqūm. Our lord granted me what I asked for, that is the land of Qumqūm, and dispatched[95] the *malik* Bishāra from his entourage to me. He made over possession of this aforesaid land to me. We know [nothing] about any gift of my brother."

*Examination and judgment*

We demanded the charter of the Commander [of the Faithful];[96] he produced it and it was read publicly (*'alā ru'ūs al-ashhād*). [The charter] promulgated the gift of the land of Qumqūm, it being clearly defined in all directions. We said to 'Alī, "Are you within these boundaries, or outside them?" He said that [his land] was within them. We therefore ordered him to hand over the area under dispute there inasmuch as it was within the assignment of the Commander [of the Faithful].

*Appeal and second hearing*

But he would not obey [our judgment] and took his complaint again to the Commander [of the Faithful].[97] He claimed that their place was[98] outside the land of Qumqūm, which the sultan had assigned to [the] *bāsī*.

*Second plea and testimony of the defendant*

Then [the] *bāsī* said, "This place of theirs is part and parcel of the land which is included under the name 'Qumqūm'." We then charged him to bring proof of this.

He absented himself[99] and then came with seven men who gave testimony that the place under dispute was part and parcel of the land of Qumqūm as it is [described] in our lord's charter.

*Second judgment*

We then gave 'Ali an opportunity to reject them [the witnesses] and their probity.[100]

We thereupon awarded judgment to [the] *bāsī* in accordance with what was in the charter of the Commander [of the Faithful], and dismissed the suit of 'Alī and those he represented and have denied them [the right of] appeal following this [judgment]; no claim by them is to be heard [again].

*The witnesses*

[Given] in the presence of the witnesses of the court; *malik* Luqmān Rīḥ, *malik* 'Abd al-Ṣādiq, *malik* Muḥammad Bōsh,[101] the [maternal] uncle[102] *faqīh* Muḥammad Dūd, *malik* Ādam *jarr lā baḥr*,[103] *malik* Muḥammad Ṣaḥnī, *malik* Muḥammad Dūd, *malik* 'Umar al-Qafā, *faqīh* Isḥāq Markaz, *faqīh* 'Abdallāh Sallāṭa, *faqīh* Ḥasan 'Ammār, *malik* Duqū, *malik faqīh* Ḥammād, Ṣuddayq w. Jābir, Muḥammad Tūt, 'Abd al-Ṣādiq, *malik* Ḥasan Siqīrī and Bukr.

And this was [enacted in] the year 1243.[104]

# XXXV

A dispute between *bāsī* Nūr al-Dīn, representing *malik* Maydōb, and *al-ḥājj* 'Umar heard before the *wazīr* Yūsuf b. Fiṭr.

*seal* The *amīn*, *maqdūm* Yūsuf.

Concerning a judgment by the one so-authorized, the *wazīr*, the aforesaid *amīn* Yūsuf b. Fiṭr,[105] acting for the Commander of the Faithful and Caliph of the community of the Lord of the Messengers, who trusts in the solicitude of the Glorious King, Sultan Muḥammad al-Faḍl, the victorious, son of our lord Sultan 'Abd al-Raḥmān al-Rashīd, may the mercy of God be upon him.

This [judgment concerns a dispute which] arose between *bāsī* Nūr al-Dīn, representing the *malik* Maydōb, and *al-ḥājj* 'Umar.

*Plea by the plaintiff*

*al-ḥājj* 'Umar made his plea: our lord Sultan Muḥammad Tayrāb gave Nu'mān [some] land and sent out to him the *khabīr* Muftāḥ[106] to assign it to him. He demarcated it for him; then [Nu'mān] died and [*al-ḥājj* 'Umar] took over ownership of it,[107] and our lord confirmed for him the land (*al-ḥadd*) [which] the *khabīr* Muftāḥ had demarcated. But the *malik* Maydōb kept him from his land. Then he presented to us our lord the sultan's charter [which was] a confirmation [of the land] for him.

*Plea by the defendant*

Then we looked at it and the defendant was asked about this. *Bāsī* Nūr al-Dīn, representing the *malik* Maydōb upon his authorization, answered in rebuttal of [the plaintiff's] plea, "Our lord Sultan Muḥammad Tayrāb sent the *khabīr* Muftāḥ to [Nu'mān] to establish him in one [particular] place,[108] not to demarcate the land for him; but Nu'mān wrote down the boundaries falsely. *Malik* Idrīs Marjān[109] took his complaint to our lord Sultan Muḥammad Tayrāb, who summoned Nu'mān and invalidated [the demarcation] of the place which Nu'mān had written down (*al-Nu'mān katabahu*) falsely. The *malik* Marjān took possession of this area and had full disposal of it until he died, when [the land] passed to the *malik* Maydōb. Our lord the sultan said to [Maydōb], 'Give [Nu'mān] sufficient land (*ḥadd kifāya*) and take charge of the rest of the land'. So he gave him sufficient land and took over the additional [land] and had had full disposal of it from Sultan Tayrāb's time until now in his possession; no one (has disputed with him) over this."

*Examination*

Having comprehended the pleas of the two of them and having looked exhaustively into both their claims submitted before me, I took counsel with the *'ulamā'* and then instructed *al-ḥājj* 'Umar to substantiate the boundary that the ***khabīr*** Muftāḥ had demarcated. And upon our own initiative,[110] we allowed him a deferrment again and again, but he was unable to find proof (***bayyina***, i.e. witnesses) that would provide testimony for him in this [matter]. Four months elapsed, but he persisted in absenting himself. Then, upon our own initiative, we warned him on the twenty-first day,[111] but he would not come but persisted in absenting himself.

*The judgment*

Thereafter, the *'ulamā'* advised us and so we awarded judgment to ***bāsī*** Nūr al-Dīn, the ***malik*** Maydōb's representative, over his land,[112] b.nāb.n., [that is] the additional [land], in accordance as the Author[113] says;

> He [the judge] shall grant a delay [to the plaintiff to present proof] upon his own initiative. Then [if no proof is brought forward at the stipulated time], he shall award judgment.[114]

Inasmuch as *al-ḥājj* 'Umar claimed that he had proof but did not produce it, we have therefore disallowed [any further plea by him] lest he should claim that no such invalidation (***al-ta'jīz***) was imposed, because an estate (*iqṭā'*) needs to be taken possession of [to render it legally valid] just like any other gift, according to the predominant view (***al-mashhūr***, i.e. of the Mālikī School of Law).[115]

Therefore the land of b.nāb.n. has been established as the property of ***malik*** Maydōb, and to him is [the] oath.[116] We have dismissed *al-ḥājj* 'Umar's suit inasmuch as he does not have a claim that can be heard.

*The witnesses*

Among our witnesses to our judgment were *faqīh* Ḥāmid, *faqīh* 'Umar, *faqīh* Jādallāh, *faqīh al-ḥājj* Sirāj,[117] *bāsī* 'Āmir, *malik* Jum'a Tānā and *al-ḥājj* (Anbarāk); and the gathering was so large [that it was not possible] to prolong [the list] by recording them [all here].

# XXXVI

A rescript from Sultan Muḥammad al-Faḍl confirming the judgment given in XXXV.

*seal* Sultan Muḥammad al-Faḍl, son of Sultan ʻAbd al-Raḥmān al-Rashīd, son of Sultan Aḥmad Bukr, son of Sultan Sulaymān. The year 1218.[118]

What God Wills.

With blessings. In the name of God, the Compassionate, the Merciful: may the blessing and peace of God be upon our lord Muḥammad and his family.

From the presence of the Sultan of the Muslims and Caliph of the community of the Lord of the Messengers, servitor of the Law and Religion, who trusts in the Most High God, the One, Incomparable, Just and Patient, our lord and majesty Sultan Muḥammad al-Faḍl, the victorious, may the Most High God preserve and watch over him, defend his realm, befriend him through His aid and annihilate his enemies, Amen; son of the late Sultan ʻAbd al-Raḥmān al-Rashīd, may God bless his noble soul and illumine his exalted tomb, Amen.

To all who encounter this rescript,[119] namely, the leading notables, sultans,[120] *maliks*, *qāḍīs* and the other officials and all the people of the sultan's state.

Thereafter: inasmuch as there arose [a dispute] between *bāsī* Nūr al-Dīn, acting for Maydōb upon [his] authorization, and *al-ḥājj* ʻUmar, the aforesaid sultan sent them both the *maqdūm*, *amīn* Yūsuf. They presented their dispute concerning the land.

*Recapitulation of XXXV*

*al-ḥājj* ʻUmar made his plea that the late Sultan Muḥammad Tayrāb gave Nuʻmān [a piece of] land. He sent to him the *khabīr* Muftāḥ who assigned and demarcated it for him. Then [Nuʻmān] died and the late sultan, our father Sultan ʻAbd al-Raḥmān al-Rashīd, gave [*al-ḥājj* ʻUmar] Nuʻmān's land (*ḥadd*), which he had possessed. But *malik* Maydōb kept him from his land and showed him a charter from my late father, Sultan ʻAbd al-Raḥmān al-Rashīd [which] confirmed it to him.

Then [the judge] questioned the defendant about this. *Bāsī* Nūr al-Dīn, representing *malik* Maydōb with [his] authorization [to make] a denial of [*al-ḥājj* ʻUmar's] claim, answered that Sultan

Muḥammad Tayrāb had sent the *khabīr* Muftāḥ to [Nu'mān]; he had taken him to settle in one area, giving him enough land (*ḥadd*). But [Nu'mān] took more [land] and wrote down the boundaries falsely.[121] Then, after *malik* Maydōb came to power,[122] he took his complaint to the late Sultan Muḥammad Tayrāb, who invalidated [Nu'mān's rights] to the area which Nu'mān[123] had written down and said to [Maydōb], "Give [Nu'mān] enough land for his [needs]". *Malik* Maydōb took the additional area, but before he could take the document[124] from him, Nu'mān died.

Then [the judge] understood both of their pleas, recorded all this and consulted the *'ulamā'*. He instructed *al-ḥājj* 'Umar to provide confirmation of the boundaries which the *khabīr* Muftāḥ had delimited,[125] and granted him an adjournment in order that he could bring proof [i.e. witnesses] who testify in support of his claim. But he found no proof to support his claim. [The judge] granted him a respite, at his own discretion, time after time, [yet] he provided no proof even though four months elapsed. Although *bāsī* Nūr al-Dīn came at the appointed time, [*al-ḥājj* 'Umar] did not come but persisted in absenting himself. [The judge] granted him a [further] delay of two months,[126] but he [still] did not come and persisted in absenting himself. At this point [the judge] consulted the *'ulamā'*, then awarded judgment to *bāsī* Nūr al-Dīn, *malik* Maydōb's representative, over his additional land and [administered] an oath to him. And [the land] was b.nāb.n. [The judge] denied leave to *al-ḥājj* 'Umar to raise his claim again.

*Appeal to the sultan*

But he protested against the judge [who had been] deputed[127] [to hear the case], the *amīn*, *maqdūm* Yūsuf [and] presented the judgment [for appeal] to our lord, the aforesaid sultan, the mighty Sultan Muḥammad al-Faḍl, the victorious, may God aid him with victory, Amen.

Thereupon, [the sultan] examined it exhaustively and considered it to be correct. Then he enforced the *amīn* Yūsuf's judgment, dismissed *al-ḥājj* 'Umar's suit, awarded judgment to *malik* Maydōb over this additional land and denied leave to *al-ḥājj* 'Umar to appeal inasmuch as he had no claim. He confirmed the judgment of the *maqdūm*, *amīn* Yūsuf.

There were present as witnesses to the *amīn* Yūsuf's judgment, *al-ḥājj* Muḥammad Sirāj "shaykh of the sultan",[128] *faqīh* 'Umar, *faqīh* Ḥāmid, *bāsī* 'Āmir, *faqīh* Jādallāh, *malik* Jum'a, Tājā, *al-ḥājj* Anbarāk, Ḥajjāj, Yūsuf b. 'Umar, Ḥamad Kana Yaḥyā, *Sulṭān* Jār, Muḥammad 'Abd al-Qādir Qayba, Muḥammad Tōm, *al-ḥājj*

Ḥamad and *malik* Muḥammad Fawāz.[129] These are the witnesses of the council of the judgment of the *amīn* Yūsuf. The sultan gave judgment, then the *maqdūm, amīn* Yūsuf gave judgment.[130]

Written in the year 1223.[131]

## XXXVII

A dispute between Abū Bakr b. *al-ḥājj* 'Umar and *bāsī* Nūr al-Dīn heard before 'Ubaydallāh Muḥammad al-Sanūsī Abu'l-Ḥasan.

*seal* Sultan Muḥammad Faḍl, son of Sultan 'Abd al-Raḥman al-Rashīd, son of Sultan Aḥmad Bukr, son of Sultan Mūsā, son of Sultan Sulaymān. The year 1218.[132]

The cause of recording and the reason for writing [the words arise] from a judgment by the one so-authorized, 'Ubaydallāh Muḥammad al-Sanūsī Abu'l-Ḥasan, acting as judge for (*bi-taḥkīm min*) the Commander of the Faithful, our lord Muḥammad al-Faḍl, in a case between *bāsī* Nūr al-Dīn and Abū Bakr b. *al-ḥājj* 'Umar, representing his brothers and sisters upon their authorization.

*Plea by the plaintiff*

[Abū Bakr] first made his plea, that our lord, Sultan 'Abd al-Raḥmān, had assigned/and given/[133] to their father a place which had first belonged to *al-ḥājj* Nu'mān [and which] had been assigned to him by our lord Sultan Muḥammad Tayrāb. When Nu'mān died, their father asked for it and our aforesaid lord gave it to him – "But our uncle, [the] *bāsī*, acted unjustly towards us and took part of it".[134] He concluded his plea.

*Plea by the defendant*

Nūr al-Dīn replied by agreeing that the sultan's gift to their father had been *al-ḥājj* Nu'mān's place – "Which you now have, but [as for] the additional [land] to which you are now referring, I do not accept that [it belonged] to *al-ḥājj* Nu'mān nor that your father [received] it from the sultan. Moreover, when I, acting for the *malik* [Maydōb], took the dispute with your father/over this additional [land]/[135] before our judge of the Commander of the Faithful,[136] the *āb shaykh* Yūsuf."[134] The Law rejected his claim to the additional [land] and gave judgment to the *malik* Maydōb. And it was established as being his property.

"Then I myself asked our lord for a place in *malik* Maydōb's district. He assigned and had [an estate] demarcated for me; and [the place] to which you are referring was included within my estate. You have no case against me." He concluded [his plea].

*Examination by the judge*

I cross-examined Abū Bakr about the court-hearing of his father with [the] *bāsī* before the *āb shaykh*, and whether it had rejected his claim. But he denied this.

Thereupon we instructed [the] *bāsī* to produce his judgment.[137] He produced it; we examined it and found that it appeared to be authentic. In accordance with the advice of the *faqīhs*, who [also] examined it, we adjudged it to be authentic. Therefore, we put the judgment into force in accordance with [the document] after its confirmation.[138] We have denied leave to Abū Bakr and those he represents to raise the claim after this. We have dismissed their claim, being guided by [the Author's] statement,

> [The sentence of an unjust judge or an ignorant one who is '*adl* shall be annulled unless he has consulted the men of learning.] If he has done so, [his judgment] shall be reviewed [if necessary] and confirmed insofar as it is not unjust.[139]

*The witnesses*

There were present as our witnesses to the judgment, the *imām* Miṣrī,[140] *faqīh* Zarrūq, *faqīh* Muḥammad Tāma, *faqīh* Maḥmūd, *faqīh* Muḥammad al-Nūr, *malik* Ḥamad Darōk, *malik* 'Abd al-Ṣādiq, *al-ḥājj* Hilikī,[141] *malik* Ḥasan Siqīrī,[142] *faqīh* Sa'īd, *faqīh* 'Abd al-Qādir s.r.bī; but God is Sufficient as a Witness.

This was [written] in the month of God, Sha'bān; the year twelve hundred and forty-five,[143] from the Emigration of him who merits prayers and the most pure blessings.

## XXXVIII to XLI: The Princesses Fāṭima Umm Dirays and Zahra[1]

> He (Muḥammad al-Ḥusayn) provided at the country's expense extravagant dowries for the marriages of the girls among his children, and among his cousins and grandchildren.[2]

Nachtigal's comment is well illustrated by the documents here concerning, directly and indirectly, the *mayram* Fāṭima and her daughter, Zahra. The maintenance of the royal clan was an obvious burden on the state and with the growth of "*ḥarīm*" government in the nineteenth century the burden grew greater. The royal sons and daughters were also an unproductive burden, since by the same century they took little part in the running of the state. As a consequence, estates were carved out in increasing numbers to provide for the royal clan, particularly in western Dār Fūr.[3]

The first document, XXXVIII, is a charter granting the estate, Niʿama, otherwise unidentified, to the sultan's son-in-law, *al-ḥājj* Aḥmad b. *al-ḥājj* ʿIsā, likewise unidentified. *al-ḥājj* Aḥmad was probably a *faqīh*, and there are other instances of *faqīhs* marrying into the royal family. Ṭāhir Jāmūs, a famous eighteenth century *faqīh* of the Borno community of Manawāshī, married Fetessa, daughter of Sultan Tayrāb, while Nūr al-Anṣārī married Ḥawwā', daughter of Sultan ʿAbd al-Rahmān.[4] This intermarriage of particular interest groups, here *faqīhs*, but also merchants (see below, p. 107), into the royal family is part of discernable patterns of socio-political change within the ruling elite, patterns cut off abruptly by the invasion of 1874. However, Browne's comments, although from an earlier period, on the hazards of marrying a *mayram* indicate the distance, a relic perhaps of sacral ideas of royalty, between royals and commoners;

> Whoever, impelled by vanity, (for no profit attends it,) receives to his bed the daughter of a king or powerful Melek, (women of this rank are *Miram*,) finds her sole moderatrix of his family, and himself reduced to a cipher. Of his real or reputed offspring he has no voice in the disposal, government or instruction. The princess, who has honoured him with the limited right over her person, becomes not the partner, but the sole proprietor, of all that he possessed; and her most extravagant caprices must not be thwarted, lest her displeasure should be succeeded by that of the monarch.[5]

The estate granted to *al-ḥājj* Aḥmad had had four previous owners, the last named being the *ḥabbōba* Umm Būṣa. Although Umm Būṣa was evidently dead by 1263/1846–47, the date of our charter,[6] the owner before her, the *maqdūm* ʿAbd al-ʿAzīz, was not, since he is ordered in the charter to send an official to assist in demarcating the estate. And with its fifty slaves, Niʿama was probably a wealthy and desirable property (on estate slavery, see above, pp. 19–20).

# XXXVIII

Sultan Muḥammad al-Ḥusayn grants the estate, Niʿama, to his son-in-law, *al-ḥājj* Aḥmad b. ʿIsā.

*seal*[7]

From the presence of the Commander of the Faithful, the essence of the most noble ones, the servant of the Law and Religion, who trusts in the Lord of the Universe, our lord and master Sultan Muḥammad al-Ḥusayn al-Mahdī, son of Sultan Muḥammad al-Faḍl may the clouds of [God's] beneficence and good pleasure [cover] his tomb, Amen.

To all who encounter this charter and examine its truthful contents, the *amīrs*, *wazīrs*, *maliks*, sons of the sultans, *mayrams*, *ḥabbōbas*, *qāḍīs*, *jabbays*, *shartays*, *makkas*-s, *dimlijs* and the rest of the people of this state who hold authority.

Thereafter: we bring to you honourable attention with regard to the estate (*ḥākūra*), Niʿama, which was formerly in the hands of the *malik* Kartakayla as his possession, and then in the hands of the *malik* ʿAbdallāh Karqāsh as his possession, and then in the hands of the *maqdum* ʿAbd al-ʿAziz[8] as his posession, and then in the hands of our grandmother, the *ḥabbōba*, the mother of our late lord [Muḥammad al-Faḍl], as her possession. Now I have shown favour to and have given, bestowed and donated it to our son-in-law, *al-ḥājj* Aḥmad b. ʿIsā, with its slaves as a choice gift and have made it "her" property in absolute ownership.[9] Then I sent Ibrahim, the official (*al-maqām*) from the *amīn* Ṣāliḥ's entourage, to assign possession of it, and ordered the *maqdūm* ʿAbd al-ʿAzīz to send someone to him [Ibrāhīm] from his entourage to go[10] with him. He sent the *malik* Hārūn b. *al-faqīh* ʿAbdallāh who went[10] to this estate. They went around it in all directions and demarcated it . . .[11] and this land, which is enclosed by these boundaries, I have assigned it to our son-in-law, *al-ḥājj* Aḥmad b. *al-ḥājj* ʿIsā as an allodial concession, have given "her"[9] absolute possession and have made it over to "her"[9] as a property in full ownership with its slaves who number fifty.

He has disposal over it and its slaves [just as] an owner has disposal of his property, [with rights of] cultivation, causing to be cultivated, sale, demolition, building, alms and purchase; it is for him and his descendants after him. Let no sultan after me alter or change it. I have relinquished to "her"[9] the *fiṭr and zakāh*, that is the Sharīʿa taxes, and we have likewise forgiven [him] the customary taxes, namely the great and small *dam*, *fisq*, *hāmil*, *nār*, *quwwār* and *daraqa*. Let no *malik*, *jabbay* or *maqdūm* or any of the servants [of the state] encroach upon them.

We have relinquished it to "her"[9] for "her"[9] spiritual and temporal [benefit]. God is the Guardian of what we say. "He is sufficient for us; How good [a Keeper] is He."[12]

This was written in the year 1263.[13]

## XXXIX

*Al-ḥājj* Aḥmad has given the estate, Ni'ama, to his wife, *mayram* Fāṭima Umm Dirays. The sultan issues a decree confirming the gift.

*seal*

From the Commander of the Faithful, our lord, master and majesty Sultan Muḥammad al-Ḥusayn al-Mahdī, victorious through the Most High God, Amen.

To all who encounter this charter and examine its truthful contents.

Thereafter: our daughter, *mayram* Fāṭima Umm Dirays, presented to us a document from her husband, *amīn*[14] *al-ḥājj* Aḥmad 'Isā. I read that he had given to her the estate (*ḥākūra*), Ni'ama, which I had previously given to him and which he has now given to his wife. I have confirmed her husband's gift to her. It has become her property and possession; it is at her disposal, both [the estate] and its revenues, Sharī'a and customary, for herself and her descendants after her.

This is my letter and seal for him who knows it.

Written on 7 Sha'bān 1269.[15]

On an earlier occasion, Sultan Muḥammad al-Ḥusayn gave his son-in-law ten nomads. Now *al-ḥājj* Aḥmad has given the nomads to his baby daughter, Zahra. The present is occasioned by "the shaving of her hair", *ziyānat rāsihā*, on the fortieth day after her birth. The custom, which is not confined to Dār Fūr, is widely practised in the province;

> A public ceremony called *mushāṭ arba 'īn* (lit. binding the hair into braids of forty) signs the end of the next period [in the birth cycle]. During this period the woman is not allowed to leave the village. On the fortieth day a large quantity of millet beer is prepared by the women of her household. This is served to the female

neighbours, who undo the mother's hair and plait it into new braids. At the same time the child's hair is shaved for the first time.[16]

In XL, the sultan confirms the gift.

## XL

Sultan Muḥammad al-Ḥusayn confirms the gift of ten nomads by *al-ḥājj* Aḥmad to his daughter Zahra.

*seal*

From the presence of the Sultan of the Muslims and the Caliph of the lord of the messengers, our lord and master Sultan Muḥammad al-Ḥusayn al-Mahdī, victorious through the Most High God, Amen.

To all who encounter this decree, namely, the leading notables, *amīrs*, *wazīrs*, *maliks*, *shartays*, *dimlijs*, sons of the sultans, *mayrams*, *jabbays*, *maliks* of the nomads, shaykhs, *kursīs*, the servants [of the state] and their officials,[17] and all the people of the state [who are] servants.

Thereafter: previously I had shown favour to and had given to our son-in-law, *al-ḥājj* Aḥmad 'Isā, [some] nomads from the Māhriyya,[18] of Shaykh Dalam's community. Their names were 'Abd al-Na'īm, Nu'mān, al-Dānī, Aḥmad, Ḥusayn, Ḥāmid, Zarzār, Ṭāhir, '.j.z., and Aḥmad. I had rendered these said men as cripples [to the tax-collectors][19] and placed them under the authority of our son-in-law, *al-ḥājj* Aḥmad 'Isā. I had relinquished [lit. forgiven] to him all their revenues (*manāfi'him*). They had been established as attendants for him (*taba'an lahu*, lit. to follow him) and his descendants.

Now my aforesaid son-in-law has given them to his daughter, *mayram* Zahra, [on the occasion of] the shaving of her hair, and has informed me. Therefore I have confirmed [the gift] for her and have made over (*qābaltuhā*) to her all the taxes, both Sharī'a and customary, *zakāh* and *fiṭr*, *dam*, *fisq*, *hāmil* and the other [taxes]. No harassment, ill-treatment or service [should be offered to or demanded from] them; their affairs have been made over to our granddaughter (lit. our daughter's daughter), *mayram* Zahra. Let no one interfere or dispute with her over them, since they have become her nomads and herders; for her and her descendants after her.

This is my letter, decree and seal for him who knows it. Written in the year 1268.[20]

In XLI Sultan Muḥammad al-Ḥusayn gives his daughter, *mayram* Fāṭima Umm Dirays (whose husband is not mentioned), an estate in al-Dōr (or al-Dawr) district. The location of the estate is uncertain; it may have bordered the estate whose boundaries are given in XLV, which was probably to the west of Kobbei (see below p. 115 and map). Neither is it certain that it is the same estate as the one mentioned in the report quoted below; this latter arose from a meeting held in 1924 to determine the boundary between the districts of Suwaynī and Furok. It throws interesting light on how estates were created.

> In Sultan Mohd Fadl's time, the sultan took part of Dar Sueini and part of Dar Furnung and gave it to Ibrahim, *malik* of the Jellaba.[21] Later Sultan Husein divided this hakura into three, one to Fiki Abida (father of Shams al Din), one to Meram [*mayram*] Um Dereis his daughter, one to his son Abu el Baashr [Abu'l-Bashar]. Later still the Sultan Hussein gave part of Abu el Bashr's dar to one Fiki Isagha wad Bedein a Gimrawi [i.e. from Dār Qimr]. When Meram Um Dereis died, her sister Meram Arifa (who died recently in Fasher) took her sister's dar and put in Mohd. Daldum, Ahmad Mohd. Again's father, to run the dar.
>
> Abu el Bashar put Saadalla Gelam in to run his hakura. When Abu el Basher died Saadalla carried on as a Shartai dealing direct with the Sultan. He was followed by Hasab el Karim elected by the people of the hakura (He was killed by the people of Osman Gano in the Mahadia). The whole of these hakuras then became deserted owing to wars etc....
>
> Dar Abu el Basher contained 25 villages...[22]

## XLI

Sultan Muḥammad al-Ḥusayn grants an estate to his daughter, *mayram* Fāṭima Umm Dirays.

*seal*[23] The property of the Commander of the Faithful and offspring of the most noble, Sultan Muḥammad Ḥusayn, son of Sultan Muḥammad al-Faḍl, son of Sultan ʿAbd al-Raḥmān al-Rashīd, son of Sultan Aḥmad Bukr, son of Sultan Mūsā, son of Sultan Sulaymān. The year 1264.[24]

From the presence of the most mighty sultan and most noble Caliph, who unfurls the banner of justice over the heads of the nations, the Commander of the Faithful and scion of the most noble [ancestors], our lord and master Sultan Muḥammad al-Ḥusayn al-Mahdī, victorious through the Most High God, Amen; son of the late Commander of the Faithful, Sultan Muḥammad al-Faḍl, may God make the earth [over his grave] sweet-smelling, Amen.

To all who encounter this charter, namely, the *amīrs*, *wazīrs*, *maliks*, *shartays*, *dimlijs*, sons of the sultans, *mayrams*, *ḥabbōbas*, *jabbays* and all the officials, servants of this state in positions of authority and power.

Thereafter: I favoured and assigned to our daughter, the honoured and virtuous *mayram* Fāṭima Umm Dirays, some land in the district of al-Dōr [or al-Dawr]. I sent out there the commissioner ʻUmar b. *al-faqīh* Jallāb and ordered *maqdūm* Muḥammad Ḥasan[25] to send a commissioner from his entourage to join our commissioner. Accordingly he sent Ḥusayn b. *al-malik* Fīl.[26] The two commissioners went to this place, assembled the testimony [i.e. the witnesses] and administered the oath [to them] upon the Noble Book. They traced its boundaries until they had encircled it on all four sides, east, west, south and north. They recorded the boundaries and presented to us [their report which] I examined.

The boundaries begin on the northern side ⌜driving off from⌝[27] the *ḥarāz* tree and cross over the big riverbed, the riverbed of f.r.q., and run up to the other hillocks (*qiraywud*) and run to the deserted cultivation (*bōbāya*) of Khayr. From the western side, [the boundary is] with al-k.r.sī[28] . . .[29] [and] runs by the rocks of d.rū, and runs to the twin rocks, and runs to the rocks of b.r.kū, and runs to the *nabaq* tree and to the *ḥarāz* tree by [the land of] the *faqīh* ʻUbayda, and runs to the hill of Umm ʻArīf descending at the riverbed of f.r.q. at the *nabaq* tree, and runs [along] the riverbed at the twin *ḥarāz* trees, and runs to the new well and runs [along] the riverbed rising at the *nabaq* tree of j.dh.q. Jārō [where] it borders with Jabā at a well. [The boundary] runs [along] the riverbed of t.l.q.b., and runs to the white pool, and runs to the hill of al-Naḥās [lit. the copper hill], and runs to the *ḥarāz* tree of al-ʻArāīs, and runs to the *mukhīṭ* tree at the boundary of the *shartāya* of Bukr, Tayrāb and r.b.q., and runs along following the riverbed eastwards at the well of k.d.r.ā [Kadarō?] and to the pool of Ḥammād, and runs to the hill of Bōwa and to the *nabaq* tree of al-Dalam, and runs to the rocks of Ẓalīma; and the boundary runs with [the land of] *faqīh* Abu'l-Bashar at the *ḥijlīj* and *jummayz* trees at Karam j.nā, and runs to the '*arad* tree, and runs to the tomb of the Berti man (*qabr al-birtāwī*). [Then] the boundary joins with [the land of] *faqīh* Abu'l-Bashar and *al-ḥājj* 'Isā at the rock [at] the mouth of the white hillocks,[30] and runs to the *ḥarāz* and *tunḍub* trees, and joins with [the land of] *al-ḥājj* 'Isā, ⌜ending up with⌝[32] the *ḥarāz* tree. These are the boundaries of the aforesaid land which the two commissioners went over.

I have assigned and donated it to my daughter, *mayram* Fāṭima Umm Dirays: indeed, it has been established for her as a lawful allodial concession with full possession and complete ownership, as a donation and gift for her and her descendants after her. I have relinquished [lit. forgiven] to her all its Sharī'a and customary revenues, [namely] the great and small *dam*, *fisq*, *hāmil*, *nār*, *quwwār* and likewise the Sharī'a [taxes], *zakāh* and *fiṭr*, and all [the revenues] accruing from [the estate] and its inhabitants, to her and her descendants after her with [rights of] sale,[32] presentation and inheritance.

Let no one interfere with it or dispute with her. This is my letter, decree and seal for him who knows it.

Written in the month of Shawwāl, 13, in the year 1273.[33]

## XLII to XLVII: The merchants Muḥammad Kannūna and 'Alī Bey Ibrāhīm al-Tirayfī[1]

The sultanate's entrepôt for the caravan trade with Egypt along the Forty Days Road was Kobbei (written Kubay or Kubayh), roughly a day's march to the north-west of al-Fāshir. The six documents that follow concern the land of two of the leading merchants of Kobbei.

Kobbei is now deserted, in part because the wells there dried up at the end of the last century, in part because of the fall of the sultanate and consequent disappearance of the trade,[2] but in its heyday it was the most populous town in Dār Fūr.[3] Strictly speaking, Kobbei was not a town as such, but a string of settlements along the riverbed, the Wādī Kobbei, between Kofod (written Kafōt in IX) and Jabal Kobbei, a prominent landmark; outlier villages lay on either side of the main settlement. Browne estimated the town's length at more than two miles,

> And the houses, each of which occupies within its enclosure [Arabic *zarība*] a large portion of ground, are divided by considerable waste. The principal, or possibly the only view of convenience by which the natives appear to have been governed in their choice of situation and mode of building, must have been

that of having the residence near the spot rented or inherited by them for the purpose of cultivation.[4]

Kobbei was thus a trading community in contrast to the administrative capital at al-Fāshir, one of a number of such settlements created west of the Nile by merchants from the Nile valley, North Africa and Egypt.[5] A cosmopolitan community – Browne noted merchants from Upper Egypt, Tunis, Tripoli, Dongola, Nubia and Kordofan[6] – its main function was long-distance trade, centred on a market held twice a week,[7] exporting camels, slaves, ostrich feathers, ivory, gum and other items and importing a variety of manufactured goods from Egypt and North Africa. The merchants who settled in the area built up their own households (Arabic *zarība*) and cultivations, to which they welcomed their compatriots, so that the area became a patchwork of immigrant communities.

Among the merchants or *jallāba*, the elite were the *khabīrs*,[8] a title meaning literally "leader" or "guide" given to the twenty or so long-distance and large-scale traders operating between Egypt and Dār Fūr. The long-distance trade was a specialized business, requiring capital or credit, market skills and contacts (for example, with the European merchant houses in Cairo and Asyūṭ) and close links with the ruling elite in Dār Fūr. The merchants brought into the sultanate the luxury goods consumed by the elite, paying for them with goods collected under the protective umbrella provided by the same elite. Occasionally, like the holy men (see above pp. 100–1), some merchants married into the royal family, one prominent example was the *khabīr* Muḥammad Pasha Imām from Dongola who married ʻArōfa, a daughter of Muḥammad al-Ḥusayn.[9]

The merchants of Kobbei, as the following documents indicate, were also assimilated to the land-holding system of the sultanate. The charters make it clear that the land in and around Kobbei was carefully parcelled out.[10] And apart from the formal granting of land, there appears to have been a market for land as well; thus ʻAlī Bey Ibrāhīm is said to have bought land in the region.[11]

XLII to XLIV concern the land of the *khabīr* Muḥammad Kannūna,[12] who had been granted by Sultan Muḥammad al-Faḍl an estate formerly held by another *khabīr*, Khayr Abū Khādimallāh.

# XLII

Sultan Muḥammad al-Ḥusayn confirms an estate to the *khabīr* Muḥammad Kannūna.

*seal* Property of Sultan Muḥammad al-Ḥusayn, son of Sultan Muḥammad al-Faḍl, son of Sultan ʻAbd al-Raḥmān al-Rashīd, son of Sultan Aḥmad Bukr, son of Sultan Mūsā, son of Sultan Sulaymān. The year 1254.[13]

From the presence of him through whom God illumines the lands, gives relief to [His] servants and sweeps away oppression and evil, the Commander of the Faithful, Sultan Muḥammad al-Ḥusayn, may God prolong his life, Amen.

To the presence of whomsoever encounters this charter, namely, the leading notables, *amīrs*, *wazīrs*, *maliks*, *shartays*, *dimlijs*, *qāḍīs*, *wakīls*, sons of the sultans, *mayrams*, *ḥabbōbas*, *korays*, *jabbays*, *qawwārs*, *makkās*-s, and all the people of the state and the holders of power, the oppressors who trample upon the rights of the Muslims.

Thereafter: the *khabīr* Muḥammad Kannūna presented to me a charter from my father, the late Sultan Muḥammad al-Faḍl, [which] promulgated [the grant] as a present and estate to him [of] the locality [formerly belonging to] Khayr Abū Khādimallāh, which is in the district of Kubayh. He (Muḥammad al-Faḍl] sent *al-ḥājj* Arbāb from the *amīn* Ādam's entourage [and] he demarcated this locality.

The boundary begins with Bāqirmī[14] from in front of the two [areas] of pebbly (*al-zalṭāyāt*) rocks and the big *ḥarāz* tree, and runs by the main road, the market road, which goes (*al-māshā*) by Khayr's house to Kubayh market, and from there it joins the tributary of al-Wuṣṭānī riverbed,[15] [going] to where the riverbed divides into three; the eastern[16] [side of this boundary belongs] to the *khabīr* Kannūna and the western to the people of Kubayh. Then [the boundary] runs by the tributary of al-Wusṭānī riverbed[15] until a plot of ground by the road of Ḥassān's village,[17] and runs from the course (*qīf*) of the old riverbed and to where it turns away towards Tarnā.[18] Between both [Tarnā and Kannūna is] the riverbed; the eastern [side of the boundary belongs to] Kannūna, the western to Tarnā. [Then it goes] eastwards by the *ḥarāz* tree, which the sons of Barakat Allāh have marked, and runs to the date tree[19] of Ḥassān's village at the hollow (*qa'r*) of the *shōk* tree. The southern date trees [(or, south of the date tree) the land belongs to] Kannūna and the northern lies outside it. Then it runs to the *nabaq* tree at the entrance of the household compound of 'Abd al-Jabbār, and runs to the big *nabaq* tree which is in the household compound of *al-ḥājj* Muḥammad Kūk, and [goes] eastwards to the date [patch] of Qaṣdīr where the date [patch] is itself the boundary, [but some of] the date [patch] is outside [the boundary]. Then it runs through the middle of *al-ḥājj* 'Isā's fields and by the *tunḍub* and burnt *ḥarāz* trees, and runs to Dānī's village, and runs to the big *hijlīj* tree which is in the water course, and runs to the south of Dānī's village by the *hijlīj* trees, the *ḥashāb* tree and the Abū Ḥusayn rocks to where it meets at the road. Then it runs by the footpath and the *tunḍub* tree, and runs to the foot of the Kardal rocks, and runs southwards to the boundary of Ṭawīl al-Nū alongside Ṭawīl [to] the boundary [at] Mardūfa rocks, and runs to the pebbly area (*al-zalṭāyāt*), and runs by the *sayyāl* tree, and crosses the rocks at the Qanjār road, and runs by the rocks westwards to the crevice, to the big *ḥarāz* tree, and runs by Qanjār southwards to the main road to al-Fāshir, where south of Qanjār [the land belongs] to Ṭawīl al-Nū and north to Kannūna. Then it runs to the big *tunḍub* tree, and runs by the path [which] cuts the 'Azīza riverbed at the dried-up *sayyāl* tree until it rejoins, at the Ṣanānāt rocks, the boundary with Bāqirmī. These are the boundaries of the aforesaid land.

I examined [the charter] and found it [to be] an authentic estate, acceptable in Law as a donation and gift for him and his descendants after him; [there had been] relinquished to him all the Sharī'a and customary revenues. Accordingly I, the aforesaid sultan, have confirmed for him that which my father had enacted. It is established as a donation and gift for him and his descendants after him. I have completely relinquished to him all its Sharī'a and customary revenues, *zakāh* and *fiṭr*, *dam*, *fisq*, *zinā* and *ḥāmil*; all [the revenues] are his due.

Let no one dispute with him and let no sultan after me change it. This is my letter, decree and seal for him who knows it.

Written in the month of Jumāda the First, 20, in the year 1256.[20]

In XLIII one of Muḥammad Kannūna's neighbours sues him for the alleged seizure of a farm. The case illustrates the intricacies of disputes among the merchants of Kobbei; it is probably significant that the case was heard before the *wazīr* Ādam Bōsh, Sultan Muḥammad al-Huṣayn's closest confidant, who had himself served his master as a merchant in

Asyūṭ, where he left a good reputation among the trading community there.[21]

In XLIV Sultan Muḥammad al-Ḥusayn confirms the estate for Kannūna's sons and daughters, following their father's death.

## XLIII

A hearing before the *wazīr* Ādam Bōsh of a dispute between 'Abdallāh walad Dānī and *khabīr* Muḥammad Kannūna.

*seal* The *amīn* Ādam Bōsh. 1259[22]

It has been established and confirmed in a legal judgment enacted by the one so-authorized, the Grand Vizier,[23] the *amīn* Ādam Bōsh, may the Most High God show him benevolence, Amen; acting for our lord the Commander of the Faithful, Sultan Muḥammad al-Ḥusayn, may the Most High God cause him to prosper, Amen; concerning [a dispute] which arose between two sane, mature and orthodox men, both [being] of sound body and sane mind, and both free of any legal impediment, and both willing that the judgment be enacted and completed.[24] Pleas were made by both 'Abdallāh walad Dānī[25] and the *khabīr* Muḥammad Kannūna.

*Plea by the plaintiff*

First 'Abdallāh w. Dānī made his plea, "The *khabır* Kannūna has usurped my farm. I seek justice from." Thus his plea was concluded after examination [by the judge].

*Plea by the defendant*

We requested the *khabīr* Kannūna [to answer]. He answered, "I know nothing about any farm other than [those] which our lord the late Sultan Muḥammad al-Faḍl gave me, [namely] the *khabīr* Khayr's land which is near to Kubay and includes the farm of the sons of Labbād and the farm of Arqā. [The sultan] sent a commissioner to me who went there and demarcated it for me. Then [the commissioner] presented [his report on the boundaries] to our lord Sultan Muḥammad al-Faḍl who confirmed and ratified it for me as our property. And I took possession of it. Some days afterwards, it became clear to me that Dānī, the aforementioned 'Abdallāh's father, had business dealings with the sons of Labbād and Arqā; they had concealed from me [the fact that] their farms fell within that which had been possessed by *khabīr* Khayr. So I complained to my lord Sultan Muḥammad al-Faḍl and he agreed to send a commissioner to me to confirm my possession of this farm. But he was overtaken by fate.[26] So I referred my affair to my lord Sultan Muḥammad al-Ḥusayn. He sent me *al-ḥājj* Muḥammad/Faraḥ/[27] from the *wazīr* Ādam's entourage. He went to this place and assembled the owners of the farms and their neighbours. They took the oath upon the Book of the Most High God and delimited the boundary of the *khabīr* Khayr's [property], including this aforesaid farm, according to its boundaries as shall be mentioned. I presented [the report of the commissioner] to [the sultan]. He ratified and confirmed it for me as our property and I took posession and enjoyed full disposal of it. I am not aware that 'Abdallāh w. Dānī has any part in this farm." Thus was concluded his plea after examination [by the judge].

*Examination by the judge*

Then we directed our examination towards 'Abdallāh w. Dānī, "Have you any charter from our lords the sultans [that can serve] as evidence for you in any way?" Accordingly, he produced a charter of our lord Sultan Muḥammad al-Faḍl. We scrutinized it and found that it made no reference to this farm, but instead referred to widely-scattered lands, some being there, some in Barr Bōja and some in the south.[28] So we rejected it and demanded proof (*bayyina*),[29] but he could not come with anyone who could testify for him in any way about this farm. We granted him a delay several times, but he came with no witnesses. So he disqualified himself.

Then we requested *khabīr* Kannūna [to produce] our lord Sultan Muḥamad al-Faḍl's charter and that of our lord Sultan Ḥusayn. He showed us both of them. We found that our lord Sultan Muḥammad al-Faḍl's charter promulgated to him a gift [of the property] possessed by *khabīr* Khayr including this farm and that our lord Sultan Ḥusayn's charter recorded that it accorded to him the power (*tamkīn*) to become the possessor of this right of possession (*tamlīk tilka'l-ḥiyāza*) in the same way as it had been accorded to *khabīr* Khayr.

Then 'Abdallāh said to *khabīr* Kannūna, "What evidence (*bayyina*) have you that will testify for you in support of your claim that this aforesaid farm falls within that which had been possessed by *khabīr* Khayr?" [Kannūna] then came with nine men who testified for him in support of his claim. Then ['Abdallāh] said to *khabīr* Kannūna, "Swear on oath that [your witneses] are not in any way related to you and that you have not hired them!"[30] And he swore to this.

## *Judgment*

Thereupon, we took counsel with the *'ulamā'* of the [Mālikī] School; they were in complete agreement with our opinion and with our rendering null and void the claim of /'Abdallāh/[31] w. Dānī and with our dismissal of his suit. I have given judgment in favour of *khabīr* Muḥammad Kannūna over his land [namely that] demarcated as having been possessed by *khabīr* Khayr, including the farm of the sons of Labbād and the farm of Arqā, in accordance as the Law has given judgment to him. We have dismissed 'Abdallāh w. Dānī's suit over the farm and have denied him [the right] to appeal again. As Shaykh Khalīl says,

> [The judge] shall reject [the suit of the party who fails in the period of delay to produce counter testimony] except in [cases involving] bloodshed.[32]

Thereafter, the farm's boundaries; the boundary begins from the direction [of the land] of the sons of Labbād alongside [the land of] Muḥammad Dānī. [The boundary is made up by the following trees]; *kolkol*, *hashāb*, a big *sayyāl*, two *hashāb*, *kolkol*, *siriḥ*, *hijlīj*, three *hashāb*, *mukhīṭ*, *hijlīj*, *siriḥ*, *mukhīṭ*, *nabaq*, *hashāb*, *mukhīṭ*, *hashāb*, a big twin *hijlīj*, nine ⌜growing⌝[33] *hashāb*, *mukhīṭ*, *hashāb* and *siriḥ* – this is the boundary of the farm of the sons of Labbād.[34] And running from the east alongside [the land of] *al-ḥājj* Aḥmad – these are the boundaries of the farm under dispute there.

There were present as witnesses to our judgment, *naqīb* Barakāt, *faqīh* Ismā'īl b. *al-faqīh* Aḥmad al-Ḍawī, *faqih* Ḥusayn b. *al-faqīh* Izayriq Birtāwī,[35] *faqīh* Aḥmad Qandā, *faqīh* 'Abd al-Qādir, *malik* Muḥammad Thānī, *malik* Abb(a), *malik* 'Alī w. Ḥabīb, "the son of the sultan" Aḥmad Tūtū, *faqīh* Abū Bakr w. Kabbāshī, *faqīh* Hārūn, Aḥmad Kūnū, *faqīh* Ibn w. al-Khaṭīb, *al-ḥājj* al-Shafī', *al-ḥājj* Muḥammad Ṣāliḥ w. Tharwa, Shāībū grandson of *bāsī* Nūr al-Dīn, *faqīh* Madanī, *malik*, 'Aṭiyyat Allāh, *malik* Aḥmad b. *al-faqīh* Aḥmad w. al-Taḥāwi and his brother 'Abdallāh, *faqīh* Jalāl al-Dīn and the gathering was numerous. And God is the Best of Witnesses.

Written on Saturday the blessed, 18 Rabī'a II, 1262.[36]

# XLIV

Sultan Muḥammad al-Ḥusayn confirms the grant of Muḥammad Kannūna's estate to his children.

*seal*

From the Commander of the Faithful and Caliph of the community of the lord of the messengers, our lord and master Sultan Muḥammad al-Ḥusayn al-Mahdī, victorious through the Most High God, Amen.

To all who encounter this charter, namely, *amīrs*, *wazīrs*, *maliks*, *shartays*, sons of the sultans, *mayrams*, *ḥabbōbas*,[37] *jabbays*, *qawwārs*, *makkās*-s, and all the officials, the oppressors who trample upon the rights of the Muslims.

Thereafter: the sons of the *khabīr* Muḥammad Kannūn[a], [namely] Aḥmad, 'Abd al-Majīd, Muḥammad, Ibrāhīm, Muṣṭafā; they and their brothers and sisters presented to us a charter from our father, the late Sultan Muḥammad al-Faḍl, [which] I examined. It promulgated to their father, the *khabīr* Kannūn[a], as a gift and an estate the locality of *khabīr* Khayr Abū Khādimallāh, which is in the district of Kūbay and which the commissioner, *al-ḥājj* Arbāb from *amīn* Ādam's entourage, demarcated.

[There follows the description of the boundaries as given in XLII with a few minor differences.]

These are the boundaries of the land which my father, the late Sultan Muḥammad al-Faḍl, assigned to *khabīr* Kannūn[a] as a gift and donation and [which] we had confirmed for him.[38] Now, following the *khabīr* Kannūn[a's] death, I have confirmed this aforementioned land with its recorded boundaries to his children referred to in the body of the charter. Indeed it has become a gift and donation for them, both male and female, I have relinguished all its revenues, both *zakāh* and *fiṭr* and all its customary taxes which accrue from it and its inhabitants, to them and their descendants after them. Let no sultan after me change or alter it.

This is my letter and seal for him who knows it.

[Written] in the year 1267.[39]

The *khabīr* 'Alī Bey Ibrāhīm is described in XLVI and XLVII as a servant, *khaddām*, of Sultan Muḥammad al-Ḥusayn.[40] He appears to have belonged to the Ṭirayfiyya, sections of whom are to be found among the Bidayriyya and Jawāmi'a peoples of central Kordofan and to which several prominent Kobbei merchants belonged.[41] He seems to have served as a royal merchant, trading for the sultan between Dār Fūr and Egypt. Shuqayr, who evidently knew the *khabīr* in Egypt, gives a story that illustrates his relationship with the sultan,

> Shaykh 'Alī Bey the *khabīr*, one of the best known merchants in Dār Fūr, and a contemporary, told me [Shuqayr]; "I went one day to the sultan [Muḥammad al-Ḥusayn] to greet him, taking with me a valuable present of Egyptian goods worth 9,000 piastres and he presented me with two hundred of the finest camels".[42]

'Alī was thus an influential figure both at Kobbei and at court, of a generation slightly later than Kannūna; it was indeed Muḥammad al-Ḥusayn's preference for such men that led him to be despised by his Fur notables for his close involvement with commerce and traders.[43] The German traveller, Robert Hartmann, met at Asyūṭ in 1859 an 'Alī b. Ibrāhīm, who described himself somewhat improbably as a general, *ser'asker*, to the sultan, but possibly the same person as our 'Alī here.[44] When Nachtigal passed through Kobbei in 1874 he met a *khabīr* 'Alī; he must have been one of the leading figures there, since of the two mosques in Kobbei one was the mosque of the *faqīh* Sa'd, "the *'ālim*", from the *khabīr* 'Alī's people.[45]

Although nothing further has been discovered of his subsequent career, 'Alī evidently retired to Egypt sometime after the downfall of the sultanate (although his family still live on their property in the Kobbei region) and was awarded the title of "Bey" (like Hamza and Muḥammad al-Imām, see p. 147 n. 9).

The first of the three documents here, XLV, is the report (*nasab*) of the two commissioners sent by the sultan to demarcate the village of n.q.r. or n.q.r.ī,[46] "with its fields both fallow and cultivated".[47] Following the presentation of the report, the sultan grants the village to the *khabīr* in XLVI. Our final document reiterates the grant, adding the detail that the land at n.q.r. had been "bounded by their axe (or hoe)", that is that it had been opened up to cultivation by the *khabīr*'s people. In fact H. S. Umar reports from 'Alī's grandson, Ḥamad al-Fūr, that his grandfather grew corn, probably for export on his estate.[48] It is thus probable that n.q.r. (like Ḥassān's village, see p. 147, n. 17) had been settled by the *khabīr* and his followers before being formally granted to him by the sultan.

# XLV

Two commissioners demarcate the boundaries of the village of n.q.r.

*seal* Property of the *amīn* ʻAbdallāh. 1268.[49]

Whereas it was on Thursday, in the month of God Dhu'l-ḥijja, the daytime of the eighth day, the year 1268.[50]

The Commander of the Faithful, our lord, has shown favour to the *khabīr* ʻAlī and has given him the village of n.q.r. with its fields both fallow and cultivated. He sent to him from himself a commissioner, *amīn* ʻAbdallāh, to deliver the place into his possession. The other commissioner was a person (*zōl*) [from the entourage of] *amīn*, *malik* ʻAbdallāh Kūr [or Kawr], Ibrāhīm,[51]

They were present on the said day and that place and the people of the boundaries [i.e., the neighbours] and *khabīr* ʻAlī assembled. There were with him two men whom we did not know;[52] they swore upon the Book of God and we set off and encircled this place with them.

First, the boundary begins at Jabal n.q.r. *al-kabīr* ["the big n.q.r. hill"][53] and runs towards the pebbly area (*al-zalṭāya*) known as Tawraq, and runs to the water course (*khōr*), and towards the *qafal* tree and towards the *sayyāl* tree which is inside the riverbed, and towards the *nabaq* tree, and meets the path there; and then towards the *hijlīj* [written *hijlīd*] tree which is in the torrent-bed (*al-sayl*), and then runs along the path to the pebbly area, ending on the western side at [the land of] the people of the *bayt al-jibāya*[54] and on the eastern side at [the land of] the *khabīr* ʻAlī.

From the southern side, [the boundary] runs eastwards along the path which [goes] between the two pebbly areas, and towards the crooked *ṭunṭub* tree which is in the rain-pool,[55] and towards the lake which is known as the lake of Fūrū, and towards the stump[56] of the *hijlīj* [written *hijliyya*] tree, and towards the *nabaq* tree, and to the *ṭunṭub* tree which is inside the household compound (*al-zarība*); and [the boundary] runs to the *inḍirāb* tree, and towards the stump[56] of the *ḥarāz* tree, and to the *mukhīṭ* tree, and it runs along the old path which traverses the household compounds; and it runs along the path which comes from Uzbān,[57] and towards the twin *hijlīj* [written *hijliyya*] trees, and ending [there] in respect to the south; the southern [land belongs] to the people of the *bayt al-jibāya* and the northern to *khabīr* ʻAlī.

Then it runs eastwards with [the land of] the Awlād Bās[ī]

towards the anthills (*al-quanṭūr*), and runs to the *hijlīj* [*hijliyya*] tree which is inside the torrent-bed, and towards the *ṭunṭub* tree which is in marshy ground [*al-naqa*ʿ*a*] and towards the tall *ṭunṭub* tree which is in the marshy ground and towards the *nabaq* tree of the nomads (*nabaqāyyat al-*ʿ*arab*) which is inside the household compound of Timm; and the boundary runs to the waterholes[58]

Document XLV

of Umm Sayyāla, and towards the *nabaq* tree which is in the riverbed, the meeting place of the boundaries, ending with [the land of] the Awlād Bāsī; the western [land belongs] to *khabīr* 'Alī and the eastern to the Awlād Bāsī, and lying on the northern side [is the land of] the *mayram* Fāṭim[a] Umm Dirays,[59] from the *qaraḍ* tree which is in the riverbed, and towards the *nabaq* tree which is inside the household compound of the elder Muṣṭafā, and towards the *hijlīj* (*hijliyya*) tree, and towards the *nabaq* tree which is at the junction of the two riverbeds, a *nabaq* tree, and towards the *ṭunṭub* tree which is inside the household compound.

Then it runs to the *kolkol* tree, and towards the *ṭunṭub* tree which is inside Ḥāmid's compound; and it runs to the *qaraḍ* tree which is in Yāsīn w. Ḥimār's compound, and towards the stump (*jidal*) of the *qaraḍ* tree which is by Raḥm's compound, and towards the stump (*jidal*) of the *qaraḍ* tree which...[60] and towards the *ṭunṭub* tree which is by Muḥammad Dardūq's fields; and it runs towards the anthills, and towards the crooked *sayyāl* tree, and towards the *nabaq* tree which is by 'Uthmān's compound, and towards the *nabaq* tree which is in the old open sandy area [*al-fardl*]; and it runs towards the *qaraḍ* tree, and towards the *mukhīṭ* tree; and it comes up to the big rock. The boundary comes back to the pebbly area known as Tawraq.

This brings to an end the boundaries of this locality called n.q.r. The northern [land belongs] to the *mayram* Umm Dirays and the southern to *khabīr* 'Alī, [namely] the two villages of n.q.r.

## XLVI

Sultan Muḥammad al-Ḥusayn gives *khabīr* 'Alī the village of n.q.r.ī.[61]

*seal*

From the presence of the most mighty sultan and most noble Caliph, the Commander of the Faithful and scion of the most noble, our lord and master Sultan Muḥammad al-Ḥusayn al-Mahdī, victorious through the Most High God, Amen.

To all who encounter this decree, namely, the *amīrs*, *wazīrs*, *maliks*, *shartays*, *dimlijs*, sons of the sultans, *mayrams*, *ḥabbōbas*, *jabbays* and all the officials.

Thereafter: I have shown favour to and have given our servant (*li-khaddāminā*), khabir 'Alī Ibrāhīm, the village of n.q.r.ī. with its fields both fallow and cultivated, the estate of...[62] I sent there

Ibrāhīm from *malik* 'Abdallāh Kūrī [or Kawrī]'s entourage and I ordered the *malik* 'Abdallāh ⌜to deliver the place into his possession⌝.[63] They were present; and there were present two men as witnesses. They swore upon the Book of God and walked around the fields of this village. They [the commissioners] then presented the report (*nasab*) of the boundaries to us [which] I examined.

The boundaries begin from Jabal n.q.r.ī *al-kabīr*. . .

## XLVII

Sultan Muḥammad al-Ḥusayn gives (or confirms) to the *khabīr* the village of n.q.r.ī.

*seal* . . .

. . .

1268.[64]

From the Commander of the Faithful, our lord and master Sultan Muḥammad al-Ḥusayn al-Mahdī, victorious through the Most High God, Amen.

To all who encounter this decree, namely, the *amīrs*, *wazīrs*, *maliks*, *shartays*, *dimlijs*, sons of the sultans, *jabbays* and all the officials.

Thereafter: I have shown favour to and have given our servant *khabīr* 'Alī Ibrāhīm the village of n.q.r.ī. with its land bounded by their hoe,[65] both fallow and cultivated, as a donation and gift to him and his descendants. I have relinquished to him all the Sharī'a and customary revenues, so that he has full disposal of it as a thing [in his possession].

Let no one interfere with him there; let no-one quarrel with him. This is my letter, decree and seal for him who knows it.

In the year 1284.[66]

# SOURCES AND BIBLIOGRAPHY

The following contains only those references cited in the book. For a more comprehensive bibliography on the Dār Fūr sultanate, see O'Fahey (1980). All references are cited in full on first occurrence and thereafter by author and year of publication.

### (a) Oral and archival sources

Unless otherwise indicated, all references to oral and archival sources come from O'Fahey's field-notes. Copies of the oral material will in due course be deposited at the Institute of African and Asian Studies, University of Khartoum, and the Department of History, University of Bergen.

The Province archives (PA) are located in the provincial administration headquarters, al-Fāshir.

The papers of the Rev. Dr A. J. Arkell are deposited (in two batches, here cited as AP[1] or [2]) at the School of Oriental and African Studies, University of London (accession no. 210522).

### (b) Theses and unpublished or forthcoming papers

Barkan, Omer Lutfi. "Social and economic aspects of Vakifs in the Ottoman Empire in the 15th and 16th centuries". Forthcoming in *Social and Economic Aspects of the Waqf*, ed. G. Baer.

(Bence Pembroke). "Darfur 1916: Geographical and Tribal Distribution upon Reoccupation". Unpaginated MS., Sudan Collection, University of Khartoum Library.

Hales, J. "The pastoral economy of the Meidob". Unpublished Ph.D. thesis, University of Cambridge, 1978.

MacMichael, H. A. "Notes on Darfur 1915". Typescript, Sudan Collection, University of Khartoum Library.

O'Fahey, R. S. "The growth and development of the Keira Sultanate of Dār Fūr". Unpublished Ph.D. thesis, University of London, 1972.

O'Fahey, R. S. "Slavery and society in Dār Fūr." Paper presented to the Conference, "Slavery and Related Institutions in Islamic Africa", Princeton 1977.

O'Fahey, R. S. "Endowment, privilege and estate in the Central and Eastern Sudan". Forthcoming in *Social and Economic Aspects of the Waqf*, ed. G. Baer.

Umar, H. S. "Al-Tunisi, Travels in Darfur: Translation, collation and annotation of *Tashhid al-adhhan bi sirat bilad al-Arab wa-l-Sudan* [*sic*]." Unpublished M.A. thesis, Abdullahi Bayero University, 1976.

### (c) Printed works


Abū Salīm, M. I. (1967). *Al-Funj wa'l-arḍ: Wathā'iq tamlīk*. Khartoum.

Abū Salīm, M. I. (1970). *Al-arḍ fi'l-Mahdiyya*. Khartoum.

Abū Salīm, M. I. (1975). *al-Fūr wa'l-arḍ: wathā'iq tamlīk*. Khartoum.

'Alī Dīnār, Sultan. (1331/1913). *Dīwān al-madīḥ fī-madḥ al-nabī al-milīḥ*. Khartoum.

Auriant, A. (1926). "Histoire d'Ahmed Aga le Zantiote. Un projet de conquête (1796–99) du Darfour". *Revue de l'histoire des colonies françaises*, XIV, 181–234.

'Awn al-Sharīf Qāsim. (1972). *Qāmūs al-lahja al-'āmiyya fi'l-Sūdān*. Beirut.

Baumer, M. (1975). *Noms Vernaculaires Soudanais Utiles à l'Ecologiste*. Paris.

Beaton, A. C. (1948). "The Fur". *SNR*, XXIX, 1–39.

Bivar, A. D. H. (1959). "Arabic documents from Northern Nigeria". *Bulletin of the School of Oriental and African Studies*, XXII, 324–49.

Brenner, L. (1973). *The Shehus of Kukawa*. Oxford.

Brockelmann, C. (1937–49). *Geschichte der Arabischen Literatur*. 5 vols. Leiden.

Browne, W. G. (1806). *Travels in Africa, Egypt and Syria from the Years 1792 to 1798*. 2nd edn. London.

Burckhardt, J. L. (1822). *Travels in Nubia*. 2nd edn. London.

Cadalvène, E. de and Breuvery, J. de (1841). *L'Egypte et la Nubie*. 2nd edn. Paris.

Cahen, C. (1962). "Contribution à l'étude des impôts dans l'Egypte médiévale". *Journal of the Economic and Social History of the Orient*, V/3, 244–78.

Cahen, C. (1963). "Notes de diplomatique arabo-musulmane". *Journal Asiatique*, CCLI, 311–25.

Cambridge History of Africa. (1975). Vol. IV, *c. 1600–c. 1790*, ed. Richard Gray. Cambridge.

Cunnison, I. (1966). *Baggara Arabs*. Oxford.

Cuny, C. (1854). "Notice sur le Darfour". *Bulletin de la Société de Géographie*, 4e série, VIII, 81–120.

Cuny, C. (1858). "Observations générales sur *La Mémoire sur le Soudan* de M. le Comte D'Escayrac de Lauture". *Nouvelles Annales des Voyages*, mars, 3–28.

Cuny, C. (1863). *Journal de Voyage de Siout à el-Obeid*. Paris.

Deny, J. (1930). *Sommaire des Archives Turques au Caire*. Cairo.

Douin, G. (1944). *Histoire du Soudan Egyptien*. Vol. 1 only. Cairo.

Dozy, R. (1881). *Supplément aux Dictionnaires Arabes*. 2 vols. Leiden.

Ebeid, R. Y. and Young, M. J. L. (1976). *Some Arabic Legal Documents of the Ottoman Period*. Leiden.

*Encyclopedia of Islam* (1963–00).

Ernst, H. (1960). *Die Mamlukischen Sultansurkunden des Sinai–Klosters*. Wiesbaden.

Fagnan, E. (1923). *Additions aux Dictionnaires Arabes*. Paris.

Felkin, R. W. (1884–85). "Notes on the For tribe of central Africa". *Proceedings of the Royal Society of Edinburgh*, XIII, 205–65.

Fourcade, J. F. (1968). "Documents arabes intéressant l'histoire du Dār Fūr". *Dossiers de la R.C.P. no. 45*, C.N.R.S., Paris, I, 34–53.

Fraccaroli, A. (1880). "Gita commerciale nel Cordofan e Darfur". *L'Esploratore*, IV, 205–6.

Gillan, J. A. (1929). "Darfur 1916". *SNR*, XII, 1–25.

Goody, J. (ed.). (1968). *Literacy in Traditional Societies*. Cambridge.

Hartmann, R. (1863). *Reise des Freiherrn Adalbert von Barnim durch Nord-Ost-Afrika in den Jahren 1859 und 1860*. Berlin.

Hill, R. (1967). *A Biographical Dictionary of the Sudan*. 2nd edn. London.

Hillelson, S. (1925). *Sudan Arabic: English–Arabic Vocabulary*. London.

Holt, P. M. (1969). "Four Funj land-charters". *SNR*, L, 2–14.

Holt, P. M. (1970). *The Mahdist State in the Sudan*. 2nd edn. London.
Holt, P. M. (ed.). (1977). *The Eastern Mediterranean Lands in the Period of the Crusades*. London.
Holý, L. (1974). *Neighbours and Kinsmen : a Study of the Berti People of Darfur*. London.
Humbsch, R. (1976). *Beiträge zur Geschichte des Osmanischen Ägyptens*. Freiburg.
Khalīl b. Isḥāq. (1956–62). *Mukhtaṣar = Abrégé de la loi musulmane selon le rite de l'imâm Mâlek*. Trans. G. H. Bousquet. 4 vols. Algiers.
Kropàček, L. (1970). "The confrontation of Darfur with the Turco-Egyptians". *Asian and African Studies* (Bratislava), VI, 73–86.
Kropàček, L. (1971). "Title-deeds in the fief system of the sultanate of Darfur". *Acta Universitatis Carolinae, Philologica*, IV, 33–50.
Labarre, E. (1952). *Dictionary and Encyclopedia of Paper and Paper-Making*. Amsterdam.
Lane, E. W. (1863). *An Arabic–English Lexicon*. 8 vols. London.
Last, M. (1967). *The Sokoto Caliphate*. London.
Lauture, P. H. S. D'Escayrac de (1855–56). *Mémoire sur le Soudan*. Paris.
Lejean, G. (1865). *Voyage aux Deux Nils*. Paris.
MacMichael, H. A. (1912). *The Tribes of Northern and Central Kordofan*. Cambridge.
MacMichael, H. A. (1922). *A History of the Arabs in the Sudan*. 2 vols. Cambridge.
Mitchener, M. (1977). *Oriental Coins and Their Values : The World of Islam*. London.
al-Muftī, Ḥusayn Sīd Aḥmad. (1378/1959). *Taṭawwur niẓām al-qaḍā' fi'l-Sūdān*. Vol. 1. only, Khartoum.
Nachtigal, G. (1971). *Sahara and Sudan*, vol. IV: *Wadai and Darfur*, Trans. A. G. B. and H. J. Fisher. London.
O'Fahey, R. S. (1971). "Religion and trade in the Kayra Sultanate of Dār Fūr". In *Sudan in Africa*, ed. Yūsuf Faḍl Ḥasan, 87–97. Khartoum.
O'Fahey, R. S. (1973). "Slavery and the slave trade in Dār Fūr", *Journal of African History*, XIV/1, 29–43.
O'Fahey, R. S. (1976). Review of Holý (1974), in *International Journal of African Historical Studies*, IX, 668–71.
O'Fahey, R. S. (1977a). "The office of *qāḍī* in Dār Fūr: a preliminary enquiry". *Bulletin of the School of Oriental and African Studies*, XL, 110–24.
O'Fahey, R. S. (1977b). "The Awlād 'Alī: a Fulani holy family in Dār Fūr". *Gedenkschrift Gustav Nachtigal 1874–1974 : Veröffentlichungen aus dem Ubersee-Museum, Bremen*, C, 1, 147–66.
O'Fahey, R. S. (1980). *State and Society in Dār Fūr*. London.
O'Fahey, R. S. and Abu Salim, M. I. (1983). *al-Arḍ fī-Dār Fūr*, Occasional Paper no. 6, Middle Eastern Section, Department of History, University of Bergen, Norway.
O'Fahey, R. S. and Spaulding, J. L. (1972). "Hāshim and the Musabba'āt". *Bulletin of the School of Oriental and African Studies*, XXXV/2, 316–33.
O'Fahey, R. S. and Spaulding, J. L. (1974). *Kingdoms of the Sudan*. London.
Petherick, Mr and Mrs J. (1869). *Travels in Central Africa*. 2 vols. London.
*Pièces Diverse et Correspondance Relatives aux Opérations de l'Armée d'Orient en Egypte* (messidor an XI/June, 1801). Paris.
Poliak, A. N. (1939). *Feudalism in Egypt, Syria, Palestine and the Lebanon, 1250–1900*. London.
Poncet, C.-J. (1709). *A Voyage to Ethiopia in the Year 1698, 1699 and 1700*. London.
al-Qalqashandī, Ahmad b. 'Abdallāh. (1913–14). *Ṣubḥ al-a'shā fī-sinā'at al-inshā'*. 14 vols. Cairo.
Quézel, P. (1969). "Flore et Végétation des plateaux du Darfur Nord-occidental et du jebel Gourgeil [= Kurge]", *Dossiers de la R.C.P. no. 45*, C.N.R.S. v. Paris.

Reid, J. A. and MacLaren, J. F. P. (1936). "Arab court procedure and customary law". *SNR*, XIX, 158–61.

Reychman, J. and Zajaçskowski, A. (1968). *Handbook of Ottoman–Turkish Diplomatic*. The Hague.

al-Rahūnī, *al-imām*. (1398/1978). *Ḥāshiyyat al-imām al-Rahūnī 'alā sharḥ al-Zurqānī li-Mukhtaṣar Khalīl*. 8 vols. Cairo.

Risciani, N. (1931). *Documenti e Firmani*. Jerusalem.

Sāmī Amīn. (1334–55/1916–35). *Taqwīm al-Nīl*. 6 vols. Cairo.

Santillana, S. (1926–38). *Istituzioni di Diritto Musulmano Malachita, con Riguarda anche al Sistema Sciafiita*. 2 vols. Rome.

Sarsfield-Hall, E. G. (1922). "Darfur". *The Geographical Journal*, LX/5, 359–68.

El Sayed el-Bushra. (1971). "Towns in the Sudan in the eighteenth and early nineteenth centuries". *SNR*, LII, 63–70.

Schacht, J. (1964). *An Introduction to Islamic Law*. London.

Seetzen, U. J. von. (1816). "Wörterverzeichnis aus der Sprache der Neger von Dâr-Fûr". In J. S. Vater (ed.), *Proben Deutscher Volks-Mundarten*. Leipzig.

Serjeant, R. B. (1962). "Haram and Hawtah, the sacred enclave in Arabia". In *Mélanges Taha Husain*, ed. Abd al-Rahman Bedawi, 41–58. Cairo.

al-Shāṭir Buṣaylī 'Abd al-Jalīl. (1955). *Ma'ālim ta'rīkh Sūdān wādī'l-Nīl*. Cairo.

Shuqayr, N. (1903). *Ta'rīkh al-Sūdān al-qadīm wa'l-ḥadīth wa-jughrāfiyatuhu*. 3 vols. Cairo.

Slatin, R. C. (1896). *Fire and Sword in the Sudan*. London.

Stern, S. M. (1965). *Documents from Islamic Chanceries*. First series. Oxford.

*Ta'rīkh al-Fattāsh*. (1913–14). Ed. and transl. O. Houdas and M. Delafosse. Paris (repr. 1964).

Theobald, A. B. (1965). *'Alī Dīnār : Last Sultan of Darfur, 1898–1916*. London.

Thomas, E. S. (1923). "The ethnographical collection of the Royal Geographical Society, Cairo". *Bulletin de la Société Royale de Géographie*, XII, 1–36 and 137–85.

Tubiana, M.-J. (1964). *Survivances préislamiques en pays Zaghawa*. Paris.

Tubiana, M.-J. and J. (1977). *The Zaghawa from an Ecological Perspective*. Rotterdam.

Tubiana, M. J. and J. (1967). "Mission au Darfour", *L'Homme*, VII, 89–96.

al-Tūnisī (El Tounsy), Muḥammad b. 'Umar. (1845). *Voyage au Darfour*. Trans. N. Perron. Paris.

al-Tūnisī (El Tounsy), Muḥammad b. 'Umar. (1851). *Voyage au Ouadây*. Trans. N. Perron. Paris.

al-Tūnisī, Muḥammad b. 'Umar. (1965). *Tashḥīdh al-adhhān bi-sīrat bilād al-'Arab wa'l-Sūdan*. Ed. Khalīl Maḥmūd 'Asākīr and Muṣṭafā Muḥammad Mus'ad. Cairo.

Tyan, E. (1945). "Le notariat et le Régime de la preuve par écrit dans la pratique du droit musulman". *Annales de l'Ecole Française de Droit de Beyrouth*. Université de Lyon, no. 2, Lyon.

Tyan, E. (1960). *Histoire de l'Organisation Judiciare en Pays d'Islam*. 2nd edn. Leiden.

'Umar al-Naqar. (1972). *The Pilgrimage Tradition in West Africa*. Khartoum.

'Uthman b. Fudi. (1978). *Bayān wujūb al-hijra 'ala'l-'Ibad*, ed. and transl. F. H. Elmasri, *Fontes Historiae Africanne, Series Arabica*, vol. 1. Khartoum.

Vassel, Philipp. (1922). "Uber marokkanische processpraxis". *Mitteilungen des Seminars für Orientalische Sprachen*, 170–232.

Vater, J. S. (1816). *Proben Deutscher Volks-Mundarten*, pp. 319–33. (U. J. Seetzen's Fur word-list). Leipzig.

Walz, T. (1978). *Trade between Egypt and Bilād as-Sūdān, 1700–1820*. Textes Arabes et Etudes Islamiques, VIII, Institut Français d'Archéologie Orientale du Caire. Paris.

Watin, L. (1954). *Recueil de Textes Marocains: Style Administratif*. Paris.
Wickens, G. E. (1976). *The Flora of Jebel Marra (Sudan Republic) and its Geographical Affinities*. London.
Wright, W. (1967). *A Grammar of the Arabic Language*. Cambridge.

# NOTES

## 1. The Dār Fūr sultanate

1 A brief survey is given in R. S. O'Fahey and J. L. Spaulding, *Kingdoms of the Sudan* (London, 1974), pp. 107–86. Greater detail will be found in O'Fahey's Ph.D. thesis, "The growth and development of the Keira Sultanate of Dār Fūr", (University of London, 1972), and in his *State and Society in Dār Fūr* (London, 1980). On Dār Fūr's wider milieu, see *The Cambridge History of Africa*, vol. IV, *From c. 1600–c. 1790*, ed. Richard Gray (Cambridge, 1975), chapters 1 and 2.

2 A brief ethnographic description is given in A. C. Beaton, "The Fur", *Sudan Notes and Records*, XXIX (1948), 1–39.

3 For ethnographic surveys of Dār Fūr, see A. B. Theobald, *'Alī Dīnār: Last Sultan of Darfur, 1898–1916* (London, 1965), pp. 1–16, and H. A. MacMichael, *A History of the Arabs in the Sudan* (Cambridge, 1922), I, pp. 52–128.

4 See the brief account in R. S. O'Fahey, "Religion and trade in the Kayra Sultanate of Dār Fūr", *Sudan in Africa*, ed. Yūsuf Faḍl Ḥasan (Khartoum, 1971), pp. 87–97. This is now superseded by T. Walz, *Trade between Egypt and Bilād as-Sūdan, 1700–1820*, Textes Arabes et Etudes Islamiques, VIII, Institut Français d'Archéologie Orientale du Caire (Paris, 1978), and O'Fahey (1980), 131–44.

5 Muḥammad b. 'Umar al-Tūnisī, *Tashḥīdh al-adhhān bi-sīrat bilād al-'arab wa'l-sūdān*, ed. Khalīl Maḥmūd 'Asākīr and Muṣṭafā Muḥammad Mus'ad (Cairo, 1965), p. 201; and in the French translation, *Voyage au Darfour*, tr. N. Perron (Paris, 1845), p. 194 (hereafter the translation will be cited in parentheses after the Arabic).

6 L. Kropàček, "The confrontation of Darfur with the Turco-Egyptians", *Asian and African Studies* (Bratislava, 1970), VI, 73–86.

7 For a more detailed discussion, see O'Fahey (1980), 69–114.

8 On the *fāshir*, see further O'Fahey and Spaulding, (1974), 146–51, and O'Fahey (1980), 14–28.

9 On the office, see al-Tūnisī (1965), 95 and 116 (78 and 105), and G. Nachtigal, *Sahara and Sudan*, tr. A. G. B. and H. J. Fisher (London, 1971), IV, pp. 328–9.

10 Written thus in the documents; al-Tūnisī and other sources write *takanyāwī*, which is the way it is pronounced.

11 The family, a Fur section called Konyuŋa, claim to be of Tunjur origin; Arkell Papers (see bibliography; hereafter cited as AP[1] or [2]), second batch, 10/48, f.

222. On the wider use of the title, see M.-J. Tubiana, *Survivances préislamiques en pays Zaghawa* (Paris, 1964), *passim*.

12 See further, al-Tūnisī (1965), 100–1 (a reference to several *takanāwīs*), 150–1 and 182 (87–8, 137–8 and 173), and Nachtigal (1971), IV, 277, 291–2, 324, 332, 349–50 and 358–9.

13 Nachtigal (1971), IV, 309. Neither W. G. Browne, the earliest traveller to write on Dār Fūr (*Travels in Africa, Egypt and Syria from the years 1792 to 1798*, 2nd edn., London, 1806), nor al-Tūnisī, in his Dār Fūr volume, refer to the title. al-Tūnisī (1851) mentions it in passing in his *Voyage au Ouadây* (Paris, 1851), p. 144.

14 Nachtigal (1971), IV, 330–1, and PA (al-Fāshir), file DP. FD. 66 K. 15 El Fasher District, Azagarfa Omodia, note by Bredin, 22 February 1931.

15 On Ḥasan, see P. H. S. D'Escayrac de Lauture, *Mémoire sur le Soudan* (Paris, 1855), p. 95; C. Cuny, "Observations générales sur *Le Mémoire sur le Soudan* de M. le Comte D'Escayrac de Lauture", *Nouvelles Annales des Voyages* (Mars, 1858), 13, and Nachtigal (1971), IV, 306 and 310. On Muḥammad, who appears to have governed only briefly, see Cuny, (1858). On Ādam, see AP[1], 3/14, ff.54–5, and G. Lejean, *Voyage aux Deux Nils* (Paris, 1865), p. 189, who has an Ādam wad Ḥasan ruling at Mellīt and, erroneously, ʻAbdallāh Ruŋa (Rôma) as governor of the north; ʻAbdallāh, a Dinka slave, was a *maqdūm* in the west. A document of Ādam (DF147.18/7) has the seal-date of 1277/1860–61.

16 DF269.33/2, 22 Jumāda I 1317/28 September 1899. The Condominium Government tried twice, from 1926 to 1929 and 1930 to 1946, to revive the province under Yūsuf Muḥammad Ādam.

17 Province archives (al-Fāshir), DP. FD. 66 K. 15 El Fasher District, Azagarfa Omodia, note by Bredin, 22 February 1931.

18 On the Berti, see L. Holý, *Neighbours and Kinsmen: a Study of the Berti People of Darfur* (London, 1974), and on the Meidob, J. Hales, "The Pastoral Economy of the Meidob", unpublished Ph.D. thesis (University of Cambridge, 1978).

19 al-Tūnisī (1965), 152 and 182 (138 and 173), and AP[1], 4/13, ff. 48–50. The number of *shartāyas* varied between 12 and 15.

20 This was less true of some of the Fur *shartays* of the west and south-west, whose distance from the capital and the ethnic homogeneity of their districts gave them considerable power and independence.

21 al-Tūnisī (1965), 152 (138); see further, O'Fahey (1980), 69–91.

22 On military developments, see O'Fahey (1980), 93–100.

23 As explicitly stated in V.

24 The same distinction was observed in Borno; see L. Brenner, *The Shehus of Kukawa* (Oxford, 1973), pp. 109–11. Sixteenth-century Ottoman charters granting *mülk*-rights also distinguish between *hukuk-i şerʻiyye* and *rüsûm-i ʻörfiyye*, the Islamic and customary taxes; Omer Lutfi Barkan, "Social and economic aspects of Vakifs in the Ottoman Empire in the 15th and 16th centuries", conference paper, Jerusalem, 1979 (to be published).

25 Browne (1806), 345–6; al-Tūnisī (1965), 184 (176); Nachtigal (1971), 358; PA (al-Fāshir), Western Darfur District Handbook, and Ibrāhīm and Muḥammad ʻAbdallāh ʻAbd al-Rasūl (al-Ṭawīla, 31.7.1976).

26 Nachtigal (1971), 358, and D176.18/36, undated.

27 Nachtigal (1971), 359.

28 al-Tūnisī (1965), 106 and 184 (93 and 175); Nachtigal (1971), 331, and *shartay* Ḥasaballāh Abu'l-Bashar (Tarnī, 9.4.1974).

29 In VIII, X and XXVIII, *al-jabbāyyīn al-'aysh wa'l-quṭn wa'l-ḥabb*; *quṭn* presumably refers to the *takkiyya* tax, but the exact meaning of *ḥabb* is uncertain in this context.

30 D199.19/1, undated.

31 al-Tūnisī (1965), 183–4 (175); Nachtigal (1971), 334, and Riḥaymtallāh Maḥmūd al-Dādinqāwī (al-Fāshir, 7.6.1970).

32 See further, R. S. O'Fahey, "The office of *qāḍī* in Dār Fūr: a preliminary enquiry", *Bulletin of the School of Oriental and African Studies*, XL (1977), 112–13.

33 The scale of fines in the Fur *shartāyas* are given in PA (al-Fāshir), Western Darfur District Handbook; see also the more general comments in N. Shuqayr, *Ta'rīkh al-Sūdān al-qadīm wa'l-ḥadith wa-jughrāfiyatuhu* (Cairo, 1903), II, pp. 137–9; Ḥusayn Sīd Aḥmad al-Muftī, *Taṭawwur niẓām al-qaḍā' fi'l-Sūdān* (Khartoum 1378/1959), I (only one volume published), pp. 60–1, and O'Fahey (1980), 109–14. For examples of the gap between custom and the Sharī'a Law of Inheritance, see I. Cunnison, *Baggara Arabs* (Oxford, 1966), pp. 198–200.

34 DF170.18/30, 1279/1862–63.

35 PA (al-Fāshir), Western Darfur District Handbook. The fines and fees were usually divided half and half.

36 Khalīl's *Mukhtaṣar* is the most widely-used lawbook in Dār Fūr. On these authors, see C. Brockelmann, *Geschichte der Arabischen Literatur* (GAL) (Leiden, 1937–49), II, p. 83 and *suppl.*, I, 96 (Khalīl); and II, 318 and *suppl.*, II, 438 (al-Zurqānī).

37 On the custom of the Berti people, see Holý (1974), 94–110; but see a review of the latter by O'Fahey in *International Journal of African Historical Studies*, IX (1976), 668–71.

38 On procedure in the Sudan, especially with reference to the oath, see J. A. Reid and J. F. P. MacLaren, "Arab court procedure and customary law", *SNR*, XIX (1936), 158–61. A useful article on Mālikī procedure is Philipp Vassel, "Uber marokkanische processpraxis", *Mitteilungen des Seminars für Orientalische Sprachen* (1902), 170–232.

39 Classically the *qāḍī*'s judgments should be written in two copies, "One of which is kept in the records (*dīwān*) of the tribunal", J. Schacht, *An Introduction to Islamic Law* (London, 1964), pp. 188–9.

40 The formal elements may be listed as follows: (a) introduction, (b) plaintiff's plea, (c) defendant's plea, (d) judge's examination and witnesses, (e) counsel of the *'ulamā*, (f) judgment, and (g) witnesses to the judgment.

41 The three *sijills*, XIII to XV, illustrate very well the evolution of a land/communal leadership dispute over several hearings.

42 This was the normal practice in Muslim lands; see E. Tyan, *Histoire de l'Organisation Judiciaire en Pays d'Islam*, 2nd edn (Leiden, 1960), p. 101.

43 These proportions reflect the whole Dār Fūr corpus; see further, O'Fahey (1977a), 110–24.

44 Ibid., 120–1.

45 Which did not prevent the dispute being revived later in XXXVIII. On *maẓālim* in Sharī'a theory, see Schacht (1964), 51 and *passim*.

46 For the details, see O'Fahey (1977a), 116–18.

47 PA (al-Fāshir), Western Darfur District Handbook (adultery punished by hanging), and DF221.28/2, undated.

## 2. Estate and privilege

1 The growth of the title-holding class in the period 1800 to 1870 may be charted by comparing the list given in al-Tūnisī (1965), 181–4, with that in Nachtigal (1971), 324–38. See further, O'Fahey (1980), 29–48.

2 For example, the move from military estate to "charitable" estate (*rizqa*) in Mamluk Egypt; see A. N. Poliak, *Feudalism in Egypt, Syria, Palestine and the Lebanon, 1250–1900* (London, 1939), pp. 30–3.

3 Shuqayr, II, 137.

4 See XI. Other examples include a charter from ʻAbd al-Raḥmān for Tōr b. Ḥāfiẓ, a grandson of Aḥmad Bukr, confirming the latter's original grant (DF92.11/6 Rajab 1200/April–May 1786), and a letter from Muḥammad al-Ḥusayn confirming the authenticity of a charter from Bukr which had been queried in court (DF120.13/5; 1271/1854–55)

5 DF142.18/2 and DF160.18/20; both are undated. Nachtigal (1971), 282–3 in fact records that Dawra inherited and used his father's seal.

6 A similar development occurred in Borno; see Brenner (1973), 105–10.

7 Browne (1806), 314.

8 Browne (1806), 323–4; Nachtigal (1971), 339 and R. W. Felkin, "Notes on the For tribe of Central Africa", *Proceedings of the Royal Society of Edinburgh*, XIII (1884–85), 225–6.

9 The usual meaning of *rɔ*, pl. *rɔta*, is "well" or "farm", while *ḥākūra*, pl. *ḥawākīr*, has as its usual meaning, "small vegetable garden, or plot". In some parts of Dār Fūr, *ḥākūra* is also used to mean the communal land of a clan (*khashm al-bayt*). This latter meaning raises the question of the interaction between local custom and central administrative practice, a question that cannot be pursued solely through the documents, but requires investigation on the ground.

10 Browne (1806), 345–6; al-Tūnisī (1965), 152 (138); Lauture (1855–56), 98; Nachtigal (1971), 326, and PA (al-Fāshir), Western Darfur District Handbook.

11 al-Tūnisī (1965), 152 (138), and E. de Cadalvène and J. de Breuvery, *L'Egypte et la Nubie*, second edn (Paris, 1841), II, p. 206 note.

12 al-Tūnisī (1965), 184–5 (176–7); compare, C. Cuny, "Notice sur le Darfur", *Bulletin de la Société de Géographie*, iv[e] série (1854), 91–2.

13 al-Tūnisī (1965); of the taxes he names, ***hāmil*** "stray(s)", ***dam*** "bloodmoney" and ***khidma*** "service" appear in the charters, while ***taqādum*** represents ***ḍiyāfa*** "hospitality" and ***khaṭiyya*** "judicial fee" or ***ḥukm***.

14 (Bence Pembroke), "Darfur 1916: Geographical and Tribal Distribution upon Reoccupation", unpaginated manuscript, Sudan Collection, University of Khartoum Library. A *maqdūm* would, for example, bring between 100 to 200 armed retainers.

15 On the Konyuŋa, see O'Fahey (1980), 35–6.

16 Sabīl Ādam Yaʻqūb (al-Fāshir, 1 and 4.6.1970); see also Nachtigal (1971), 288.

17 ʻAlī Ṣāliḥ Bidayn (al-Fāshir, 30.3.1974); on Aḥmad, see Shuqayr (1903), II, 125–6.

18 DF252.29/1.

19 DF121.13/6, 1281/1864–65; DF116.13/1, 1283/1866–67, and DF123.13/8.

20 *Shartay* Ḥasaballāh Abu'l-Bashar (Tarnī, 9.4.1974).

21 DF271.33/4.

22 H. A. MacMichael, "Notes on Darfur, 1915", typescript, Sudan Collection, University of Khartoum Library, p. 62, and (Bence Pembroke), "Geographical...Distribution", on the Zayyādiyya.

23 PA (al-Fāshir), DP. K. I(9) Gedid el Seil Omodia; note, C. Dupuis, 10 July 1928.
24 See further, R. S. O'Fahey, "Endowment, privilege and estate in the Central and Eastern sudan", in *Social and Economic Aspects of the Waqf*, ed. G. Baer (forthcoming).
25 R. B. Serjeant, "Haram and Hawtah, the Sacred Enclave in Arabia", in *Mélanges Taha Husain*, ed. Abd al-Rahman Bedawi (Cairo, 1962), pp. 41–58. Professor Serjeant traces the concept back to pre-Islamic and early Islamic times.
26 Physical sanctuary appears in at least one Dār Fūr charter: a chief "sought from us (the sultan) inviolability (for) his house", *ṭalaba minnā ḥaram manzilih*; DF305.44/5, issued in 1278/1861–62 by Sultan Muḥammad al-Ḥusayn for Ādam Daw.
27 The recipient is described as *ṣāḥib ḥurma wa-ṣāḥib jāh* in DF123.13/8 (1283/1866–67) and as *ahl ḥurma wa-karāma* in DF199.19/1 (undated). In another charter we find *huwa wa-māluhu ṣārū ḥurr min bayt al-jibāya*, "He and his property have been made free of the palace (lit. 'House of Taxation')", DF121.13/6 (1281/1864–65). More expressively the recipients could be described as "cripples to the *dīwān*", *maksūrīn al-'aẓm min al-dīwān*; DF294.41/3, 5 Sha'bān 1257/22 September 1841.
28 Namely nos. I, II, III, V, VI, XI, XXIX, XXX, XXXVIII, XXXIX, XLI, XLII, XLIV, XLVI and XLVII.
29 XXIV, XXV, XXVI, XXVII and XL.
30 L. Kropàček, "Title-deeds in the fief system of the sultanate of Darfur", *Acta Universitatis Carolinae, Philologica*, IV (1971), 33–50. However, no charters have been found to support Kropàček's suggestion of a Dār Fūr parallel to *iltizām*, i.e. tax-farming in the strict sense of the term.
31 Nachtigal (1971), 290 and 299, and O'Fahey (1980), 57.
32 O'Fahey (1980), diagram 5, "The charters of the Awlād Jābir", for an example of one of these chains.
33 XVI, XVII, XVIII, XX, XXI, XXIII, XXXI, XXXIV, XXXV, XXXVI, XXXVII and XLIII all concern various types of boundary disputes.
34 In XXXVIII, the rights are listed as, "cultivation, causing to be cultivated, sale, demolition, building, alms and purchase", and in XLI, "sale, presentation and inheritance".
35 On slavery within the sultanate, see R. S. O'Fahey, "Slavery and the slave trade in Dār Fūr", *Journal of African History*, XIV/1 (1973), 29–43, and *idem*, "Slavery and society in Dār Fūr", Conference paper, Princeton 1977 (to be published).
36 DF92.11/6 (undated).
37 On the size of Zaghawa herds, see M-J. and J. Tubiana, *The Zaghawa from an Ecological Perspective* (Rotterdam, 1977), pp. 39–45.
38 DF280.37/1: the recording of his own boundaries by Sharīf Thābit is unusual.
39 DF193.18/53 (undated); see below p. 149, n. 47.
40 We are grateful to Jonathan Hales for information on stone-walling.

### 3. Literacy and chancery

1 We have not discussed the question of how widespread literacy was (or is) in Dār Fūr since data are lacking. It is reasonable to assume that virtually only the *fuqarā'* could read or write with ease. On literacy in general, see *Literacy in Traditional Societies*, ed. J. Goody (Cambridge, 1968).
2 The *takanāwī* Ādam accuses two local chiefs with having over-taxed a *faqīh* by

four *takkiyyas*, a comparatively small quantity of cloth (DF176 . 18/36, undated), while a *maqdūm* investigates the theft of a donkey (DF97 . 12/5, undated).

3 Browne (1806), 234, Sultan 'Abd al-Raḥmān hears a case in Fur; 341, cases are heard in both Fur and Arabic, each being translated into the other by an interpreter. Cuny, (1858), 24 says the legal language was Arabic.

4 Thus 'Abd al-Ḥamīd, a Fulani *faqīh* prominent at Muḥammad al-Ḥusayn's court, was obliged to learn Fur according to his grandson (interview Aḥmad Amīn 'Abd al-Ḥamīd, al-Fāshir, 7.5.1970).

5 *Dīwān al-madīḥ fī-madḥ al-nabī al-milīḥ*, Khartoum 1331/1913.

6 Assistant Director of Intelligence, letter 7.7.1915; box 127/3, Darfur Campaign July–September 1915, Sudan Archive, School of Oriental Studies, University of Durham.

7 J. A. Gillan, "Darfur 1916", *SNR* (1929), 18. Even 'Alī Dīnār's scribes did not make copies of all out-going correspondence, to judge by the small amount of material found in al-Fāshir upon the conquest in 1916 and now located in the Central Records Office.

8 They are described in E. S. Thomas, "The ethnographical collection of the Royal Geographical Society, Cairo", *Bulletin de la Société Royale de Géographie*, XII (Cairo, 1923), 1–36 and 137–85.

9 Nachtigal (1971), 273, but judging from the information he gives these might well have been comprehensive and detailed.

10 In Sokoto copies were not made of outgoing letters, Murray Last, *The Sokoto Caliphate* (London, 1967), p. 190. Last's description of the Sokoto chancery (190–7) is instructive. We have some hints of a formally organized secretariat in Dār Fūr; thus Aḥmad Amīn 'Abd al-Ḥamīd (interview, al-Fāshir, 7.5.1970) described the *wazīr* Salāma b. Mālikī al-Fūtāwī as being particularly responsible for land affairs.

11 One archive contains a *sijill* in two copies which vary slightly (DF278 . 37/1 and 279 . 37/2, both dated 1279/1862–63), but since we have only transcriptions, it is impossible to determine if they are contemporary.

12 'Ubaydallāh is described in the latter as "secretary to the Grand Imam"; he also wrote DF69 . 8/7 (5 Jumāda I 1230/15 April 1815).

13 Cuny (1854), 113.

14 Shuqayr (1903), II, 132. al-Tūnisī's father met a Shaykh Ḥasan 'Ammārī al-Azharī in Dār Fūr; al-Tūnisī (1965), 117 (108).

15 DF145 . 18/45, and 150 . 18/10. All are undated but bear the same seal.

16 DF90 . 11/4 (1220/1805–6) and 199 . 19/1.

17 Who also wrote the letter from the sultan to John Petherick reproduced in Mr. and Mrs. Petherick, *Travels in Central Africa* (London, 1869), as the frontispiece to the second volume.

18 In a notebook among the papers of P. J. Sandison, there is a suggestion that certain officials were entrusted with certain seals; unfortunately no details are given (uncatalogued papers, Sudan Archive, University of Durham).

19 See discussion in Walz (1978), 74–8.

20 One of the original letters from 'Abd al-Raḥmān is at Vincennes; Service Historique de l'Armée Française, pièces B 6 54, 8 and 13 octobre 1800, and pièce B 6 60. The earliest printing of the translation is in *Pièces Diverses et Correspondance Relatives aux Opérations de l'Armée d'Orient en Egypt*, Paris messidor an XI (June, 1801), p. 187. The various letters exchanged between Bonaparte and his successors in Egypt and the rulers of Dār Fūr and Sinnār are given (but without adequate references) in A. Auriant, "Histoire d'Ahmed Aga

le Zantiote. Un projet de conquête (1796–99) du Darfour", *Revue de l'histoire des colonies françaises*, XIV (1926), 181–234.

21 For the letter to the Pethericks, see above, and on Vogel, C. Cuny, *Journal de Voyage de Siout à el-Obeid* (Paris, 1863), pp. 198–201.

22 Reproduced in al-Shāṭir Buṣaylī 'Abd al-Jalīl, *Ma'ālim ta'rīkh Sūdān wādi'l-Nīl* (Cairo, 1955), p. 261.

23 See further J. Deny, *Sommaire des Archives Turques au Caire* (Cairo, 1930). Some of these are copied or précised in Sāmī Amīn, *Taqwīm al-Nīl* (Cairo 1334–55/1916–35), 6 vols.

24 G. Douin, *Histoire du Soudan Egytien* (Cairo, 1944), I, pp. 55–6.

25 'Umar al-Naqar, *The Pilgrimage Tradition in West Africa* (Khartoum, 1972), p. 113. The original letter is on exhibit at the History Museum, University of Zaria, Nigeria. We are grateful to Dr al-Naqar for a transcription. See also Nachtigal (1971), 394–5 and facsimile.

26 Nachtigal (1971), 310.

27 Thus in DF15.5/1 (15 Rabī' I 1318/13 July 1900) 'Alī Dīnār appoints Muḥammad 'Alī Ṣāliḥ Shaykh of the 'Irayqāt and defines the boundary of their lands.

28 See Deny (1930), plate LIII; Walz (1978), 24–5 and O'Fahey (1980), 44–6 and 141–4.

29 al-Tūnisī (1851), 468–9. The context in which these letters were issued is discussed in O'Fahey (1980), 135.

### 4. A diplomatic commentary

1 Unfortunately no attempt was made to examine documents in the field for watermarks. Browne (1806), 348, gives in his list of imports, "writing paper (papier des trois lunes), a considerable item", and J. L. Burckhardt, *Travels in Nubia*, 2nd edn (London, 1822), p. 270, lists "paper (papier de trois limes, from Genoa and Leghorn)" among the exports to Dār Fūr. The water-mark, "three crescents in a horizontal row", appears on paper made in or near Venice from 1725 onwards (E. Labarre, *Dictionary and Encyclopedia of Paper and Paper-Making*, 2nd edn (Amsterdam, 1952), p. 342). See also Walz (1978), 30–1.

2 Burckhardt (1822).

3 The comments here are cursory both because no study of Dār Fūr Arabic has yet been undertaken and because the whole corpus needs to be studied in detail. Some discussion of Sudanese Arabic may be found in S. Hillelson, *Sudan Arabic: English–Arabic Vocabulary* (London, 1925), and in the dictionary, 'Awn al-Sharīf Qāsim, *Qāmūs al-lahja al-'āmmiyya fi'l-Sūdān* (Beirut, 1972).

4 A comparable formula is *ilā kulli wāqif 'alayhi min...*; see the Mamluk and Ottoman examples in Hans Ernst, *Die Mamlukischen Sultansurkunden des Sinai–Klosters* (Wiesbaden, 1960), XXVI, and Robert Humbsch, *Beiträge zur Geschichte des Osmanischen Ägyptens* (Freiburg, 1976), *passim*.

5 This usage of the definite article is noted in W. Wright, *A Grammar of the Arabic Language* (Cambridge, 1967) (many editions) I, pp. 269–70.

6 Compare the *sijill* translated in Walz (1978), 215–21, where the same shift from formal to colloquial speech is found.

7 A. D. H. Bivar, "Arabic documents from Northern Nigeria", *Bulletin of the School of Oriental and African Studies*, XXII (1959), 329 and plate 1.

8 Brenner (1973), 53, says, on the authority of Borno mallams, that it represents "five".

9 The form is listed as appearing on Islamic coins in M. Mitchener, *Oriental Coins and Their Values* (London, 1977), p. 12.
10 Claude Cahen, "Notes de diplomatique arabo-musulmane", *Journal Asiatique*, CCLI (1963), 311–25.
11 By 'Alī Dīnār's time the distinction in the use of the seal placed above on a decree and placed below by the name of the witnesses or official was regularly observed; see (B. Björkman), "Diplomatic", *Encyclopedia of Islam*, 2nd edn, II, p. 307.
12 DF176.18/36; 184.18/44 and 186.18/46 (undated). The use of camel-brands (*wasm*) is reminiscent of the *damgha* on Uyghur–Turkic documents, "The origin of the *tamga* is traced back to primitive family symbols which were once branded on cattle", Jan Reychman and Ananiasz Zajączkowski, *Handbook of Ottoman–Turkish Diplomatics* (The Hague, 1968), p. 157.
13 However, excellent seals are still made in al-Fāshir.
14 al-Tūnisī (1965), 51 (32).
15 This is exaggerated; safe-conducts bearing the sultan's seal were given to foreigners, including Nachtigal, who made no attempt to conceal that he was a Christian.
16 Cuny (1854), 94–5.
17 On the typology of the seals, see M. I. Abu Salim, *al-Fūr wa'l-arḍ: wathā'iq al-tamlīk* (Khartoum, 1975), pp. 25–46 and facsimiles at end. This listing is incomplete.
18 Shuqayr (1903), II, 141; his general description of the seals is based only on those of Muḥammad al-Ḥusayn that he saw in Cairo.
19 DF166.18/26 and 173.18/33 (both are otherwise undated).
20 (G. S. Colin), "Diplomatic", *EI*², p. 307; DF142.18/2 has the ligature of the *hā'* and *dāl* in *waḥdah* noted by Colin.
21 The charter given in al-Tūnisī (1965), 68–9 (50–1) lacks an *invocatio*, but it may simply have been omitted in transcription.
22 M. I. Abū Salīm, *al-Funj wa'l-arḍ: wathā'iq tamlīk* (Khartoum, 1967), p. 11.
23 But XVII and XXIX both begin with the *basmala*.
24 Perhaps the clearest published Mamluk examples are to be found in N. Risciani, *Documenti e Firmani* (Jerusalem, 1931).
25 On Mahdist diplomatic, see P. M. Holt, *The Mahdist State in the Sudan, 1881–1898*, 2nd edn (London, 1970), p. 269.
26 See further *Documents from Islamic Chanceries*, first series (Oxford, 1965), ed S. M. Stern, p. 21 and n. 52.
27 See Abū Salīm (1967), *passim*, and P. M. Holt, "Four Funj land-charters", *SNR*, I (1969), 2–14, for Sinnār. The provenance of the Borno charters (called *maḥrams*) granting privileged or exempt status is discussed in O'Fahey, "Endowment, privilege and estate", forthcoming, in *Social and Economic Aspects of the Waqf*, ed. G. Baer.
28 Similar listings are found in the Funj charters. For a comparative perspective, see the discussion of the Ayyubid al-'Ādil's titles in Stern (1965), 18–24.
29 They appear in the charter transcribed in al-Tūnisī (1965), 68–9 (50–1) and in the letter sent to Napoleon (see p. 129, n. 20). Ottoman examples are given in Humbsch (1976), *passim*.
30 See Holt (1969), 9.
31 Shuqayr (1903), II, 121; see also Browne (1806), 237–8. It appears in DF92.11/6 and 150.18/10.
32 And in a charter (dated 19 Dhu'l-ḥijja 1220/30 March 1806) transcribed in al-Muftī (1378/1959), I, 52–3.

33 The former appears in Shuqayr (1903), II, 131–2; the latter is reproduced in al-Shāṭir (1955), 261.

34 III, V, XIX, XXXVIII, XXXIX, XL, XLI, XLIV, XLVI, and XLVII. Perhaps, indeed, it was no less than a claim to be the expected Mahdi.

35 Last (1967), 46–7; its earliest appearance is in a letter from a Kānem Sultan dated 1391–92 (the letter appears in Aḥmad b. 'Abdallāh al-Qalqashandī, *Ṣubḥ al-a'shā fī-sinā'at al-inshā'* (Cairo, 1913–14), VIII, p. 155), a clue perhaps to Kanem/Borno's role as the "diplomatic" exemplar for much of the central Sudan.

36 DF85.10/10, from Sultan Muḥammad b. Muḥammad Yūsuf, 12 Muḥarram 1320/21 April 1902, and DF86.10/11, from Sultan Aḥmad al-Ghazzālī, 1319/1901–2.

37 DF142.18/2: the latter phrase (and its alternative form, *wulāt umūr al-islām*) has a long history, see Humbsch (1976), 177, n. 2.

38 *Wa-jumlat al-ṭughāt al-mutamarridīn bi-ḥuqūq al-muslimīn*; see VIII, X, XI, XII, XXX (*al-mutamarridīn 'alā al-muslimīn*), XLI and XLIII.

39 *Ta'rīkh al-fattāsh*, ed. and transl. O. Houdas and M. Delafosse, (Paris, 1913–14) (repr. 1964), pp. 72–4 (transl. 138–41); *wa-yamsik kull jā'ir wa-fājir jawrah wa-fujūrah min jundinā wa-ahl jayshinā wa-khadaminā al-jā'irin...fa-lā yaqrubhum bi-ḍaym*.

40 Transcribed in al-Muftī (1378/1959), I, 52–3.

41 Almost identical phrasing appears in III and XXXVIII; all are from Muḥammad al-Ḥusayn. In VI, 'Alī Dīnār alludes to his re-establishing the sultanate, a very frequent theme in his charters.

42 DF125.13/10.

### 5. Translations and commentary

#### I. The *faqīh* 'Abdallah's charter

1 In the possession of 'Alī Ḥasaballāh (al-Fāshir); the text is given in Abū Salīm (1975), 124–5.

2 Ādam Muḥammad Muḥammadayn (al-Fāshir, 16.6.1970); the informant possesses the original charter, as yet unphotographed.

3 Qur'ān, LV, 60.

4 The text reads *awqa'tu; awqaftu* makes better sense.

5 A clan who are traditionally said to have been the original owners of the site that became al-Fāshir (we are grateful to G. M. La Rue for this note).

6 I.e. Jadīd al-Sayl, see below pp. 37–8.

7 The recipient of IV below.

8 Here and throughout we have added "tree(s)" for the sake of clarity.

9 Qur'ān, XXXVIII, 38.

#### II to VI. The Jawami'a *fuqarā'* of Jadīd al-Sayl

1 Now in the possession of Naṣr al-Dīn 'Izz al-Dīn (Jadīd al-Sayl).

2 See further MacMichael (1922), I, 225–8.

3 On Kerio, see O'Fahey "The Awlād 'Alī: a Fulani holy family in Dār Fūr". *Gedenkschrift Gustav Nachtigal, 1874–1974 : Veroffentlichungen ans den Ubersee – Museum, Bremen* (1977), Reihe C., Band l, pp. 147–66.

4 Browne (1806), 271.

5 Nachtigal (1971), 283; Theobald (1965), 191–3.

6 Nachtigal (1971), 292; PA, DP 66 K 1(9), Gedid el Seil Omodia, note 10 July 1928.

7 See further O'Fahey (1977a), 120–1.
8 PA, DP 66 B 28, Tungur, note 17 November 1930. The name may really be Dhu'l-Nūrayn.
9 1799–1800.
10 *al-'izz* repeated.
11 But Muḥammad al-Faḍl's grandfather was Aḥmad Bukr, not Muḥammad Dawra.
12 Conjectural emendation; what can apparently be read is *al-mutawalli al-imārah min ba'd al-sulṭān Aḥmad Bukr*...
13 Ibrāhīm b. 'Abd al-Qādir was the *abbo daadiŋa* (see glossary), a descendant of a man from Dār Tāma called Wīr. Wad Wīr became the family patronymic, see Nachtigal (1971), 334.
14 What follows is evidently a direct quotation from Muḥammad al-Faḍl's charter.
15 *khuddām al-daraqa*, a term that does not appear elsewhere; it may possibly mean "soldiers" except that *junūd* appears earlier in the list.
16 "The builders", which does not appear elsewhere; its meaning is unknown.
17 Cf. Qur'ān, III, 173.
18 10 February 1807.
19 1844–45.
20 Thus a number of charters include the formula, "There is due from them [i.e. the recipients] nothing except intercessory prayer."
21 On Qur'ānic recitations as part of the preparations for war, see Nachtigal (1971), 285–6.
22 158.18/18, from the Awlād Jābir Archive.
23 Alternatively, the threat may have been the raid on northern Dār Fūr by an Egyptian nomad chief, 'Umar al-Miṣrī, who had been expelled from the Fayyum region in about 1855 by the Egyptian authorities; see Lejean (1865), 43 and Nachtigal (1971), 313.
24 Qur'ān, XII, 18.
25 The seal impression is given twice.
26 A Beigo slave given to Sultan 'Abd al-Raḥmān before his accession. She is also listed among the former owners of an estate in XXXVIII.
27 A tribal or clan name.
28 Correctly, *tunḍub*, but this spelling is in fact more common.
29 A son of Sultan 'Abd al-Raḥmān who is said to have been imprisoned and later executed by his brother, Sultan Muḥammad al-Faḍl; Nachtigal (1971), 298–303.
30 Reading *al-nakhla* for *al-naḥla*.
31 This passage may be compared with XXXVIII.
32 1846–47.
33 Zakariyyā is invariably described as "sultan" in his son's documents although he never reigned. The retrospective use of the title served to legitimize his son's position, since customarily only a son of a sultan could accede to the throne.
34 *Aḥbābunā*, an imitation of Mahdist usage that disappeared from 'Alī Dīnār's later documents.
35 17 December 1898, the day before the charter was issued.
36 *al-madhkūr* is often used where the subject has not in fact been previously mentioned.
37 Not literally, since Muḥammad al-Ḥusayn was 'Alī Dīnār's paternal uncle.
38 1844–45.
39 18 December 1898.

**VII to XXIII. The Tunjur *fuqarā'* of Khirībān**

1 From an archive of 23 documents in the possession of Ādam Rijāl 'Alī of Khirībān. Those documents not translated here come mainly from the Mahdist period (1882–98).
2 See further, O'Fahey & Spaulding (1974), 107–16. The Tunjur empire probably flourished in the fifteenth and sixteenth centuries.
3 Nachtigal (1971), 348; MacMichael (1922), II, 71.
4 Ādam Rijāl 'Alī (al-Fāshir, 23.4.1974); 'Abdallāh is said to have acted as "vizier" to one of the sultans. Although VII refers only to Tayrāb's charter, the last charter in the sequence, XI, refers to a charter from Aḥmad Bukr, while XXII refers to a charter from Abu'l-Qāsim.
5 The Awlād 'Abdallāh Maṭlūq are not directly named but according to the documents' owner were included under "the descendants of the *faqīh* 'Abd al-Raḥmān."
6 Compare with the ruling in XXIII.
7 1799–1800, or 1213/1798–99; the last number is unclear.
8 It is not clear if this is meant to represent a date.
9 The seal differs from the usual design, consisting of a central panel surrounded by two outer rings. It is not entirely legible.
10 A space has been left between the *invocatio* and the *intitulatio*.
11 *Abnā' al-shawba* (*al-shōba*); 'Awn (1972), 422 gives "a band of warriors".
12 The original date is illegible; the year 1221/1806–7 has been written in by another hand.
13 1825–26.
14 Cf. Qur'ān, I, 5.
15 *Shākir sayyidinā*; possibly "grateful to our Lord".
16 Literally, "May God make his earth [over his grave] light."
17 The scribe has transposed *ṭayyaba al-llāh tharāhu* and *zāda al-llāh ayyāmahu*.
18 *al-waḥdyān*; possibly an elision of *al-wāḥid wa'l-dayyān*.
19 *al-takānū*, the only written example of a plural for *takanāwī*.
20 The Arabic reads *f.l.ḥāṣ.l.*, which we have interpreted as *falā ḥāsal* (*shay'*).
21 Or "your protection", *dhimmatika*. Although the Tunjur of Kafōt and Khirībān were no longer to be taxed by the *takanāwī* or his officials, Sultan Shalabi would leave his people under the governor's jurisdiction in other, e.g. judicial, matters. Nevertheless, the use of *dhimma* of a Muslim community is unusual.
22 1840–41.
23 Reading *fī-kitāb* as (*mā*) *fī-kitāb*.
24 For *shaghghala*.
25 8 November 1841.
26 On the reasons for the grant, see XX.
27 The seal is identical to that on X.
28 *Iḥyā'ahum*, that is, the land brought under cultivation by 'Abdallāh and his people.
29 Amīn was probably a leader of a Kotoko community. The Kotoko, from the Shari/Logone region south of Lake Chad, are widely settled throughout Dār Fūr. "Takārīr" (a plural form of "Takrūrī") is a generic term for western immigrants in the Sudan; Amīn's title may thus indicate some general authority over western immigrants within the sultanate (or a district). Burckhardt refers to a *makk al-takarna* (an alternative plural for "takrūrī") at al-Ubayyiḍ in Kordofān; see Burckhardt (1822), 437.

30 Despite several lacunae, the description of the boundaries can be restored both by reference to a gloss in another hand in the right-hand margin and to the description given in XXII.
31 *Majarr al-wādī*, the channel or stream's bed within the *wādī*; see 'Awn (1972), 118.
32 *al-h.s.l.mās al-abyaḍ*; the first word remains unidentified.
33 Or "flowing waterholes"; compare below p. 86 (XXIX).
34 28 December 1842.
35 A word here not understood.
36 *Sharr kull madarra*; presumably the loss of rank and position.
37 *Amr karīm* is the usual expression in 'Alī Dīnār's correspondence (but not before him) for a sultanic order or charter, remotely in imitation of Ottoman and earlier practice.
38 However, no charter from Aḥmad Bukr has been referred to before.
39 Referred to in VII.
40 I.e. VII.
41 I.e. VIII.
42 I.e. X and XI.
43 *Bi'l-tafwīḍ ilayhi.*
44 *Taṣrīḥan.*
45 *'ala'l-athar.*
46 Literally, "may God make their earth (over their graves) light".
47 *La ḥujja*, "no plea" as to a court.
48 12 June 1899. We have not translated the various Condominium marks of registration written at the bottom of the document.
49 Son and nominated successor (*khalīfa*) of Sultan Muḥammad Tayrāb, on whose behalf he governed northern Dār Fūr from about 1770. He was killed in civil war with his uncle, Sultan 'Abd al-Raḥmān, in 1204/1789–90; see O'Fahey and Spaulding (1974), 135–41.
50 One of the sons of Ibrāhīm b. Ramād, who as head of the Konyuŋa clan, *malik al-naḥās* "master of the drums" and *somiŋ dogala* "chief of the cadets", was accurately described by Browne as, "The most opulent man in the empire except the sultan" (1806), 224. On the power of the Konyuŋa clan, see O'Fahey (1980), 35–6. Ibrāhīm himself appears as a witness in XXIV, a son, Fāris, in XXVI and another son, Ādam, in XXVII.
51 1773–74.
52 *Sabāb al-taḥrīr*, a formula frequently used to open the written judgments of a *qāḍī*. On these introductory formulae and others used in the *sijills*, see R. Y. Ebied and M. J. L. Young, *Some Arabic Legal Documents of the Ottoman Period* (Leiden, 1976) (Ḥanafī examples from Palestine); L. Watin, *recueil de Textes Marocains: Style Administratif* (Paris, 1954) (Mālikī from Morocco, with an extensive vocabulary), and Vassel (1902).
53 We have added these headings here and throughout for the sake of clarity, but plaintiff (*mudda'ī*) and defendant (*mudda'ā 'alayh*) must be understood in the Islamic legal sense, since the decision as to who is which is an integral and decisive part of the judicial process; see Schacht (1964), 189–91.
54 *Iḥyā* is used here and throughout loosely for "cultivations", meaning virgin land brought under cultivation for the first time, an act legally described as *iḥyā' al-mawāt*, "the revivification of the dead [lands]". See further, *EI*², III, 1053–4.
55 *Muwakkilīh*; those who had mandated Aḥmad as their *wakīl*, to represent them. See Santillana (1926–38), II, 336–7.
56 *Ilā al-muddat al-madhkūra*, that is, until the time of the hearing.

57 *Bayyina*: "by far the most important kind of evidence is the testimony (*shahāda*) of witnesses, so much so that the term *bayyina* is sometimes used as a synonym for 'witness"', Schacht (1964), 192.

58 The terms translated here as "possession", *ḥiyāza* and *ḥawz*, mean a prescriptive right of possession derived in this instance from the opening up of new land; see further Abū Salīm *Al-arḍ fi'l-Mahdiyya* (Khartoum, 1970) p. 57 for the Mahdist legal practice.

59 An ambiguous reference since the sultan could be either Muḥammad Dawra (*c.* 1720–30) or Muḥammad Tayrāb (1752/53 – 1785/86)

60 *Bi'l-ḥawz faqaṭ*: but perhaps this should be "property only" to agree with the earlier part of the witnesses' testimony.

61 By omission, 'Abd al-Raḥmān in effect rules that Muḥammad Nartaq's testimony was not legally valid (*'udūl*), as is made clear below.

62 *Nuṣūṣ al-madhhab*, i.e. consulted the Mālikī lawbooks.

63 That is, to swear to the truth of what their witnesses said.

64 The Qur'ān; in this instance, presumably one of particular sanctity.

65 The full name of the commissioner (*muwajjah*), the *faqīh* Aḥmad (not to be confused with the plaintiff), sent by the judge to administer the oath is unclear.

66 They thus gave him full authority (*wakāla mufawwaḍa*) to take the oath on their behalf; see Santillana (1926–38), II, 340.

67 It seems that Aḥmad did not take the oath; instead Muḥammad sought pardon (*'afw*) through an oath sanctioning a peaceful settlement of the dispute.

68 See also XVI, where the same officials are named; *sajjān* can mean "gaoler", but there is no other reference to such an official in the *corpus*.

69 See further, O'Fahey (1977a), 121.

70 The defendants of XIII are now the plaintiffs, although at least one person, 'Arībī (or 'Uraybī) has changed sides.

71 *Jidduhumā*, that is the grandfather (or more loosely, the ancestor) of both the plaintiffs and the defendants. Whether this was the 'Abd al-Raḥmān later referred to by the defendant or 'Abdallāh Maṭlūq is unclear.

72 On this title and *qāḍī quḍāt al-islām* (below n. 79), see O'Fahey (1977a), 119–22.

73 *F'a'dharnā lahu f'adh'ana bi-'adam al-ḥujja*: *i'dhar*, the final questioning by the judge to that party whose plea will fail if they are unable to present proof of their claim.

74 *bi-wakālat aḥmad bi-tawkīl...tafwīḍan lahu*: Aḥmad was their representative!

75 *Jiddihum*, see n. 71.

76 Kakama in XIII.

77 A word not read, possibly *ya'nī* "that is".

78 *Fa-laghāhumā al-shar'*; that is, the law set aside the two previous court rulings.

79 *al-qāḍī* (*sic*) *quḍāt al-islām*.

80 1833–34.

81 1839–40.

82 Literally "the letters".

83 Literally "its judge".

84 Neatly reversing the order of events as described in XII, where there is no mention of *al-ḥājj* 'Izz al-Dīn seizing a document.

85 "That we thought worth recording."

86 *Fa-aqarra bi'l-muḥākama wa-idda'ā 'adam al-inṣāf*: the transition of the subject seems abrupt. On *iqrār*, "confession, or acknowledgment", see Santillana (1926–38), II, 590–1, and Schacht (1965), 151.

87 The *malik* turns to the *'ulamā'* for legal advice.

88 The archive of the Fulani *faqīhs* who were (and are) neighbours of the Tunjur contains eleven documents (DF63.8/1 to 73.8/11), of which one is a detailed pedigree in five folios of the Fulani tracing their descent back to ʻUqba b. Nāfiʻ.

89 DF69.8/7, 5 Jumāda I 1230/15 April 1815.

90 The Arabic has *walad walad al-sulṭān ʻAqrab*; although this construction does occasionally appear, in DF69.8/7 he appears simply as *walad al-sulṭān*.

91 *Iḥyā' ajdādinā*; i.e. which they brought under cultivation.

92 Evidently the judge's regular entourage, see XIII.

93 1805–6.

94 The seal, which is virtually illegible, is of the same type as that on VIII.

95 There is a wide margin between the *basmala* and the first line of the intitulation.

96 *Al-ashhād al-qudam* (for *al-qudamā'*); that is, witnesses old enough for their testimony to span a long period of time, cf. the witnesses for the defendant in XIII.

97 Perhaps the person whose Qur'ān was recommended in XIII.

98 *Huwa yumallikuhum zirāʻatahum : mallaka* seemingly used in two senses, here to mean "hand over, hand back", and below *mallakūhu* "you are to transfer it to the ownership of".

99 1802–3.

100 Reading *bi-nuwwābihi.*

101 The obliques denote, here and throughout, a word or phrase written above the line in the original document.

102 *Muwajjah.*

103 Literally "has brought his complaint to us".

104 *Qirab* (sing. *qirba*), the large waterskins carried by donkeys.

105 Literally "the place of their quarrel".

106 The Fur honorific, *iriŋa*; see above, p. 5.

107 The last numeral of the date is not clear.

108 ʻAbd al-Ghanī b. Makkī came from the Juba section of the northern Fulani of Dār Fūr (Fallāta al-Rīḥ) and was *imām* to Sultan Tayrāb. His father was an immigrant from West Africa. He is mentioned in Shuqayr (1903), II, 119. His nephew, the *imām* Muḥammad al-Miṣrī, appears as a witness here and in XXXVII.

109 Reading conjecturally at end of line, *wa-lam yataʻarraḍ.*

110 S.n.f.tī in XXI.

111 *Maʻa rāḥatih*, literally "with his palm"; *rāḥa* "palm" being used of certain of the sultan's senior officials.

112 In document XI.

113 *Aʻrāḍ maʻlūma*, reading *aʻrāḍ* as an error for *arāḍī.*

114 Who are referred to in the boundary description in XI.

115 That is document XI.

116 *Istathnāhu li-sayyidih muḥammad*, which appears to mean, "Which Muḥammad had reserved for his master". The whole passage seems confused and our translation is an attempt to make sense of it. *Sayyid* almost invariably refers to the sultan.

117 *Imām* to both Sultans Muḥammad al-Faḍl and Muḥammad al-Ḥusayn; his father, al-Ṭayyib, was a brother of the ʻAbd al-Ghanī referred to above.

118 1845–46.

119 See further O'Fahey (1973), 37–43.

120 The date is written as ٤ ϕ ٢ ١, that is backwards. In Chapter 4 (p. 27), it has been suggested that ϕ represents "five", giving thus the date 1254/1838–39.

This reading of the date may be confirmed by Nachtigal who says (p. 329) that Raḥma was *āb shaykh* to Muḥammad al-Ḥusayn who acceded in that year.

121 A similar demand is made in DF 65 . 8/3, where the dispute appears to have been over who had the right to dispose of the community's land.

122 For a discussion of this point, see 'Uthman b. Fudi, *Bayān Wujūb al-Hijra 'ala' l-'Ibād*, ed. and transl. F. H. Elmasri (Khartoum, 1978), pp. 71–2.

123 Written by the side of the seal. This is probably a note attesting to the correctness of *qāḍī* Ḥammād's judgment from *shaykh al-quḍāt* Isḥāq.

124 In fact, the defendant is not named at this point.

125 This is presumably the charter from Tayrāb referred to in VII.

126 A reference to XIII.

127 This sounds like an interjection by Ādam to the effect that Muḥammadayn's claims were no greater than his own.

128 Restored from XI, from which the boundary description below is copied although with two errors or variant spellings.

129 See p. 135, n. 32.

130 Or "flowing waterholes", see p. 135, n. 33.

131 R.kh. in XI.

132 Ma'qūq in XI.

133 The scribe has rewritten this sentence, but then reverts to direct quotation from XI.

134 Two quotations appear to have been run together. The first comes from Khalīl b. Isḥāq, *Mukhtaṣar*, *bāb mawāt al-arḍ* (= G.-H. Bousquet, *Abrégé de la loi musulmane selon le rite de l'imâm Mâlek*, 4 vols. (Algiers, 1956–62), III, p. 142). The second appears to be from a commentary on the *Mukhtaṣar* by 'Abd al-Bāqī b. Yūsuf al-Zurqānī, *Sharḥ Mukhtaṣar Khalīl*. We have not found the precise quotation in the printed text of al-Zurqānī, although his discussion of Khalīl's chapter may be found in *al-Imām* al-Rahūnī, *Ḥāshiyyat al-imām al Rahūnī 'alā Sharḥ al-Zurqānī li-Mukhtaṣar Khalīl*, 8 vols. (Cairo, 1398/1978), VII, pp. 97–129. Furthermore, "the *imām*" at the end of the quotation or summary from al-Zurqānī is ambiguous; it may be part of the quotation referring to the ruler making the concession or it may preface "'Abd al-Bāqī".

135 1863–64.

136 Who was also twice sued by the Fallata holy men of Khirībān (DF63 . 8/1 and DF64 . 8/2.); on their archive, see p. 137, n. 88.

137 Nachtigal (1971), 365.

138 Or perhaps he thought in other terms, that the rights of a "son of the sultan" were stronger than those of a *faqīh*.

139 This appears to be inaccurate, since the whole point of XXII is that it was Muḥammadayn's father and brother who were the first to receive the land at Khirībān as an estate.

140 Literally "long-lived", *ṭawil al-'umr*, but evidently used here and elsewhere as an invocation for the reigning sultan.

141 Fakhr al-Dīn was one of several prominent Dār Fūr religious figures to whom al-Zubayr wrote in the spring of 1874 justifying his invasion of the sultanate. al-Zubayr describes him as a specialist in the science of tradition (*ḥadīth*); see Shuqayr (1903), III, 76.

142 1872–73.

**XXIV and XXV. The Masāmīr Arabs**

1 From an archive of fifteen documents (of which fourteen appear in the present volume, the others being XXVI to XXXVII) in the possession of *shartay* Adam Ṭāhir Nūrayn of Dōr, where they were photographed by Professor J. and Madame M.-J. Tubiana in 1965; see M.-J. and J. Tubiana, "Mission au Darfour", *L'Homme*, VII (1967), 89–96. A preliminary survey of the Dōr documents is given in J. F. Fourcade, "Documents arabes intéressant l'histoire du Dār Fūr", *Dossiers de la R.C.P. no. 45*, C.N.R.S. (Paris, 1968), I, 34–53. The texts were first published in Abū Salīm (1975), 89–118. The one document not given here is too corrupt to admit of a creditable translation.

2 The term used, *'arab*, bears no particular ethnic connotation in Dār Fūr.

3 *Dār al-ṣabāḥ* was most frequently used in Dār Fūr for the eastern province (otherwise Dār Dālī), which between *c.* 1785 and 1820 included part of Kordofān; less often it was used for the lands of the Sinnār Sultanate. On the latter usage, see U. J. von Seetzen's Fur word-list (item 59) in *Proben Deutscher Volks-Mundarten*, ed. J. S. Vater (Leipzig, 1816), pp. 319–33.

4 On the succession crisis, see O'Fahey and Spaulding (1974), 137–40. Suicide was not infrequent among Dār Fūr's political elite, see O'Fahey (1980), 46–7.

5 Nachtigal (1971), 293–7, who says he remained in confinement for thirty years. On Muḥammad in Kordofān, see R. S. O'Fahey and J. L. Spaulding, "Hāshim and the Musabba'āt", *Bulletin of the School of Oriental and African Studies*, XXXV (1972), 316–33.

6 MacMichael (1922), I, 263, lists a Misāmīr section of the Awlād Jarbū'a, one of the three main divisions of the Zayyādiyya.

7 And an ancestor of 'Alī Dīnār's general, Ādam Rijāl (interview, O'Fahey/ Muḥammad al-Faḍl 'Abd al-Raḥmān Ādam Rijāl, Nyala 26.6.1969). On Ḥāmid, see Nachtigal (1971), 301 and 333, n. 1.

8 1799–1800.

9 A wide gap.

10 The scribe began to write *al-ḥukkām*, "the governors", after *awlād*, realized his error but did not erase it.

11 Possibly a nomad caravan leader (on *khabīr*, see below p. 107). Nomad caravans from the Zaghawa or Zayyādiyya of northern Dār Fūr mainly engaged in the specialized natron trade with Egypt; see Cuny (1854), 85–6, and R. Slatin, *Fire and Sword in the Sudan* (London, 1896), p. 106.

12 Thus vowelled in the original.

13 Ḥamad al-'umyan.

14 A total of fifty-one names.

15 See p. 135, n. 50.

16 Or j.r.n.qīs.

17 A son of Sultan Aḥmad Bukr, see al-Tūnisī (1965), 96–8 (85–6).

18 Probably the son of Muḥammad Tayrāb by the *iiya kuuri* Kināna who is said to have later been imprisoned in Jabal Marra; see al-Tūnisī (1965), 125 (117), and Nachtigal (1971), 293.

19 A *faqīh* Sirāj is described as a Fallātī *imām* who was a confidant of Sultan 'Abd al-Raḥmān by Browne (1806), 206; see also 200, 221 and 240. See further al-Tūnisī (1965), 209 (203).

20 1803–4.

21 Balīlī in XXIV.

22 Ambarāk in XXIV.

23 A total of forty-seven compared with fifty-one in XXIV.

24 Since his name still appears at the head of the list, 'Alī would appear to have been reduced in status and subordinated to Qurayb.
25 *Fī-ḍirā'*, "in the grip of": in another charter of Sultan Muḥammad al-Faḍl (DF295.41/3), a *faqīh* is released by the sultan "from the authority" of a chief, *akhraja shaykh ambādī min ḍirā' bāsī awad*; the charter is given in Abū Salīm (1975), 122.
26 1806–7.

### XXVI to XXXVII. The land and followers of Nūr al-Dīn b. Yaḥyā

1 The significance of his title *bāsī* (Fur, *baasi*) is not clear. Normally, the title which means approximately "royal" was reserved for certain senior princes of the Keira clan, but it was occasionally used by others. Thus the chief of the Awlād Diggayn, a Zaghawa clan in Dār Tuer just north of Suwaynī, was given the title by 'Alī Dīnār; PA (al-Fāshir), DP/66. B. 6, vol. II, Darfur Province. Tribal Affairs – General Zaghawa.
2 On the Kaitiŋa, see MacMichael (1922), I, 58.
3 "Meidob" is mentioned in one of two abbreviated genealogies found in AP[1] 21/10–13. The Kaitiŋa are alleged to be genealogically linked to the Konyuŋa; on the latter, see p. 135, n. 50.
4 On the position of Gumgum within the seasonal movement of herds and flocks northwards from Dor, see Tubiana and Tubiana (1977), 52–3 and map 2.2, pp. 60–1.
5 An incomplete text of this letter is given in Abū Salīm (1975), 107–8.
6 1787–88: this is the earliest date to appear on a seal of 'Abd al-Raḥmān and is almost certainly the year of his accession or more accurately the year of the victorious conclusion of his struggle with the *khalīfa al-ḥājj* Isḥāq; see O'Fahey and Spaulding (1974), 140.
7 *Wa'l-'askar wa'l-jinādī.*
8 *Dār al-ṣabāh*, see p. 139, n. 3.
9 *al-shahāda* (*sic* for *al-shuhūd*) *al-ḥādirīn al-majlis*: the reference to a council in this context is unique. There is no certain evidence that the sultans had a regular council; rather the evidence of the lists of witnesses on royal documents suggests an *ad hoc* gathering of notables. See the examples from royal *sijills* given in O'Fahey (1977a), 118.
10 The *faqīh* Mālikī al-Fūtāwī (his full name is given in XXVII) was a close confidant of 'Abd al-Raḥmān and an influential figure during his reign; on his career, see O'Fahey (1977b), 147–66.
11 The charter is badly mutilated.
12 Enough remains of the intitulation to mark the difference of its phrasing from, for example, XXVI, written by the same scribe.
13 *Arbāb al-dawla*, for the more usual *aṣḥāb al-dawla.*
14 *Akhwālahu al-zaqāwī*: the form, Zaqāwa for Zaghāwa, is not uncommon.
15 *Sic*, probably for "their sons".
16 *Mamlakatī al-'arab wa'l-sūdān*: this designation of the sultanate ("Dār Fūr" appears very rarely in pre-1874 documents; here, only in II, *dārunā al-fūrāwiyya*, and XXIV) is more vivid than the commoner *sulṭān al-'arab wa'l-'ajam* stereotype that first appears in the intitulation of a charter from Tayrāb (DF173.18/33, seal-date 1172/1758–59). "The Arabs and the Blacks" recalls both the title of al-Tūnisī's travels and Poncet's reference in 1698 to Dār Fūr as "The Kingdom of *Sudan*"; C.-J. Poncet, *A Voyage to Ethiopia in the Year 1698, 1699 and 1700* (London, 1709), p. 8.

17 More accurately, the confirmation by the sultan of a gift from one member of a notable family to another, an act that always required the sultan's authorization, as XXXIX also illustrates.
18 *'abdihi*, but probably not meant literally. The more usual terms for ranking servants of the sultan were *khādim* or *tābi'*.
19 Muḥammad Rīz, one of the numerous sons of Ahmad Bukr, was one of the candidates for the sultanate during the succession crisis at Bāra; see al-Tūnisī (1965), 96–8 (85–6).
20 *Kātib al-imām al-ā'ẓam*: a title that does not appear elsewhere but probably refers to the *faqīh* appointed as *imām* to the sultan; for one example, see p. 137, n.108.
21 1801–2.
22 1803–4.
23 A wide gap between the *basmala* and the *intitulatio*.
24 M.r.mī in XXVII.
25 Nasīr in XXVII.
26 Ādā in XXVII.
27 *Jirānihim*; "neighbours" in the sense of non-kin members or followers of the privileged community.
28 *Shurūṭuhum wa-ḥabluhum al-marmī* (*'ala'l-arḍ*) *mā yanshāl*: this curious prohibition is found in only two other Dār Fūr charters, both issued also by Muḥammad al-Faḍl, DF149.18/9, dated 1222/1807–8, and a charter from Kordofān, dated 19 Dhu'l-ḥijja 1220/30 March 1806, transcribed in Ḥusayn Sīd Aḥmad al-Muftī (1387/1959), I, 52–3. A similarly-worded prohibition also occasionally appears in Funj charters; two examples are one from 1734 in Holt (1969), 4, and one from 1789–90 in Abū Salīm (1967), 78.
29 1810–11.
30 A gap following the *basmala*.
31 *Rās al-shartay*: *rās* here refers to a representative of the *shartay* Muḥammad Rīl sent to be present at the demarcation of the estate, see Chapter 2, pp. 20–21.
32 A formula much more frequently found in Funj charters than in those from Dār Fūr.
33 Probably a reference to a slave settlement, see above, p. 68.
34 For *tān(i)*, the colloquial form of *thāniyya*.
35 Literally "in".
36 *al-jarrāba*, muddy or cultivable land; an alternative translation is the *jurab* tree, *Tephrosia subtriflora*.
37 Which lie five days east of Umm Ḥaraz, see Tubiana and Tubiana (1977), 53.
38 Jabal Imām on Tubiana and Tubiana (1977), map 2, lying north-east of Qōz Qumqūm; as "Hagar Imam" on 1:250,000, Kutum ND-35-E (54-E).
39 Qur'ān, II, 181.
40 1822–23.
41 Here *kull al-ṭughāt al-mutamarridīn 'alā al-muslimīn*, instead of the more usual, *al-ṭughāt al-mutamarridīn bi-ḥuqūq al-muslimīn*.
42 Compare with *'abdihi* in XXVII, p. 141, n. 18.
43 Written here as two words, but in XXIX as one word.
44 That is, relinquished to Nūr al-Dīn the right to collect the revenues.
45 *Subul al-ḥukkām al-'ādiyya kullihā*; this would appear to mean specifically those customary taxes resulting from legal judgments (*ḥukm*), i.e. fines and legal fees.
46 This is an exceptionally explicit and precise formulation of the benefits of an estate.

47 This document contains numerous colloquialisms and orthographical errors.
48 *Girgit*, a word of uncertain linguistic origin but generally regarded as meaning the same as the Fur *sambe*, "barbed spear", was the title of a chiefly rank intermediate between a *shartay* and *dimlij*. There were at least two *girgits* within or near to Dār Suwaynī, one directly subordinate to the *maqdūm* of the north, the other to the *takanāwī*.
49 *Lā* omitted in the original.
50 It is unusual for a court transcript to open with a *basmala* and *taṣliyya*.
51 *Ḥujja sulṭaniyya*: the only appearance in a Dār Fūr document of a phrase commonly used in Funj documents, of both charters and *sijills*.
52 Ibrāhīm is thus using his father's seal.
53 Yaḥyā b. Muḥammad, the recipient of IX.
54 *Naṣara* for *naṣarahu*.
55 *Al-mursalīn* omitted.
56 The Arabic is clearly written as *al-danānī'*, this may be a deformation of a common *nisba* of the Prophet, *al-'adnānī*, "the 'Adnanite". The Prophet is sometimes called *sayyid wuld 'Adnān*, "lord of the descendants of 'Adnān".
57 *Ba'asa* for *ba'atha*.
58 It is not really clear who brought the action nor whom the judge regards as the plaintiff.
59 *Hawwazanī iyahā* for *ḥawwazanī iyyāhā*.
60 *al-falqanāwī sayyidī yaḥyā*.
61 That is, *malik* Muḥammad Rīl.
62 A conjectural translation of, *bayyina al-fāṣil iz* (*sic* for *izā'a*) *al-sharṭay bi-nawl* (perhaps for the colloquial, *bi(y)nawwil*) *min arḍī wa-ḥilālihā*.
63 Written phonetically as *s(a)ln(a)* for *sa'alnā*.
64 Written phonetically as *al-m(u)dd(a)'* for *al-mudda'ā*.
65 *al-anta* for *allatī anta*.
66 *Māhu* (*sic* for *ma'ahu*) *thalātha ḥilāl*.
67 *Hiyyāzatuka* for *ḥiyyazatuka*.
68 *Huztahā* for *ḥuztahā*; on *ḥazza*, see 'Awn (1972), 160.
69 For, *khallinā narfa' al-naẓar 'ind sayyidnā*. On *al-naẓar* "examination, referral", see above, p. 10.
70 Not literally, "my *abō*", as a respectful form of address.
71 *Natafāḥum* for *natafāhum*.
72 *al-sayyidnā*.
73 *Lahu wa-arḍahu*; the *wa* seems otiose here.
74 The following is copied from XXIX, but with several errors.
75 *Ka-taṣrīf al-mālik* omitted.
76 *Shar'an* for *shar'īan*.
77 *Hibiyya* for *hiba*.
78 The scribe has added a third Divine epithet, *baṣīr*, to the Qur'ānic verse.
79 1827–28.
80 1803–4.
81 It is unusual for the sovereign title "sultan" to be omitted.
82 *Amen* placed separately in the centre of the line.
83 This more usually refers to the district administered by a *shartay*, but is occasionally used of the office itself.
84 *Awsākh al-iqṭā'*; *wasakh* may mean, "dirt, filth, squalor". It can be used of poor soil; thus Fagnan, *Additions aux dictionnaires arabes*, 186 gives *wasakh muzdari'* "terre de culture de sixième qualité" (see also Claude Cahen,

"Contribution à l'étude des impôts dans l'Egypt médiévale", *Journal of the Economic and Social History of the Orient*, v/3 (1962), 259). Here, however, *awsākh* refers to the Shari'a taxes, *zakāh* and *fiṭra*, as the phrase, *subulihā al-'ādiyya wa-awsākhihā al-shar'iyya*, in XXXIII makes clear. The idea behind the idiom is perhaps that their payment is a form of purification (*tazkiyya*), as in the phrase, *lā ta'kul awsākh al-nās*, "Live not thou upon the alms of men", given in E. W. Lane, *An Arabic–English Lexicon*, VIII, p. 2940.

85 *Li-annahu mulāzimunā li'l-khidmat*; *mulāzim* in the sense of "courtier" was also used under the Khalifa 'Abdallāhi, as in the phrase, *al-mulāzimīna bi'l-bāb al-sharīf*, see Holt (1971), 161. However, it does not appear in any other pre-1874 Dār Fūr document. *Khidma* in Dār Fūr usually means "service", for example that owed by his tenants to an estate-holder, but here it would seem to mean "court", echoing perhaps Mamluk usage; compare, *The Eastern Mediterranean Lands in the Period of the Crusades*, ed. P. M. Holt (London, 1977), p. 48.

86 Presumably a reference to the events described in XXXI.

87 Whose dispute with Nūr al-Dīn is the subject of XXXV to XXXVII below.

88 *Yatrukū al-ziyāda wa'l-khalbāṭ*; on *khalbāṭ*, evidently a metathesis of *lakhbaṭa*, see 'Awn (1972), 207.

89 That is, XXXII; this may conceivably imply that copies were in fact kept of outgoing correspondence, a point on which we have no certain evidence.

90 That is, between obedience and disobedience.

91 It is unusual for any document to open so abruptly with *wa-ba'd*.

92 *Ladā maḥkama min amīr al-mu'minīn*: this would appear to mean that the case was heard before the sultan (or within the palace) by 'Ubaydallāh. However, the plaintiff later "takes his complaint" to the sultan, although this does not exclude the probability that the various stages of the hearing were held at court.

93 Perhaps an idiom meaning something like "by cloth and weapon"?

94 Or, alternatively, *aḥyā'*, "communities".

95 *Tawwara* = *thawwara*; literally "aroused", see 'Awn (1972), 104.

96 *al-amīr*: this is almost certainly an abbreviation for *amīr al-mu'minīn*, although it does not appear elsewhere, the usual designation for the sultan being *sayyidnā*.

97 From what follows, it would appear that the sultan ordered 'Ubaydallāh to hear the case again.

98 Or "should be".

99 Literally, he took an adjournment.

100 *Fa-a'dharnā li-'Alī fīhim wa-'adlihim*: on *i'dhār*, see XIV, p. 136, n. 73. The judge is giving 'Alī a final opportunity to refute Nūr al-Dīn's testimony by rejecting his witnesses (on grounds such as bribery or their kin relationship to Nūr al-Dīn), or by disputing their "probity", *'adl*, as witnesses. On *'adl* and the various grounds for its rejection, see Santilana (1926–38), I, 138–41, and further, E. Tyan, "Le notariat et le régime de la preuve par écrit dans la pratique du droit musulman", *Annales de l'Ecole Française de Droit de Beyrouth*, Université de Lyon, no. 2 (Lyon, 1945).

101 Whose name is repeated.

102 *al-khāl*; presumably so called to distinguish him from the other Muḥammad Dūd in the list.

103 A nickname? It might be read as *barr la baḥr*, "earth-not-sea!"

104 1827–28.

105 Yūsuf was appointed *āb shaykh* (see p. 5) sometime after 1808–9 (i.e. after the date of XXXVI) in succession to Degessa (or Dagassa) who had succeeded in 1804 the great *āb shaykh*, Muḥammad Kurra; see Nachtigal (1971), 329.

106 On *muftāḥ* "key" as a personal name, see al-Tūnisī (1965), 104–6 (92–3).

107 The sense of this passage is clearer in the précis in XXXVI: Nu'mān is given some land by Tayrāb; he dies and *al-ḥājj* 'Umar takes it over (*huwa mallakahā*), having his ownership confirmed by Tayrāb.

108 *Waqqafahu makān wāḥid*: there is evidently meant to be a distinction between this phrase and the formal demarcation of an assigned estate.

109 Idrīs was presumably Maydōb's predecessor as *shartay* of Dār Suwaynī.

110 *Bi-ijtihādinā*, see Schacht (1964), index.

111 *Talawwamnā lahu bi-ijtihādinā bi-iḥdā wa-'ishrīn*; or "we granted him [a further delay], upon our initiative, of twenty-one days". See XXXVI.

112 *Bi-bakānihi* for *bi-makānihi*.

113 *al-m.ṣ* for *al-muṣannif*.

114 *Wa-anẓarahu* (our text has *anẓara*) *lahā bi-ijtihādihi thum ḥakama*; Khalīl, *Mukhtaṣar*, *bāb al-qaḍā'* = Bousquet (1956–62), IV, 5. The passage that follows the quotation is relevant to the judge's ruling: the judge shall disallow a further plea by that party that has failed to present proof and shall record the fact.

115 The judge is referring to the various conditions that render a gift legally valid, among them *wa-ḥīza wa-in bilā idhn wa-ukhbira 'alayh*, "It [the gift] shall be taken possession of even without [the donor's specific] permission or [without] his being informed". Khalīl, *Mukhtaṣar*, *bāb al-hiba tamlīk* = Bousquet (1956–62), III, 150. See further, *Ḥāshiyyat al-imām al-Rahūnī* (1306), VI, pp. 163–72.

116 Only the party that the judge considers to have presented legally valid proof is allowed to take the oath.

117 See XXXVI.

118 1803–4.

119 *al-maktūb*; although the document opens in the same form as a charter, it is in fact a rescript confirming XXXV.

120 This rarely appears in the *inscriptio*; the sultans in question are those tribal chiefs entitled to be so addressed, see O'Fahey (1980), 83–7.

121 The point here being that the *khabīr* Muftāḥ should have written down the boundaries himself.

122 In succession to *malik* Idrīs Marjān, see XXXV.

123 *al-makān al-nu'mān* for *al-makān alladhī nu'mān*.

124 I.e. the document in which Nu'mān had allegedly written down the false boundaries.

125 *al-ḥudud al-khabīr muftāḥ* for *al-ḥudūd alladhīna khabīr muftāḥ*.

126 *Talawwama lahu bi-shahrān* (*sic*); or, "He delayed a [further] two months".

127 *Fa-'arraḍa al-muḥakkam al-munīb*; *muḥakkam* may mean here "arbitrator", which would perhaps explain the formal appeal to the sultan by *al-ḥājj* 'Umar.

128 *Shaykh al-sulṭān* is probably a variant of the title of *imām* to the sultan (see p. 137, n. 108 and n. 117); it does not appear elsewhere. Sirāj is almost certainly Browne's travelling companion; see p. 139, n. 19. Here he has been placed at the head of the list of witnesses; in XXXV he appears only midway in the list.

129 This list is longer and the names are in a different order to that in XXXV; the one was evidently not copied from the other.

130 Surely the order should be reversed! The sultan gave judgment after the *maqdūm* Yūsuf.

131 1808–9.

132 1803–4.
133 *Wahaba* is written in the margin by the side of *aqṭaʿa*.
134 Both speeches are marked by awkward and abrupt shifts from indirect to direct speech.
135 *Fī-tilka'l-ziyāda* written in the margin.
136 *Bi-maḥḍar muḥakkaminā*; alternatively, "before the one sent arbitrate between us by the Commander of the Faithful", see p. 144, n. 127.
137 I.e. XXXV; it is surprising that no mention is made of XXXVI.
138 *Wa-alzamnā al-ḥukm bi-muqtaḍāhā baʿd ithbātihi*; that is, after the confirmation (*ithbāt*) of the authenticity (*ṣiḥḥa*) of XXXV, the judge confirms (*alzamnā*) the judgment (*al-ḥukm*) itself.
139 *Wa* (*illā*, missing in our text) *tuʿuqqiba wa-maḍā ghayr al-jawr*; Khalīl, *Mukhtaṣar, bāb al-qaḍā'* = Bousquet (1956–62), IV, 6. Khalīl continues by saying that another judge cannot annul a judgment by a judge who was both learned and *ʿadl* (on the latter, see p. 143, n. 100).
140 See p. 137, n. 117.
141 Slatin (1896), 50, mentions a *faqīh* "el Hileiki" who gave him information about the history of Dār Fūr.
142 The *maqdūm* of Northern Dār Fūr.
143 January–February 1830.

## XXXVIII to XLI. The Princesses Fāṭima Umm Dirays and Zahra

1 XXXVIII to XL were first published by Shuqayr ((1903) II, 139–41). Although he does not say from where he obtained them, it is reasonable to suppose that they belonged to one of the royal captives taken to Egypt after the sultanate's conquest in 1874. XLI is SD211 . 22/7 from Archive 22, see below p. 147, n. 1.
2 Nachtigal (1971), 265.
3 Detailed lists of these estates are given in PA (al-Fāshir), Western Darfur District Handbook; see also O'Fahey (1980), diagram 6, "The estates of Dār Diima".
4 Nachtigal (1971), 293 and al-Tūnisī (1965), 116–17 (106).
5 Browne (1806), 339–40.
6 See V, p. 43
7 Shuqayr does not give a seal to any of the three documents, but reproduces separately (II, 148) a seal that may have come from one of them. It is of the same type as the seal on V.
8 Fur notable who held the title of *somiŋ dogala*; as *maqdūm* in the south, he warred in the 1840s and early 1850s against the Rizayqāt by whom he was killed. The *wazīr* Aḥmad Shaṭṭa was his son; see Nachtigal (1971), 308–10, 312.
9 *Wa-mallaktuhā iyyāhā mulkan tāman*: both here and in the places noted below, Shuqayr consistently uses the feminine form in a way that implies that the grantee was female. This is something of a puzzle; either it is a consistent error by Shuqayr (who was normally careful in the transcription of documents), or it is some form of arcane hint that the estate was really intended to go to *al-ḥājj* Aḥmad's wife, the *mayram* Fāṭima. While the latter explanation may fit Browne's remarks cited above, it seems far-fetched. XLI is clear evidence (among many other examples) that estates could be granted directly to women.
10 *Yadhhabu*: Shuqayr has probably "improved" the original; *dhahaba* appears in no other Dār Fūr document.
11 Shuqayr has evidently omitted the description of the boundary.

12 Qur'ān. III, 173 (which is also quoted in III). *al-wakīl* has been omitted from the quotation.
13 1846–47.
14 *al-ḥājj* Aḥmad has been granted the honorific, *amīn*, since XXXVIII.
15 15 May 1853.
16 Holý (1974), 161.
17 *al-khuddāmīn wa-maqādīmihim*, with *khuddāmīn* as an anomalous plural of *khādim* or *khuddām*; the meaning of "their *maqdūms*" in this context is unclear.
18 The Mahriyya (which is the usual spelling of the name) are one of the three main divisions of the Rizayqāt cattle nomads of southern Dār Fūr. However, here the name probably refers to one of the many small groups of camel nomads, most of whom relate themselves genealogically to the Rizayqāt, scattered throughout northern and eastern Dār Fūr; PA (al-Fāashir), DP. B. 3. Northern Rizeigat Arabs.
19 *Kassartu ʻaẓmahum*, literally, "I have broken their bone." Our interpretation of this phrase is confirmed by its appearance in two other charters. In DF295.41/3, dated 1257/1840–41 and published in Abū Salīm (1975), 122, it appears as... *wa-kassara ʻaẓmahu wa-adkhala baṭn baytihi*, "He [the sultan] has broken his [the recipient of a grant of privilege] bone and made him enter his [the sultan's] household"; and in the second, DF296.42/1, undated (transcription in AP², 4/16, 60–1), *ṣārū jāh allāh wa-rasūlihi* [*wa-*] *maksūrīn al-ʻaẓm min al-dīwān*, "They have been established as privileged of God and His prophet [and] broken of bone to the *dīwān* [either the tax of that name or the tax-collectors]".
20 1851–52.
21 A merchant who was appointed by the sultan to represent the trading community in legal and administrative matters; see Browne (1806), 239.
22 PA (Kutum), NDD. 66. B. 4/6 Dar Sweini; Meglis held 5 May 1924, concerning boundary between Dars Sweini and Furok.
23 The seal is given twice.
24 1847–48.
25 *Maqdūm* of northern Dār Fūr; see p. 5.
26 Probably a son of a mercenary from Baqirmī, Aḥmad Jurāb al-Fīl, who was instrumental in crushing the revolt of Muḥammad Kurra in 1804; see Shuqayr (1903), II, 124–7. The family held estates at Tarnī and Kobbei; interview O'Fahey/ʻAlī Ṣāliḥ Bidayn, al-Fāshir, 30 March 1974.
27 A tentative translation (but see below) of the phrase, *maʻa sīqan fī*, which does not appear elsewhere. R. Dozy *Supplément aux Dictionnaires Arabes* (Leiden, 1881), I, p. 704 gives the expression, *sāqa li-ḥadd*, "cheminer jusqu'a".
28 This may be the title, *kursī*, in which case it may be read as, "[the boundary with the land of] the *kursī*...".
29 One word not read.
30 A tentative translation for *ḥajar baqq al-qiraywud al-abyaḍ*; the use of *baqq* in this sense is not attested to elsewhere.
31 *Sīgan fī*; see n. 27.
32 "Sale" repeated.
33 6 June 1857.

**XLII to XLVII. The merchants Muḥammad Kannūna and 'Ali Bey Ibrahim al-Ṭirayfī**

1 From Archive 22 (ownership unknown), consisting of eight documents; one concerning *mayram* Fāṭima Umm Dirays, XLI above; three concerning Muḥammad Kannūna, and three 'Alī Bey Ibrāhīm. The remaining document is a will that does not directly concern either merchant.

2 See O'Fahey (1980), 139–44 for a more detailed description of Kobbei. On the wells, PA (al-Fāshir) DP 2D 66 K 1 27 Arab Omodias, Fasher District, and E. G. Sarsfield-Hall, "Darfur", *The Geographical Journal*, LX/5 (1922), 362. The decline was rapid; Nachtigal (1971), 255–6 noted many houses empty in 1874, six years later Fraccaroli reckoned that only 80 to 100 out of an estimated 400 or 500 houses were still inhabited; A. Fraccaroli, "Gita commerciale nel Cordofan e Darfur", *L'Esploratore* (1880), 205–6.

3 Browne (1806) estimated its population at about 6,000, "of these the greater proportion are slaves"; Perron at about 8,000 compared with 3,000 at al-Fāshir (*Voyage au Darfour*, 154; not in Arabic edition), and Nachtigal (1971), 253 at "about 2,000 hearths".

4 Browne (1806), 265, who gives (265–7 and 271–6) a vivid description of Kobbei where he spent nearly three years; see also Nachtigal (1971), 251–6.

5 El Sayed el-Bushra, "Towns in the Sudan in the eighteenth and early nineteenth centuries", *SNR*, LII (1971), 63–70.

6 Browne (1806), 271–3.

7 On Mondays and Fridays according to Browne (1806), 274; on Mondays and Thursdays according to Nachtigal (1971), 253.

8 Dozy (1881), I, 348 citing the travel literature.

9 Nachtigal (1971), 329; on Muḥammad and his brother Hamza, see R. Hill, *A Biographical Dictionary of the Sudan*, 2nd edn. (London, 1967), pp. 150–1 and Walz (1978), 76–7.

10 Two other examples of such grants are Idrīs al-Mahālī, a Nubian from Dār Mahas, who was given land by Muḥammad al-Ḥusayn, see Cuny (1854), 118, and Maḥmūd b. 'Alī who was granted land at Kofod by Muḥammad al-Faḍl (DF278.35/1, a later confirmation by 'Alī Dīnār dated 1328/1910–11).

11 PA (al-Fāshir), Beira Omodia File (number missing). There is only one reference in the Dār Fūr corpus to the purchase of land, when a *faqīh* buys a field from another (DF124.13/9, 1272/1855–56).

12 Otherwise unidentified: Cuny (1854), 111 mentions that in 1850 Muḥammad al-Ḥusayn's sister, *mayram* Zamzam, passed through Asyūṭ on her way to Mecca in the company of the *khabīr* "Kunn", possibly our Kannūna.

13 1838–39.

14 Possibly a reference to one of Aḥmad Jurāb al-Fīr al-Bāqirmāwī's estates (see p. 146, n. 26), or to a Baqirmī community in the Kobbei district.

15 A tentative translation of *bi-walad al-wādī al-wusṭānī: walad*, literally "son", is occasionally used in documents from the northern Sudan to mean a subsidiary irrigation channel (otherwise, *jadwal*). It does not appear in other Dār Fūr documents.

16 *al-ṣabānī*; in the description of the boundaries given in XLIV, which we have not translated, it appears as *al-ṣabḥānī*.

17 Browne (1806), 266 notes, "To the N.E. by N. [of Kobbei] *Hellet Hasan*, inhabited by the people of Dongola. It has been governed many years by the

*Chabir Hassan wullad Nasr*, one of the oldest of them, who had been formerly once, or more than once, *Chabir* (leader) of the jelabs on their journey to Kahira [Cairo]", author's italics.

18 Tarqā in XLIV.

19 *al-tamr*, "dates"; for its use to mean date tree, see 'Awn (1972), 99.

20 20 July 1840.

21 Cuny (1858), 11–12; on Bōsh's career, see O'Fahey (1980), 42.

22 1843–44; the seal is repeated three times in a pyramidal pattern.

23 *al-wazīr al-ā'ẓam*; an imitation of the Ottoman title, used only of Ādam Bōsh, appearing here and in one other *sijill*, DF63 . 8/1, 25 Rajab 1267/7 June 1851.

24 Compare with the formula in XXII; these legal formulae are far less common in Dār Fūr documents than those from the Nile valley.

25 Walz (1978), 204, records the arrival in Cairo in 1749 of a Muḥammad Ma'rrif (?) "of the Awlād Dānī", a slave-merchant from Dār Fūr. A. MacMichael, *The Tribes of Northern and Central Kordofan* (Cambridge, 1912), 207, also notes an Awlād Dānī section among the Shanābla of Kordofān.

26 That is, the sultan died in 1254/1838.

27 The name is written in the margin.

28 The Wādī Barr Bōja (which continues towards al-Fāshir as the Wādī Golo) lies south-east of Kobbei; see Browne (1806), 267, and Nachtigal (1971), 257. "The south", *al-ṣa'īd*, probably refers to southern Dār Fūr.

29 There were only two ways that 'Abdallāh could support his plea, either by a charter or witnesses prepared to testify on oath. His failure to produce either automatically disqualified him.

30 See p. 143, n. 100.

31 The name is written in the margin.

32 *Wa-yu'ajjazuhu īlā fī-dam*; Khalīl, *Mukhtaṣar, bāb al-qaḍā'* = Bousquet (1956–62), IV, 4. This passage comes just after that quoted above, p. 95. On the legal procedure, see Schacht (1964), 198, and Santillana (1926–38), II, 592–3.

33 For *al-muṭarrarīn*, or "sprouting".

34 This catalogue is presumably of the trees to be found encircling the Labbād farm.

35 "Izayriq", "little black one", a not uncommon Sudanese personal name; "Birtāwī", a member of the Berti tribe.

36 15 April 1846 – a Monday.

37 The title is repeated.

38 A reference to XLII.

39 1850–51.

40 A merchant, Muḥammad Abū Takkiyya, trading for 'Alī Dīnār in Wadai is described as *khādim* in a safe-conduct issued by the Wadai Sultan, DF85 . 10/10, 12 Muḥarram 1320/21 April 1902.

41 His *nisba*, "al-Ṭirayfī", is given from oral sources by H. S. Umar, "Al-Tunisi, Travels in Darfur: Translation, Collation and Annotation of *Tashhid al-adhhan bi sirat bilad al-Arab wa-l-Sudan*", MA thesis, Abdullahi Bayero University 1976, 233 and 436. On the Ṭirayfiyya as merchants, see MacMichael (1922), I, 203, and O'Fahey (1980), 141.

42 Shuqayr (1903), II, 132; see also 134 for a similar story about Sultan Ibrāhīm Qaraḍ whom 'Alī knew before his accession. Shuqayr also gives a photograph of the *khabīr* (opp. II, 134).

43 Nachtigal (1971), 261 and 308.

44 Robert Hartmann, *Reise des Freiherrn Adalbert von Barnim durch Nord-Ost-Afrika in den Jahren 1859 und 1860* (Berlin, 1863), 68.

45 Nachtigal (1971), 254, and Shuqayr (1903), II, 146.

46 This may represent the common Fur place-name, Ungorei, although no village of that name is to be found on the 1:250,000 map series in Kobbei district. Unfortunately, O'Fahey was unable to interview members of the family.

47 There is only one other report of this type in the corpus; the *faqīh* Muḥammad Shaqara is sent by *qāḍī* 'Izz al-Dīn to re-demarcate a disputed estate, DF193.18/53, undated.

48 See p. 148, n. 41.

49 1851–52; the numbers are written backwards, that is in the same direction as the writing.

50 24 September 1852.

51 The Arabic is ambiguous, but the translation here is confirmed by XLVI.

52 Meaning, "whose names we did not know".

53 There is a Jabal Ungorei on the edge of the north-eastern foothills of Jabal Marra, but this cannot be the mountain or hill referred to here.

54 Presumably a reference to some form of royal domaine; on *bayt al-jibāya*, see above p. 4.

55 *al-nagh'a*: "gh" represents the colloquial *g*; the classical form is *naq'*, see 'Awn (1972), 789.

56 *Jidal*, for the classical *jidhl*, see 'Awn (1972), 117.

57 Possibly J. Usban, which lies south-east of Kobbei below J. Kordill.

58 *Tammād* for *thammād*.

59 For whose estates, see XLI, pp. 104–6.

60 *Alladhi wa-ilā*...; a phrase has probably been omitted.

61 Since the second half of the charter is missing, we have not repeated that part of the boundary description that remains.

62 One or two words missing.

63 Restored from XLV.

64 1851–52.

65 *Ḥadd fāsihim*, lit., "the boundary of their hoe (or axe)".

66 1867–68.

# INDICES

The following indices combine the functions of index and glossary. The notes have not been indexed, although some terms that appear only there have been listed.

Definitions are based primarily upon Dār Fūr usage; for this reason, reference to the appropriate entry in the *Encyclopedia of Islam* (second edition; hereafter *EI*2) is given wherever possible.

## (a) Titles and honorifics

The titles are listed under the form most frequently used in the documents. The following titles have not been indexed: caliph, *faqīh*, *malik*, shaykh and sultan. This list by no means includes all the titles used in the sultanate; see further O'Fahey (1980), 149–53.


*āb shaykh dālī* (or *al-āb shaykh*), 5, 16, 20, 43, 68, 91, 98, 99
Chief slave eunuch; governor of the eastern province, and guardian of the palace upon the sultan's death.
*āb takanāwī*, *al-āb al-takanāwī*, 49, 88
Governor (before the rise of the *maqdum*) of the northern province.
*abbo daadiŋa*, *see malik al-qawwārīn*
*abnā' al-salāṭīn*, *see awlād al-salāṭīn*
*abnā' al-shawba*, 48, 50
Lit. "Sons of the warband"; warriors.
*abu'l-jabbāyyīn* (Fur, *abbo jubaŋa* or *jafaŋa*), 8, 16
Chief of the tax-collectors.
*'ālim*, pl. *'ulamā'*, 57, 114
Religious scholar.
*'āmil*, pl. *'ummāl*, 41
Official of unspecified rank; on its wider use, see *EI*2, i, 435–6.
*amīn*, 58, 65, 66, 74, 76–9, 81, 82, 94, 97, 98, 101, 102, 108, 113, 115
"Commander"; honorific, but perhaps with a military implication, rather than a specific office; *EI*2, i, 437.
*amīr*, 27, 39, 40–1, 43, 45, 50, 52, 87, 101, 103, 105, 108, 113, 117, 118
"Prince"; it is probably the Arabic equivalent of *bāsī* (q.v.); *EI*2, i, 438–9.
*amīr al-mu'minīn*, 31–2, 36, 40, 42, 44, 50, 52, 64, 85, 87, 90, 91, 92, 93, 94, 98, 101, 102, 105, 108, 110, 113, 117, 118
"Commander of the Faithful"; *EI*2, i, 445.
*awlād al-salāṭīn* (or *al-sulṭān*), 40, 43, 45, 47, 48, 50, 52, 61, 62, 63, 77, 78, 80, 84, 85, 87, 101, 103, 105, 108, 112, 113, 117, 118
"Sons of the sultans" (or "the sultan").
*al-bannā*, 41
Lit. "the builders"; it appears only once in the entire corpus. Its meaning is unknown.
*bāsī* (Fur, *baasi*), 61, 64, 77, 79–99
Male member of the Keira dynasty; occasionally used within other chiefly families.
*bey*, 114
Ottoman title ranking below that of *Pasha*.
"Commander of the Faithful", *see amīr al-mu'minīn*
*dimlij*, pl. *damālij* (Fur, *dilmɔŋ*), 6, 32, 40, 43, 45, 48, 49, 50, 52, 80, 81, 84, 85, 87, 101, 103, 105, 108, 117
Probably from Arabic "armlet"; sub-district chief, responsible for three to four villages, below *shartay* (q.v.).
*falqanāwī*, pl. *falāqna*, *falāqīn* (Fur, *folgɔni*), 26, 47, 63, 65, 69, 81, 84, 85, 87, 88–9
Royal messenger or herald.
*faqīh*, pl. *fuqahā'*, but with the more common Sudanese pl. *fuqarā'* (occasionally the sing. forms *faqih* and *fakī* are found).
Muslim holy man, *EI*2, ii, 756.
*ḥabbōba*, pl. *ḥabbōbāt* 18, 32, 40, 43, 45, 50, 52, 84, 100, 101, 105, 108, 113, 117
Older female members of the Keira clan.
*ḥabbōba īya* (Fur, *iiya*, "mother"), 43
Either as in the title *iiya kuuri*, the sultan's premier wife, or *iiya baasi*, his premier sister.
*ḥākim*, 32, 41, 77, 78, 86, 105, 113, 117, 118
Used in two senses, as a judicial official, and as a pl. to mean "officials, governors"; see Humbsch (1976), 160.
*imām*, 36, 38, 40–1, 65, 67, 82, 99
Local religious leader; also used of certain *faqīhs* who held an official position at court.
*iriqā*, 5, 65
The Fur title, *iriŋa*, "exalted", held by the family of the *maqdūms* of northern Dār Fūr.

*jabbay*, pl. *jabbāyyīn*, *jubāt*, 8, 32, 34, 40–1, 43, 45, 48, 49, 50, 66, 85, 87, 101, 102, 103, 105, 108, 113, 117, 118
Tax or revenue (*jibāya*) collectors; they formed a network throughout the sultanate.
*jabbāyyīn al-'asyh wa'l-quṭn*, 48
"Collectors of the grain and cotton"; "cotton" here probably refers to the tax in *takkiyya* or strips of cloth.
*jabbāyyīn al-'aysh wa'l-quṭn wa'l-ḥubb*, 50, 84
"Collectors of the grain, cotton and seed".
*jallāba*, 107
Itinerant merchant.
*jinādī*, pl. of *jindī* (classical, *jundī*), 80, 81
Soldiery.
*kātib*, 23
Scribe or secretary.
*khabīr*, pl. *khubarā'*, 25, 29, 77, 78, 94, 97, 107–18
"Expert, guide"; title of large-scale merchant.
*khaddām*, pl. *khaddāmīn*, 113
"Servant".
*khādim al-ḥaramayn al-sharīfayn*, 31
"Servitor of the two Holy Places" (i.e. Mecca and Medina); Mamluk and Ottoman sultanic title; cf. Humbsch (1976), 212, 215.
*khādim al-sharī'a wa'l-dīn*, 31, 42–3, 48, 78, 80, 84, 101
"Servitor of the Law and Religion"; sultanic honorific.
*khalīfa*, 13, 53, 54
"Successor"; specifically in Dār Fūr used of the appointed heir to the sultanate; *EI*2, iv, 936–53.
*khalīfat rabb al-'ālamīn*, 30
"Caliph of the Lord of the Universe"; sultanic honorific.
*khalīfat rasūl rabb al-'ālamīn*, 30, 47, 80
"Caliph of the prophet of the Lord of the Universe"; sultanic honorific.
*khalīfat ummat sayyid al-mursalīn*, 30, 48, 78, 84, 94, 113
"Caliph of the community of the lord of the messengers"; sultanic honorific.
*khāqān*, 31, 63, 85
"Sovereign"; sultanic honorific.
*khuddām al-daraqa*, 41
Lit. "servants of the shield"; it appears only once in the *corpus*. Its meaning is unknown, but it is probably connected with the *daraqa*-tax (see p. 102).
*koray*, *kōray*, pl. *korāyāt* (Fur, *korei*), 47, 52, 84, 85, 87, 108
"Groom"; a group of titles held by various "masters of the royal horse"; see O'Fahey (1980), 37.
*kursī*, pl. *karāsī*, 6, 32, 77, 78, 80, 81, 103
Lit. "chair"; the Arabic equivalent of the Fur *sagal*; estate-steward.
*makkās*, pl. *makkāsīn*, 32, 45, 48, 51, 52, 84, 87, 101, 108, 113
Collectors of the various market and customs dues (*maks*).
*malik*
Either those title-holders who held titles of which the first component was *malik*, e.g. *malik al-makkāsīn*, or a general term for the estate-holders; see Nachtigal (1971), 305–6, 310–11, 326, 332–3
*malik andaŋa*, 16
"Chief of the scouts (*andaŋa*, Fur)"; warlord.
*malik al-qawwārīn*, 8, 16–17
Chief of the collectors of the market and customs dues, *quwwār* and *maks*; he was also known as *malik al-makkāsīn*. The titles were held by the *abbo daadiŋa*, royal executioner and chief of the *daadiŋa* slave soldiers.
*malik saariŋa*, 16
"Chief of the swordsmen" (Fur, *saar*, "sword"); warlord.
*malik al-'urbān*, 80, 103
Chief of nomadic section or tribe.
*maqam*, 43, 101
Official.
*maqdūm*, pl. *maqādīm*, 5–6, 10, 16, 18, 25, 32, 51, 64, 65, 66, 74, 94, 97, 98, 100, 101, 102, 105
Commissioner or viceroy; title of the nineteenth century governors of northern Dār Fūr; cf. O'Fahey (1980), 87–91.
*mayram*, pl. *mayārim*, 26, 32, 40, 43, 45, 47, 48, 50, 51, 52, 71, 80, 81, 84, 85, 87, 99–106, 108, 113, 117
Younger female member of the Keira clan.
*mudarris*, 23
"Tutor."

*mulāzim*, 79, 90
Follower, courtier.
*mutakharrij*, 23
"Graduate" (of al-Azhar).
*muwajjah*, 20, 64, 85, 86, 87, 111, 115
Commissioner or official appointed to carry out a specific task; used in the documents of a man sent to demarcate the boundaries of an estate.
*nā'ib shar'ī*, 23
Deputy judge.
*naqīb*, 67, 112
Head of the local community of *ashrāf*, i.e. descendants of the Prophet.
"Officials", *see ḥākim*
*ɔrreŋduluŋ* (Fur), 4
"Master of the doorposts"; major-domo of the palace.
*qāḍī* 6, 8–11, 24, 39, 40, 43, 53, 54, 56–7, 58–61, 70, 85, 87, 101, 108
Judge.
*qāḍī al-shar' al-kabīr*, 41
"Senior judge of the Law."
*qahramān*, 31, 84
"Steward"; sultanic honorific; in modern Turkish and Persian, "hero, champion"; *EI2*, iv, 444–5.
*qawwār*, pl. *qawwārīn*, 32, 45, 48, 51, 52, 84, 108, 113
Collector of market and customs dues (synonym for *makkās*?).
*qirqīḍ* (*girgit*, of uncertain linguistic origin, but regarded as the equivalent of the Fur *sambe*, "barbed spear"), 88
Administrative chief, intermediate between *shartay* and *dimlij*.
*sajjān*, 56, 62
"Gaoler".
*shartay, sharṭay, shartaya*, pl. *sharātī, sharāṭī*, 5–6, 9, 10, 14, 26, 28, 32, 40, 43, 45, 48, 49, 50, 51, 52, 65, 71, 79, 80, 81, 84, 85, 87, 88, 89, 90, 91, 101, 103, 105, 108, 113, 117, 118
District chief.
*shaykh al-islām*, 10
Senior judge.
*shaykh al-quḍāt*, 10, 70
Senior judge.
*shaykh al-sulṭān*, 97
Probably a variant of the title, *imām* to the sultan.
*shaykh al-takārīr*, 51, 66, 71
Leader of western immigrant community.
*shaykh al-'urbān*, 77, 78, 80
Nomad chief.
*sulṭān*
Sovereign title of the Keira ruler.
*sulṭān al-'arab wa'l-ajam*, 30, 81
"Sultan of the Arabs and non-Arabs."
*sulṭān al-barrayn wa'l-baḥrayn*, 31
"Sultan of the two lands and two seas"; Ottoman title; sultanic honorific.
*sulṭān al-muslimīn*, 30, 36, 42, 47, 48, 52, 78, 80, 84, 103
"Sultan of the Muslims."
*al-sulṭān ibn al-sulṭān*, 31, 39, 84
"The sultan, son of the sultan"; Ottoman title.
*takanāwī*, pl. *takānū*, 5, 7, 28, 46, 49, 64, 85
By the nineteenth century, seemingly an honorific borne by certain senior *shartays* in northern Dār Fūr.
*'ulamā'*, pl. of *'ālim*, 53, 58, 59, 67, 97, 112
Religious scholars; used collectively for the holy men advising the judge.
*wakīl*, 6, 40, 108
"Deputy"; usually in the sense of a village headman.
*wazīr*, 10, 17, 32, 39, 40, 43, 45, 50, 52, 76, 78, 79, 80, 84, 87, 91, 92, 94, 101, 103, 105, 108, 110, 111, 113, 117, 118.
Honorific rather than a specific office
*wazīr al-ā'ẓam*, 110
Grand Vizier; in imitation of the Ottoman title.
*wulāt al-umūr*, 32, 80, 103, 108
"The leading notables."

## (b) Administrative and legal terms

*'adl*, pl. *'udūl*, 99
"Of good morals"; juridically, a witness or judge whose testimony or judgment is trustworthy; *EI2*, i, 209–10.
*al-aḥkām al-shar'iyya*, 7
"The lawful ordinances"; the Islamic taxes, *zakāh* and *fiṭr*.
*'alāma*, 30
The ruler's signature, usually placed at the top of the document.

*arenga*, 33
General statement of reasons for issuing a document.
*awsākh al-iqṭā'*, 90, 91
"The dirts of the estate"; the Islamic taxes, *zakāh* and *fiṭr*.
*basmala*, 30, 35
The formula, "In the name of God, the Compassionate, the Merciful"; *EI2*, i, 1084–5
*bayt al-jibāya*, 4, 18, 115
"The house of tribute"; a synonym for the *fāshir* or palace.
*bayyina*, 53, 95, 111
"Proof, evidence"; hence often "witnesses".
*dam, dam ṣaghīr, dam kabīr*, 11, 44, 47, 48, 50, 51, 52, 72, 84, 85, 87, 102, 103, 106, 109
Lit. "blood", or "little blood" and "big blood"; levy by sultan's representative on a community where a homicide or injury has occurred. After its payment, the bloodprice, *diya* (q.v.), can be arranged.
*dār dālī*, 4–5
The eastern province, governed by the *āb shaykh dālī*.
*dār diima*, 4
The south-western province, governed by the *aba diima*; see O'Fahey (1980), 76–80.
*dār al-ṣabāḥ*, 4, 76, 77
"The land of the east"; alternative name of *dār dālī* province, but also used occasionally for Kordofān and Sinnār.
*dār al-takanāwī*, 4
The northern province governed in the eighteenth century and earlier by the *āb takanāwī* and in the nineteenth by a line of *maqdūms*.
*dār umɔ*, 4
The south-eastern province, governed by the *abbo umɔ*.
*darb al-arba'īn*, 3, 6
"The forty days road"; caravan route across the desert from Kobbei to Asyūṭ in Upper Egypt.
*daraqa*, 102
Lit. "shield", a tax the nature of which is unknown.
"The dirts of the estate"; *see awsākh al-iqṭā'*
*dīwān*, 23
A general term for the taxes or the institution to which they were paid; *EI2*, ii, 323–37.
*diya*, 8
Bloodprice; *EI2*, ii, 340–3.
*du'ā'*, 42
Intercessory prayer; appears frequently in charters of privilege as the motive for making the grant; *EI2*, ii, 617–18.
*farmān*, 24
Decree, edict; *EI2*, ii, 803–6.
*fāshir* (linguistic origin unknown), 1, 4, 12, 14, 27
Open area before royal compound; by extension, the royal compound itself; and then the capital, al-Fāshir, from the end of the eighteenth century; see O'Fahey (1980), 23–5.
*fisq*, 9, 41, 44, 47, 48, 50, 51, 52, 72, 84, 85, 87, 102, 103, 106, 109
"Adultery"; fine, paid usually in rolls of cloth or animals; *EI2*, ii, 833–5.
*fiṭr, fiṭra*, 7, 36, 41, 44, 50, 51, 72, 80, 82, 84, 85, 86, 87, 90, 101, 103, 106, 109, 113
Polltax, paid at the rate of one *midd* (q.v.) per head.
*ghazwa*, 25
Slave-raid; *EI2*, ii, 1055–6.
*ḥadd*, 94, 96, 97
"Boundary", and by extension the defined land; *EI2*, iii, 20–2.
*ḥākūra*, pl. *ḥawākīr*, 14, 20, 73, 101, 102, 104
Commonly a vegetable garden or plot; in Dār Fūr, a farm or estate; in the latter sense, it is the equivalent of the classical *iqṭā'* (q.v.).
*ḥākūrat al-sulṭān*, 14
Royal domain, mainly Jabal Marra and certain lands in south-western Dār Fūr.
*ḥamdala*, 35, 38
The formula, "Praise be to God"; *EI2*, iii, 122–3.
*hāmil, hāmila*, also *ḥāmil*, 36, 41, 44, 47, 50, 52, 82, 84, 85, 87, 102, 103, 106, 109
"Stray" (from *hamala*); a tax paid to chief or estate-holder from the sale of stray animals or slaves.
*ḥaram*, 17
"Forbidden, taboo."
*ḥawṭah*, 17

*ḥawṭah* (*cont.*)
A sacred enclave in South Arabia; *EI*2, iii, 294.
*ḥawz*; *see ḥiyāza*
*hiba*, 33
Donation, gift; see Schacht (1964), 157–8, and *EI*2, iii, 342–51.
*ḥiyāza*, or *ḥawz*, 53, 111
A prescriptive right of possession, derived for example from the clearing of virgin land, *iḥyā' al-mawāt* (q.v.), as opposed to *milk* (q.v.).
*ḥubs*, 39
Religious bequest.
*ḥujja*, pl. *ḥujaj*, 24
Deed (of purchase, property etc.), or "argument, plea", in court; *EI*2, iii, 543–5.
*ḥukm*, 9, 46, 53
A legal judgment (*ḥukm shar'ī*), or fees paid to judge or estate-holder for rendering justice; *EI*2, iii, 549–51.
*ḥurma*, 8, 17–18, 80, 84
"Being forbidden"; an occasional synonym for *jāh* (q.v.).
*ḥurr*, 17
"Free"; a synonym for *jāh* (q.v.).
*iḥyā'*, from *iḥyā' al-mawāt*, 46, 65, 67, 68, 69, 73, 74, 92
"Cultivation", from the phrase, "the revivification of the dead (lands)"; the clearing of wasteland by which the settler obtains rights of property (Santillana (1926), i, 419), but which in Dār Fūr could be overridden by an allodial concession (*iqṭā'*, q.v.); *EI*2, iii, 1053–4.
*ijtihād*
Judicial discretion; for example, that of a judge to grant an adjournment; *EI*2, iii, 1026–7.
*iltizām*
Tax-farming (Egyptian); *EI*2, iii, 1154–5.
*iqrār*
Acknowledgment, confession; *EI*2, iii, 1078–81.
*iqṭā'*, 13, 14, 18, 20, 33, 46, 69, 71, 73, 74, 75, 95
Concession of public domain by the ruler; *EI*2, ii, 1988–91.
*iqṭā' al-istighlāl*, 18
Concession by ruler of rights of usufruct.
*iqṭā' nājiz*
Allodial concession.
*iqṭā' al-tamlīk*, 18
Concession by ruler of property (*milk*).
*jāh*, pl. *ajwāh*, 12, 17–18, 46, 69, 70, 80
Privileged status granted by ruler, giving the recipient tax-exemption but not direct rights over land; see 'Awn (1972), 146.
*jawāb*, 32
Letter, document.
*jibāya*, 8, 47
Revenue.
*karāma*, 8, 17
Sanctity; *EI*2, iv, 615–16; used of those granted privileged status.
*kharāj*, 38
Land-tax; *EI*2, iv, 1030–56.
*khatma*, 42
Recitation of the entire Qur'ān.
*khidma*, 8, 81
Used in two senses; service owed by the tenants to the estate-holder; and for the court.
*kitāb*, 32, 38
Document, charter.
*maḥram*
The term used for the charters of privilege granted by the rulers of Kānem/Borno to various holy clans.
*majlis*
Court, both in the judicial and administrative sense.
*maks*, 8
customs duties.
*maktūb*, 24, 32
Document, charter.
*maṭmūra*, 8
Clay-lined pit for the storage of grain.
*midd* (*mudd*), 7
Unit of dry measure used for grain; approximately 8.25 litres.
*milk*
Freehold property, property-rights.
*mithqal*, 25
Unit of weight for gold and precious stones; approximately 8 grammes.
*mudda'ā 'alayh*
Defendant.
*mudda'ī*
Plaintiff.
*muḥakkam*
Arbitrator.
*muwakkil*
Person or persons who mandate

*muwakkil* (*cont.*)
another (*wakīl*) to represent them in court upon their authorization (*tafwīḍan lahu*).
*naḥās*, 6
"Copper"; copper kettle-drum; symbol of sovereignty in the Dār Fūr sultanate.
*nār*, 41, 44, 47, 102, 106
"Fire"; fine levied by chief or estate-holder for causing bush-fires.
*al-naẓar fi'l-maẓālim*, 10
"Investigation of complaints"; appeal to the ruler of a disputed judgment.
*qānūn* (or *kitāb*) *dālī*, 8
Name of the code of Fur customary law.
*quwwār*, 41, 44, 47, 82, 87, 102, 106
Market-dues payable to chief or estate-holder; see MacMichael (1922), ii, 79.
*rasm*, 24, 32
Decree.
*rayka*, 7
A dry measure of 30 *midd* (q.v.); more commonly in Dār Fūr called *umm thalāthīn*.
*rizqa*, 18
Estate granted as a pension or for a charitable purpose (Mamluk).
*rɔ kuuriŋ*, 14
Royal domain; see *ḥākūrat al-sulṭān*.
*ṣadaqa*, 13, 25, 33
Charitable gift.
*ṣadaqa wa-hiba*, 13, 18
"Gift and donation"; a formula frequently used in the charters.
*ṣadr*, 32
The "body" of a document.
*salamāt*, 17
Presents paid by holy men to the notables whose estates encompassed their own.
*ṣalatiyya*, 25
Broad-bladed lance; also used of a state-sponsored slave-raid.
*shahāda*
"Testimony"; thus occasionally "witnesses".
*shurūṭ*
"Stipulations"; exemplary legal formulae.
*sijill*, 9, 23–4, 28
Transcript of a court hearing.
*al-subul al-ʿādiyya*, 7, 14
"The customary ways"; the traditional or non-Sharīʿa taxes.
*takkiyya*, pl. *takākī* (sometimes written *taqqiyya*), 7
A long narrow strip of locally-produced cloth, widely used as a unit of exchange or taxation; a tax of the same name.
*ṭaliba*, 8
"Reckoning"; tax-returns sent to the capital by the *jabbāyyīn*.
*taṣliyya*, 30
The formula, "May the blessings and peace of God be upon our lord Muḥammad and his family."
*timar*, 18
Land originally granted in return for military service (Ottoman).
*umm thalāthīn*, 7
"Mother of thirty"; a dry-weight measure of 30 *midd* or one *rayka*; since *zakāh* was not paid on a harvest of less than 30 *midd*, *umm thalāthīn* was also a synonym for the tax.
*waqfiyya*, 41
A document granting a *waqf* or pious endowment.
*wathīqa*, 24, 32
Document, charter.
*zakāh*, 7, 14, 36, 41, 44, 50, 51, 52, 72, 80, 82, 84, 85, 86, 87, 90, 101, 103, 106, 109, 113
The tithe tax on grain and animals.
*zinā*, 9, 82, 102–3
"Fornication"; fine payable to chief or estate-holder for making an unmarried girl pregnant.
*ziyānat rāsihā*, see pp. 102–3.

## (c) Botanical and topographical terms

Botanical names are given here according to Wickens (1976) where stated, or Baumer (1975). For a general description of the flora and vegetation of north-western Dār Fūr see also Quézel (1969).


*'arad*, 43, 106
  *Albizia amara* (Wickens).
*'aysh*, 7
  Lit. "life", general term for "grain".
*bīr*, classical *bi'r*, pl. *abyār*
  Well.
*bōbāya*, *bōbāī*, 85, 105
  Land formerly cultivated but now left deserted.
*dabba*, 85
  A low dune of yellow or clayey sand (Baumer).
*daldūm* = "Rounded", 36
  See 'Awn (1972), 249.
*dhurra*, 7
  Common millet.
*dukhn*, 7
  Bullrush millet.
*fardal*, 43, 117
  Open sandy depression. 'Awn (1972), 552 gives *ghardal/fardal* as a western Sudanese usage, meaning "row or furrow in a field". This meaning is not supported by oral sources. The word is possibly Nubian (it is found in the Birged language).
*habīl*, 36, 43
  A word covering several species of *Combretaceae* (Wickens).
*ḥarāz*, 43, 105, 106, 108, 109, 115
  *Acacia albida* (Wickens).
*ḥashāb*, *hashāb*, 86, 109, 112
  *Acacia senegal*, which produces the commercial "gum arabic" (Wickens).
*ḥaskanīt*, 43
  *Cenchrus biflorus* (Wickens).
*hijlīj*, *ḥijlīj*, 43, 44, 85, 106, 109, 112, 115, 116, 117
  *Balanites aegyptiaca*; a tree with many uses, see Wickens.
*hijlīj al-na'sh*, 36
  As above.
*inḍirāb*, 51, 115
  *Vangueria venosa*; edible fruit (Wickens).
*jarrāba*, 85
  Muddy or cultivable land; 'Awn (1972), 119.
*jidal*, classical *jidhl*, 117
  "Stump" of a tree; see 'Awn (1972), 117.
*jummayz*
  *Ficus sycomorus*; edible fruit, but see Wickens (1976), 119.
*karkar* = "Rocky outcrop", 36
  See 'Awn (1972), 448.
*khōr*, pl. *khayrān*, 115
  Water course.
*kolkol* (not Arabic?), 112, 117
  *Bauhinia rufescens*; "a browse shrub for all stock" (Wickens).
*majarr* = "channel of the riverbed", 51
  The channel or stream's course within the riverbed itself; 'Awn (1972), 118.
*mukhīṭ*, 43, 105, 112, 115, 117
  *Boscia senegalensis*. 'Awn (1972), 732 gives *mukhīt*.
*nabaq*, 43, 105, 109, 112, 115, 116, 117
  *Ziziphus spina-christi*; edible fruit (Wickens).
*nakhl* = date-palm, 43
*naqa'a*, 43, 116
  Marshy ground; cotton soil temporarily flooded after the rains; 'Awn (1972), 602.
*qadd*, pl. *qidūd*, 86
  Crack or fissure in rock; 'Awn (1972), 602.
*qafal*, 115
  *Commiphera africana*; "the resin is believed to have medicinal properties. The root is sweet and edible" (Wickens).
*qanṭūr*, 116
  Anthills; 'Awn (1972), 636.
*qaraḍ*, 117
  *Acacia adansonii*; the pods and seeds are used for tanning" (Wickens).
*qarqūr* = "Depression", 36
  See 'Awn (1972), 611.
*qiraywud*, 105
  Hillocks; 'Awn (1972), 624.

*qōz*, 6
Stabilized sand-dunes, favoured as agricultural land.
*rahad* = "rain pool", 39
*sallam*, 85
*Acacia tortilis* or *Acacia ehrenbergiana* (Baumer).
*sayl*, 37, 115
"Floodbed"; 'Awn (1972), 382.
*sayyāl*, 36, 44, 71, 109, 112, 115, 117
*Acacia tortilis* (Wickens).
*shōk*, 109
*Oxygonum sinuatum* (Wickens).
*siriḥ*, 43, 112
*Asparagus flagellaris* (Wickens).
*tabaldī*, 39–40, 43
*Jatropha curcas* (Wickens); widely used in eastern Dār Fūr to store water.
*taqur* = "thicket", 36
See 'Awn (1972), 91
*thamad*, pl. *thammād* (more usually written *tammad*, *tammād*), 85, 86.
Water-holes; "To obtain water the Zaghawa dig holes (Z./kúnấ/, Ar. tamada) somewhat at random in the wadi beds. As they are shallow, such rough and ready wells require no timbering. A calabash is used to draw the water, which oozes onto the sand at the bottom. Such draining wells serve during the rains and afterwards" (Tubiana and Tubiana (1977), 37).
*tunṭub*, *ṭunṭub* (both are more frequent than the classical *tunḍub*), 43, 85, 106, 109, 115, 116, 117
*Capparis decidua* or *Capparis fascicularis*; the first produces an edible fruit, the second a fruit eaten by camels (Wickens).
*zalṭāya*, *zalṭāyāt*, 108, 109, 115
Stony or pebbly outcrops or patches; 'Awn (1972), 324.
*zarība*, pl. *zarā'ib*, 85, 106, 115
Thorn enclosure; household and gardens enclosed by such; 'Awn (1972), 317.

### (d) Personal and place-names

The following abbreviations are used:

*ami.* = *amīn*
b. = *ibn* "son of"
*bās.* = *bāsī*
bt. = *bint* "daughter of"
desc. = descendant(s)
*faq.* = *faqīh*
gra. = grantee
lit. = litigant
loc. = locality
*mal.* = *malik*
*maq.* = *maqdūm*
*muw.* = *muwajjah*
nom. = nomad
par. = partner (in estate etc.)
*qāḍ* = *qāḍī*
scr. = scribe
sha. = shaykh
sul. = sultan
vil. = village
*waz.* = *wazīr*
wit. = witness
*zar.* = *zarība*

Abb(a); *mal.*, wit., 112
Abbakr al-Sanūsī; *faq.*, scr., 23
'Abd al-'Āl; *faq.*, wit., 75
'Abdallāh; *faq.*, lit., 58
'Abdallāh; lit., "another", 58
'Abdallāh; *ami.*, *mal.*, *muw.*, 115, 118
'Abdallāh b. Abu'l-Ḥasan; *faq.*, gra., 35–6
'Abdallāh b. Aḥmad w. al-Taḥāwī; wit., 112
'Abdallāh w. Dānī; lit., 110–12
'Abdallāh Ibrāhīm, *al-ḥājj*; wit., 58
'Abdallāh b. Ibrāhīm Ramād; *mal.*, 53, 58–60
'Abdallāh Karqāsh; *mal.*, gra., 101
'Abdallāh Kūr (or Kawr); *ami.*, *mal.*, 21, 115, 118
'Abdallāh Maṭlūq al-Tunjurāwī; *faq.*, gra., 46–8, 51, 53, 66, 71, 74
'Abdallāh al-Naw; wit., 81–2
'Abdallāh Sallāṭa; *faq.*, wit., 93
'Abdallāh al-Ṭayyib; *faq.*, 62
'Abd al-'Azīz; *maq.*, 25, 100–1
'Abd al-Bāqī b. Yūsuf al-Zurqānī; commentator, 9, 73
'Abd al-Bārī Muḥammad Jurāb; *faq.*, wit., 62
'Abd al-Fattāḥ, desc. of. . ., 49
'Abd al-Ghanī b. Makkī; *imām*, 65
'Abd al-Jabbār, *zar.*, of. . . 109
'Abd al-Mājid; wit., 61
'Abd al-Majīd b. Muḥammad Kannūna; gra., 113
'Abd al-Manān; *faq.*, wit., 61

'Abd al-Na'īm; nom., 103
'Abd al-Nūrayn; *faq.*, 38
'Abd al-Qādir; *faq.*, wit., 112
'Abd al-Qādir s.r.bī; *faq.*, wit., 99
'Abd al-Raḥmān; par., 56
'Abd al-Raḥmān; Fulani, 65
'Abd al-Raḥmān; *faq.*, wit., 68
'Abd al-Raḥmān; *faq.*, desc. of..., 49
'Abd al-Raḥmān; sul., 5, 20, 24, 29, 30–2, 35, 38–40, 46–7, 52, 57–9, 62, 76–8, 80–2, 96, 98
'Abd al-Raḥmān Kākama (or Kawma); *faq.*, 53–5, 57–8
'Abd al-Ṣādiq; lit., 54
'Abd al-Ṣādiq; *mal.*, wit., 93
'Abd al-Ṣādiq; wit., 93
'Abd al-Ṣādiq; *mal.*, wit., 99
'Abd al-Salām; *faq.*, Fulani, 65
'Abd Ṣāliḥ; *faq.*, wit., 75
"Abida"; *faq.*, gra., 104
Abō; Zaghāwa of Kawra vil., 82
Abū Bakr; lit., 58
Abū Bakr; sha., wit., 51
Abū Bakr; *qāḍ.*, wit., 61, 65–7
Abū Bakr w. Kabbāshī; *faq.*, wit., 112
Abū Bakr b. *al-ḥājj* 'Umar; lit., 91–2, 98–9
Abu'l-Bashar; *walad al-sulṭān*, gra., 104
Abu'l-Bashar; *faq.*, 106
Abū Dawra; rain pool, 39
Abū Hajūra; fields, 39
Abū Ḥasan; *bās.*, *muw.*, 64
Abū Ḥusayn; rocks, 109
Abu'l-Qāsim; sul., 38–9, 40, 70
Adā; Zaghāwa of Kawra vil., 82, 84
Ādam; lit., 69–73
Ādam; lit., "another", 70
Ādam w. 'Awadallāh; wit., 61
Ādam Bōsh; *ami.*, *waz.*, 108–13
Ādam Bōsh; *mal.*, wit., 77
Ādam b. Ḥasan; *maq.*, 5
Ādam b. Ibrāhīm Ramād; *mal.*, wit., 82
Ādam *jarr lā baḥr*; *mal.*, wit., 93
Ādam r.t.f.l.; wit., 62
Ādūma; par., 56, 63
Aḥmad; *faq.*, wit., 73, 75
Aḥmad; lit., 54, 57, 58–9
Aḥmad; lit., 70
Aḥmad; nom., 103
Aḥmad; nom., "another", 103
Aḥmad, *al-ḥājj*; land of..., 112
Aḥmad b. Aḥmad w. al-Taḥāwī; *mal.*, wit., 112
Aḥmad Bukr; sul., 1, 5, 13, 20, 29, 40, 46, 52, 54–5, 56–9, 62, 76
Aḥmad w. walad Bishāra; wit., 61
Aḥmad b. 'Īsā, *al-ḥājj*; gra., 100–4
Aḥmad Jaraf; lit., 56
Aḥmad Jurāb al-Fīl; soldier, 14
Aḥmad b. Kabbāsh, Fulani, 64–5
Aḥmad Kūnū; wit., 112
Aḥmad Majdhūb; *faq.*, wit., 62
Aḥmad b. Muḥammad Kannūna; gra., 113
Aḥmad Qandā; *faq.*, wit., 112
Aḥmad Ṣāliḥ; *faq.*, wit., 67–8
Aḥmad Tūtū; *walad al-sulṭān*, wit., 112
Aḥmad Zarrūq; *faq.*, wit., 73
al-'Ajūz; waterpool, 86
'Alī; sha., nom., 77–8
'Alī Dīnār; sul., 4–5, 10, 16, 19, 22–3, 30–1, 37, 44, 47, 52–3
'Alī w. Ḥabīb; *mal.*, wit., 112
'Alī b. Ibrāhīm al-Ṭirayfī; *khabīr*, gra., 21, 106–18
'Alī b. Jāmi'; *waz.*, 76
'Alī b. Muḥammad; wit., 81
Alī b. Muḥammad Nartaq; *faq.*, lit., 58–60
'Alī Tōm; lit., 91–3
'Alwa; par., 56
'Amāra; *muw.*, 40–1
Ambarāk; nom., 77–8
Amīn; *faq.*, wit., 68
Amīn al-Katakāwī; *muw.*, 51, 66, 71
'Āmir; *bās.*, *wit.*, 95, 97
Anbarāk; *al-ḥājj*; wit., 95, 97
'Aqrab; *walad al-sulṭān*, lit., 61–2, 73
Arabic, language, 26–7
'Arafa ("Arifa") bt. Muḥammad al-Ḥusayn; *mayram*, gra., 104
al-'Arāis; loc., 105
Arbāb, *al-ḥājj*; *muw.*, 108, 113
'Arībī; lit., 56
'Arōfa bt. Muḥammad al-Ḥusayn; *mayram*, 107
Arqā; farm of..., 110–12
Asyūṭ, 28, 107, 114
'Atiyya; nom., 77–8
'Aṭiyyat Allāh; *mal.*, wit., 112
Awlād 'Abd al-Raḥmān; Tunjur clan, 53
Awlād Bāsī, 115–16
Awlād Darash; Fulani clan, 65, 67
Awlād Dardūq; clan, 36
Awlād Diyāt; vil. of..., 86
Awlād Jābir; Zayyādiyya clan, x, 13, 42
Awlād Jāmi'; Jawāmi'a clan, 37
Awlād Khamīs and Bilāl; clan, 36
Awlād Mūrunj; Jawāmi'a clan, 37
Awlād Rashdān; *faq.*, clan, 86
Awlād Sulaymān; Jawāmi'a clan, 37
Awlād Zaydān; *faq.*, clan, 16
Aydām; nom., 77–8

'Ayn; nom., 77–8
Azagarfa/Arārī; loc., mosque, 38
Azbāba; hillocks, 51, 71
al-Azhar; university, 23
'Azīza; riverbed, 109

Badawī b. 'Abdallāh Maṭlūq; gra., 46–8, 50, 54, 57, 61–4
Baḥrī; Zaghāwa of Kawra vil., 84
Balilī; nom., 77, 78
Balūla; nom., 77, 78
Baqirmi; state and people, 14, 108–9
Baqqāra; cattle nomads, 3
Bāra; town, 76
Barakāt; *naqīb*, wit., 67, 112
Barakat Allāh; sons of..., 108
Barr Bōja; riverbed, 148
Bashīr, *al-ḥājj*; wit., 82
Bātī; Zaghāwa of Kawra vil., 82, 84
Bayd; estate, 18, 42–4
Berti; people, 6
Bidayriyya; people, 114
Bilayla; *faq.*, wit., 62
Biringia; battle, 37
Birged; people, 14
Bishāra; *muw.*, 85, 87, 92
Bivar, A. D. H., 27
b.nāb.n.; loc., 91, 95
Bonaparte, Napoleon, 24
Borno; state and people, 27, 31, 37, 100
Bōwa; hill, 105
b.q.t.; Zaghāwa of Kawra vil., 84
Browne, W. G.; traveller, 37, 100, 106–7
b.r.kū; rocks, 105
Bukr; *bās.*, wit., 81
Bukr; par., 56
Bukr; wit., 93
Bukr, Tayrāb & r.b.q; *shartāya* of..., 105
Bulawla; nom., 77, 78

Cairo, 23–4, 28–9, 107
Cuny, C.; traveller, 28

Daali; sultan, 8
al-Dabba; town, 25
Dabirtu; loc., 51, 71
Dābō; Zaghāwa of Kawra vil., 84
Daḥm; lit., 54
Daju; people, 1, 26
Dalam; *sha.*, nom., 103
al-Dalam; tree of..., 105
Dānī; nom., 77, 78
al-Dānī; nom., 103
Dānī's vil., 109
Dār Fongoro; *shartāya*, 14
Dār Furnung; *shartāya*, 104
Dār Marārīt, 79
Dār Qimr, 5
Dār Suwaynī; *shartāya*, 79, 104
Dār Zaghāwa, 6
*darb al-arba'īn*, 3, 6
Dhiyāb; *faq.*, wit., 51
Dongola; town, 31, 107
Dōr; loc., 79, 104–6
d.r.fī; Zaghāwa of Kawra vil., 84
d.rū; rocks, 105
Duhaysh; nom., 77, 78
Duqū; *mal.*, wit., 93
Duwwār; nom., 77, 78

Egypt, 3, 12, 24, 26, 28, 107

Faḍl; nom., 77
Faḍl; Zaghāwa of Kawra vil., 82, 84
Fāiq; nom., 77
Fakhr al-Dīn; *faq.*, wit., 68
Fakhr al-Dīn b. Muḥammad Sālim; *faq.*, wit., 75
Fallāta; people, 37, 61
Fāris b. Ibrāhīm Ramād; wit., 81
al-Fāshir, 4–5, 8, 12, 23, 36–7, 106, 109
Fāṭima Umm Dirays bt. Muḥammad al-Ḥusayn; *mayram*, gra., 99–106, 117
Fazārī; *mal.*, wit., 62
Fetessa bt. Muḥammad Tayrāb; *mayram*, 100
al-Filfil, waterpool, 86
al-Firsh; mosque, 38
f.r.q.; riverbed, 105
Fulani, see Fallāta
Funj; state, 30, 33–4
Fur; people & language, 22, 79
Furok; loc., 104
Fūrū; lake, 115

Ghadīr; nom., 81
Ghanamiyya; Jawāmi'a clan, 37

Habābīn; clan, 43
Ḥabīb; *faq.*, 51, 71
Ḥabīb; wit., 61
Ḥabīb b. 'Abd al-Raḥmān; *walad al-sulṭān*, wit., 77
Hadī; *faq.*, wit., 68
Ḥajjāj; nom., 97
Ḥallūf; water course, 37
Ḥamad, *al-ḥājj*; wit., 98
Ḥamad Abū Zayd; nom., 77, 78
Ḥamad "the blind"; nom., 77, 78
Ḥamad Darōk; *mal.*, wit., 99
Ḥamad al-Fūr; informant, 114
Ḥamad Kana Yaḥyā; wit., 97

Ḥāmid; *faq.*, wit., 95, 97
Ḥāmid; nom., 77, 78
Ḥāmid; *zar.* of..., 117
Ḥāmid; nom., 103
Ḥāmid b. Aḥmad Sakīn; *ami.*, *waz.*, gra., 17, 76–9, 92
Ḥāmid Muḥammad Kamar Daw, *zar.* of..., 85
Ḥammād; desc. of..., 49
Ḥammād; *mal.*, *faq.*, wit., 93
Ḥammād; pool of..., 105
Ḥammād; *qāḍ.*, 69–73
Hartmann, Robert; traveller, 114
Hārūn; *faq.*, wit., 112
Hārūn; nom., 77, 78
Hārūn; par., 56
Ḥasab al-Karīm; *shartay*, 104
Ḥasab al-Karīm; *walad al-sulṭān*, 43
Ḥasan; *faq.*, wit., 61
Ḥasan; *faq.*, wit., 73
Ḥasan; par., 56
Ḥasan 'Ammār; *faq.*, wit., 93
Ḥasan Siqīrī; *maq.*, 5, 51, 65–8, 71, 93, 99
Ḥassān's vil., 108–9
Ḥawwā' bt. 'Abd al-Raḥmān; *mayram*, 100
Hilikī, *al-ḥājj*; wit., 99
al-Ḥimyar; loc., 40, 41
Hīrān; nom., 77, 78
Ḥusayn; *maqām*, 43
Ḥusayn; nom., 103
Ḥusayn b. Fīl; *muw.*, 105
Ḥusayn b. Izayriq Birtāwī; *faq.*, wit., 112
h.w.l.; nom., 77, 78

Ibn w. al-Khaṭīb; *faq.*, wit., 112
Ibrāhīm; *faq.*, wit., 73
Ibrāhīm; *muw.*, 21, 115, 118
Ibrāhīm; par., 56
Ibrāhīm; *malik al-jallāba*, gra., 104
Ibrāhīm b. 'Abd al-Qādir; *abbo daadiŋa*, 40, 41
Ibrāhīm Kaiti, 79
Ibrāhīm b. Khalīl; *qirqīḍ*, 88–90
Ibrāhīm b. Muḥammad Kannūna; gra., 113
Ibrāhīm Qaraḍ; sul., 3, 25, 42
Ibrāhīm w. Ramād; *abbo konyuŋa*, 46, 77
Ibrāhīm b. Sa'd al-Dīn; *imām*, gra., 38, 40
Ibrāhīm Tītī; *mal.*, wit., 82, 85
Idrīs; par., 56
Idrīs Marjān; *mal.*, 94
Idrīs Sanbal; *faq.*, 55
Imām; rock, 86
Inqirī, or n.q.r.; vil., 19, 21, 114–18
'Īsā; par., 56
'Īsā, *al-ḥājj*, 106, 109
'Īsāwī; *mal.*, wit., 81
'Īsāwī w. b.r.n.; wit., 62
Isḥāq; par., 56
Isḥāq; *shaykh al-quḍāt*, 70
Isḥāq; wit., 61
Isḥāq Markaz; *faq.*, wit., 93
Ishạq b. Muḥammad Tayrāb, *al-ḥājj*; *khalīfa*, 53–4
Isḥāqa ("Isagha") w. Bidayn; *faq.*, gra., 104
Isirra; clan, 36
Ismā'īl; *bās.*, wit., 77
Ismā'īl, *al-ḥājj*; *faq.*, wit., 58
Ismā'īl; par., 56
Ismā'īl b. Aḥmad al-Ḍawī; *faq.*, wit., 112
Italy, 26
'Iyyād; nom., 77, 78
'Izz al-Dīn; *faq.*, 42–4
'Izz al-Dīn; *faq.*, Fallāta, 51, 71
'Izz al-Dīn; wit., 61
'Izz al-Dīn b. Mūsā; *qāḍ.*, 10, 38, 53–6, 57, 58–60, 61–3, 70

Ja'afiriyya; Jawāmi'a clan, 37
Jabā; loc., 105
Jabal 'Arā, 51, 71
J. Ḥarāza, 6
J. Ḥurayz, 46
J. Jadīd, 37
J. Marra, 1, 4, 7, 8, 14, 29, 76
J. Martabū, 51, 71
J. Meidob, 5
J. al-Samū', 51, 71
J. Sarāya, 51, 71
J. sh.q.r al-kabīr, 51, 71
J. Sī, 5
J. Umm 'Arīf, 51
al-Jabbay; *falqanāwī*, 65
Jādallāh; *faq.*, wit., 95, 97
Jadīd Rās al-Fīl; town, 38
Jadīd al-Sayl; town, 6, 17, 36–45, 53
Jāīd; nom., 77, 78
Jalāla; *faq.*, Fallāta, 66
Jalāl al-Dīn; *faq.*, wit., 112
Jāmi'; lit., 56
Jamal; field of..., 86
Jamīl; *faq.*, wit., 73
Jamīlallāh; *faq.*, wit., 51
Jāmūs; wit., 61
Jār; sul., wit., 97
Jawāmi'a; people, 6, 17, 37–45, 114
Jawdatallāh; nom., 77, 78

j.dh.q. Jārō; loc., 105
Jiddaw w. Bukhārī; gra., 44–5
Ji'rān; nom., 77, 78
Jum'a; deserted land of..., 85
Jum'a; nom., 77, 78
Jum'a Tānā; *mal.*, wit., 95, 97
'.j.z.; nom., 103

Kabbāsh b. 'Abd al-Salām; *faq.*, lit., Fallāta, 64–8
Kabkābiyya; town, 5
Kaitiŋa; clan, 79
Kalwa; riverbed, 51
Kamala (or Kamāl) Keirei (or Kīrī); loc., 19, 46, 51–2, 61, 63, 68, 70–1, 74
Kanuri; language, 27
Karam j.nā; loc., 106
Kararī; battle, 4
Kardal; rocks, 109
Kartakayla; *mal.*, gra., 101
Kawra; vil., 80, 81–2
k.d.r.ā.; well, 105
Keira; dynasty, 1, 45
Kerio; vil., 37, 38
Khabīr; *faq.*, wit., 51
Khādimallāh; *mayram*, 51, 71
Khalīl; *faq.*, wit., 58, 61
Khalīl; par., 56
Khalīl b. Isḥāq; jurisconsult, 9, 69, 73, 95, 99
Khalīl b. Ramaḍān; *qirqīḍ*, 88
Khamīs; par., 56
Khamīs b. Ma'īn; wit., 77
Khartoum, 25
Khayr; deserted land of..., 105
Khayr Abū Khādimallāh; *khabīr*, gra., 107–13
Khayr Khanaqa; loc., 36
Khidr; par., 56
Khirībān; loc., 6, 46–75
al-Khurashī; *faq.*, wit., 58
Kirātī; Tunjur clan, 46
Kobbei; town, 6, 38, 104, 106–18
Kofod (Kafōt); vil., 106
Konyuna; Fur clan, 14
Kordofān, 3, 5, 6, 32, 37, 76, 107, 114
k.sī; *sajjān*, 10, 56, 62
Kurqā Khayrbān; estate, 65
Kutum, 5, 79

Labadī; loc., 45
Labbād; sons of..., 110–12
Last, Murray, 31–2
"Leathering of the Drum"; festival, 14
Luqmān Rīḥ; *mal.*, wit., 93

Maba; people, 45
Madanī; *faq.*, wit., 58
Madanī; *faq.*, wit., 112
Madanī b. 'Abdallāh Maṭlūq; gra., 46, 49–51, 52, 57, 58–60, 68–9, 71
Mahdi, the, 3
Maḥmūd; *faq.*, wit., 68
Maḥmūd; *faq.*, wit., 99
Maḥmūd; lit., 56
Maḥmūd 'Alī; *abbo daadiŋa*, 16
Māhriyya; people, 103
Majāzī; nom., 77, 78
Makkī, *al-ḥājj*; wit., 58
Makkī; *faq.*, wit., 68
Mālikī; School of Law, 8
Mālikī al-Fūtāwī; *faq.*, wit., Fallāta, 81, 82
Mamluk, 30
Manān; nom., 77, 78
Manawāshī, 3 (battle), 37, 38, 100
Mānṣar Abū Ādam; *zar.* of..., 85
Manzil; nom., 77, 78
Ma'qūq; fields, 51, 71
Maqābil; hillocks, 51, 71
Marbūṭa; loc., 20
Mardufa; rocks, 109
Masāmīr; Arab clan, 76–9
Mauritania, 17
Maydōb b. Yaḥyā; *mal.*, *shartay*, 19, 79–80, 82, 85, 91–2, 94–5, 96–8
m.b.d.; nom., 77, 78
m.'.d.; nom., 77, 78
Meidob; people, 6
m.h.l.; nom., 77, 78
Millīṭ; town, 37
Mīma; people, 35
Mirāq; nom., 77, 78
Mītī; *falqanāwī*, 69
m.n.h.l.; nom., 77, 78
Mosques, 37–45
m.r.jī; *khabīr*, nom., 77, 78
m.r.mī; Zaghāwa of Kawra vil., 82, 84
m.sīl; nom., 77, 78
m.s.l.; nom. "another", 77, 78
m.tiyya; nom., 77, 78
Mufriḥ; nom., 77, 78
Muftāḥ; *khabīr*, *muw.*, 94–9
Muḥammad; *faq.*, wit., 51
Muḥammad, *al-ḥājj*; wit., 68
Muḥammad; lit. "and another", 58
Muḥammad; lit., 70
Muḥammad; *mal.*, wit., 73
Muḥammad; *faq.*, Mīma, 35
Muḥammad; nom., 77, 78
Muḥammad; *takanāwī*, 64–5
Muḥammad 'Abdallāh, *al-ḥājj*; wit., 67

Muḥammad 'Abd al-Qādir Qayba; wit., 97
Muḥammad Abū Isḥāq; *zar.* of..., 85
Muḥammad 'Alī Pasha, 23, 25, 31
Muḥammad w. 'Ammārī; scr., 23
Muḥammad al-Barnāwī; pilgrim, 25
Muḥammad w. Bishāra, wit., 61
Muḥammad Bōsh; *mal.*, wit., 93
Muḥammad Daldūm; *kursī*, 104
Muḥammad Daqīsān; *faq.*, wit., 51
Muḥammad Dardūq; fields of..., 117
Muḥammad Dashāsh; lit., 54
Muḥammad Dawra; sul., 13, 29, 30, 32, 37, 38, 40
Muḥammad Diyā; judicial officer, 10, 56, 62
Muḥammad Dokkumi b. 'Alī Jāmi'; *ami.*, 76–8, 79
Muḥammad Dūd; *faq.*, wit., 93
Muḥammad Dūd; *mal.*, wit., 93
Muḥammad al-Faḍl; sul., 4, 8, 16, 18–19, 23–5, 29–31, 35–6, 38, 40, 42, 46, 48, 52, 63, 69, 74, 78–9, 80, 82–8, 90–2, 94, 96–8, 99, 104, 107–13
Muḥammad Faraḥ, *al-ḥājj*; *muw.*, 111
Muḥammad Fawāz; *mal.*, wit., 98
Muḥammad Gharbāwi, 40, 41
Muḥammad Hārin; nom., 77
Muḥammad al-Ḥārith b. 'Izz al-Dīn; *qāḍ.*, 53, 56–8, 59–60
Muḥammad b. Ḥasan; *maq.*, 5, 105
Muḥammad Hūd b. Muḥammad al-Faḍl; *walad al-sulṭān*, 61, 73–5
Muḥammad Ḥumaydī; *faq.*, wit., 51
Muḥammad al-Ḥusayn; sul., 18, 23–5, 29–31, 33, 35–6, 38, 40–3, 46, 49–51, 52, 64–6, 69, 71, 73–5, 80, 87–8, 99–106, 113–18
Muḥammad al-Imām; *khabīr*, 107, 114
Muḥammad 'Izz al-Dīn; *faq.*, gra., 38–41
Muḥammad Junqīs; *mal.*, wit., 77
Muḥammad Kadūk, 40
Muḥammad Kannūna; *khabīr*, 18, 106–13
Muḥammad Kawn; lit., 54, 56, 57
Muḥammad Kayka; *takanāwī*, 85, 86
Muḥammad Kūk, *al-ḥājj*; *zar.* of..., 109
Muḥammad Kurra; *āb shaykh dālī*, 14, 18, 76
Muḥammad b. Madanī; gra., 19, 46, 51, 64–8, 71
Muḥammad al-Miṣrī; *imām*, Fallāta, 67, 99
Muḥammad b. Muḥammad Kannūna; gra., 113
Muḥammad b. Muḥammadayn; gra., 47, 52–3
Muḥammad Nartaq; lit., 53–7, 59
Muḥammad Nīl; wit., 75
Muḥammad n.l. mū (n.j.l.mū); *shartay*, 51, 65, 71
Muḥammad al-Nūr; *faq.*, wit., 99
Muḥammad Rīl; lit., 70
Muḥammad Rīl b. Maydōb; *shartay*, 79, 85–6, 88–91
Muḥammad Ṣaḥnī; *mal.*, wit., 93
Muḥammad Ṣāliḥ w. Tharwa, *al-ḥājj*; wit., 112
Muḥammad Sālim; *faq.*, wit., 67
Muḥammad Sālim; *faq.*, wit., 75
Muḥammad Shalabī; Tunjur sul., 6, 17, 49
Muḥammad Sharīf b. Ādam; *maq.*, 5, 16
Muḥammad Shinā; lit., 56, 58–9
Muḥammad Sirāj, *al-ḥājj*; *faq.*, wit., 95, 97
Muḥammad Tāma; *faq.*, wit., 99
Muḥammad al-Ṭayr; nom., 77, 78
Muḥammad Tayrāb; sul., 14, 29–30, 38–40, 46–8, 52, 65–6, 70, 74, 76, 94, 96–8
Muḥammad Thānī; *mal.*, wit., 112
Muḥammad Tōm; wit., 97
Muḥammad t.sh.ī; wit., 63
Muḥammad Tūt; wit., 93
Muḥammad Yarwa; lit., 56
Muḥammad Ziyād, *al-ḥājj*; wit., 77
Muḥammadayn b. Madanī; lit., 69–75
al-Muḥayr; loc., 39, 41
Mujāwwir; nom., 77, 78
*Mukhtaṣar*; lawbook, 9, cited: 69: 73, 95, 99
Munīr; nom., 77, 78
Murād; *mal.*, 43
Mūsā; *jabbay*, 8
Mūsā; sul., 1, 13, 46, 66
Mūsā b. Ab(o); wit., 77
Mūsā 'Anqarīb; *khalīfa*, 37
Mūsā b. Muḥammad Rīz; *mal.*, wit., 82
Musabba'āt; people, 8
Musallim; *faq.*, wit., 51
Musallim b. Muḥammad 'Izz al-Dīn; sha., gra., 38, 40
Muṣṭafā, "the elder"; *zar.* of..., 117
Muṣṭafā b. Muḥammad Kannūna; gra., 113

Nachtigal, Gustav; traveller, 23, 25, 73, 76, 114
al-Naḥās; hill, 105
Na'īm; nom., 77, 78
Najjār; *faq.*, wit., 67

Na'ma; *bās.*, wit., 81
Nasīr; Zaghāwa of Kawra vil., 82, 84
Ni'ama; estate, 18, 19, 100–3
n.q.r., see Inqirī
Nubia, 107
Nūl; nom., 77, 78
Nu'mān; *faq.*, 19
Nu'mān; nom., 77, 78
Nu'mān; nom., 103
Nu'mān, *al-ḥājj*; gra., 94–9
numerals, 27
Nūr al-Anṣārī; *faq.*, 100
Nūr al-Dīn; *bās.*, wit., 61
Nūr al-Dīn b. Yaḥyā; *bās.*, gra., ix, 17, 18, 19, 79–99
Nūr Wīr; wit., 68

Omdurman, 4
"Osman Gano", ('Uthmān Janū), 104
Ottoman; diplomatic, 31

Paper, 26
Petherick, J.; traveller, 25

Qabūsh; nom., 77, 78
Qanjār; path, 109
Qiraywud al-Wayka; hillocks, 39, 41
Qiraywud al-Zaraf; estate, 38–41
Qōz Bayna; loc., 8, 16
Qum qum (Qumqūm, Gum Gum) 17, 19, 79–99
Qurayb; sha., nom., 79

Rafīda; riverbed, 85
Raḥma (or Raḥm); *āb shaykh dālī*, 43, 68–9, 74–5
Raḥm; *zar.* of..., 117
Ramaḍān; month, 7
Ramla; riverbed, 85

"Saadalla Gelam"; *kursī*, 104
Sabīl; lit., 58
Sa'd; *al-'ālim*, 114
Sa'd; Fallāta, 64–5
Sa'd; *faq.*, wit., 67
Sa'd al-Dīn; *imām*, *faq.*, gra., 36, 42
Sa'īd; *faq.*, wit., 99
Sa'īd; *qāḍ.*, 53–4
Sa'īd Taw; *ami.*, wit., 82
Ṣalāḥ (or Ṣāliḥ); scr., 23
Ṣāliḥ; wit., 75
Ṣāliḥ al-Jābirī; sons of..., 81
Sallām al-Musmārī; ancestor of the Masāmīr, 76–8
Sanānāt; rocks, 109
Sanbal; wit., 62
Sanbal; *falqanāwī*, 63
Seal, 28–9
Selei; loc., 37
Shabāb; loc., 45
al-Shafī', *al-ḥājj*; wit., 112
Shaībū, grandson of *bās.* Nūr al-Dīn; wit., 112
Sharaf; *faq.*, wit., 56
Sharāf; *mal.*, wit., 62
al-Sharāk; loc., 39, 41
Sharīf Thābit; *faq.*, gra., 20
Shikāb; nom., 77, 78
Shōba; loc., 16
sh.q.r.; *falqanāwī*, 51, 71
Shuqayr, Na'ūm, 13, 114
Sijill; *faq.*, 43
Simayn; loc., 35
Sinnār, 31, 32
Sirāj; wit., 68
Sirāj: *faq.*, wit., 77
s.n.f.tā (s.n.f.tī); slave leader, 66, 68–9
s.nō; Zaghāwa of Kawra vil., 84
Sōmfatā; *rās al-shartay*, 85, 86
South Arabia, 17
Ṣuddayq w. Jābir; wit., 93
Sulaymān; par., 56
Sulaymān; sul., 1, 29
Sulaymān b. Aḥmad Jafdāl; gra., 14
Sulaymān Jubayr; *imām*, wit., 67
Surian Shinuda; Coptic merchant, 28–9

Ṭāhir; nom., 103
Ṭāhir; wit., 58
Ṭāhir b. Aḥmad Bukr; *bās.*, wit., 77
Ṭāhir Jāmūs; *faq.*, 100
Ṭāhir b. Maydōb; *shartay*, 79, 88, 91
Ṭāhir b. *al-qāḍī*; wit., 77
Tājā; wit., 81, 82, 97
Taka; *faq.* wit., 82
*Ṭarīq al-sūdān*; pilgrim route, 25
Tarnā; loc., 108
Tarnī; loc., x, 8, 16
Ṭawīl al-Nū; loc., 109
al-Ṭawīla; loc., 16
Tawraq; *zalṭāya*, 115–17
Tayrāb; nom., 77
Timm; *zar.* of..., 116
Ṭirayfiyya; people, 113–14
Tōr b. Ḥāfiẓ b. Aḥmad Bukr; gra., 20
Tripoli, 107
Tubu; people, 27
Tūm k.m.r.j.; loc., 40, 41
Tunis, 107
al-Tūnisī, Muḥammad b. 'Umar; traveller, 6, 14, 25, 28, 39
Tunjur; people, 1, 6, 45–75, 79
Tūrā; waterhole, 51, 71

al-Tuwānis; loc., 86
Tūwār; path, 86

Ubayḍ; nom., 77, 78
'Ubayd; par., 56
'Ubayda; *faq.*, land of..., 105
'Ubaydallāh Muḥammad al-Sanūsī Abu'l-Ḥasan; judicial officer, 92–3, 98–9
'Ubaydallāh 'Uthmān; scr., 23, 81
'Ujayl; nom., 77, 78
'Ujayna; nom., 81
Umar, H. S., 114
'Umar; *faq.*, wit., 95, 97
'Umar, *al-ḥājj*; lit., 90, 91, 94–5, 96–8
'Umar b.l.mī; Tunjur sul., 49
'Umar b. Jallāb; *muw.*, 105
'Umar Lel; sul., 37, 38, 39, 40, 55
'Umar al-Qafā; *mal.*, wit., 93
Umm Būṣa; *ḥabboba, iiya kuuri*, 18, 42, 43, 100, 101
Umm 'Arīf; hill, 105
Umm Qad; loc., 40
Umm Rajī; field, 51, 71
Umm Sayyāla; waterholes of..., 117
'Uthmān; *zar.* of, 117
'Uthmān; lit., 54, 56, 57
'Uthmān; par., 56
'Uthmān; desc. of...,49
'Uthmān Jundī; *faq.*, 51, 71
'Uthmān Qandūla; lit., 58
Uzbān; loc., 115

Vogel, Eduard; traveller, 25

Wadā'a; loc., 35
Wadā'a; *faq.*, Fallāta, 51, 66, 71
Wadai; state, 3, 25, 32, 45
Wāday (or Wādī); *al-ḥājj*, 61, 63–4
Wādī; nom., 77, 78
Wana; hills, 5
White Nile, 3
al-Wusṭānī; riverbed, 108

Yaḥyā b. Muḥammad; *takanāwī*, 49, 88–9
Yāsīn w. Ḥimār; *zar.* of..., 117
Yawma; loc., 53, 58–60
Yūsuf Hadī; *faq.*, wit., 62
Yūsuf b. Fiṭr; *waz.*, *āb shaykh dālī*, 91, 94–5, 96–8
Yūsuf Ḥāmid; Zaghāwa of Kawra vil., 82, 84
Yūsuf b. 'Umar; wit., 97

Zaghāwa; people, 6, 16, 18, 79, 81–4
Zahra; *mayram*, gra., 80, 99–106
Zakariyyā b. Muḥammad al-Faḍl; *walad al-sulṭān*, 44
Ẓalīma; rocks of..., 105
Zarrūq; *faq.*, wit., 99
Zarrūq, *al-ḥājj*, 62
Zarzār; nom., 103
Zayyādiyya; people, 6, 13, 16, 76
al-Zubayr Pasha Raḥma, 3, 42

Printed in the United Kingdom
by Lightning Source UK Ltd.
129480UK00003B/84/A

9 780521 545631